concrete5 Beginner's Guide
Second Edition

Create and customize your own feature-rich website in no time with concrete5!

Remo Laubacher

BIRMINGHAM - MUMBAI

concrete5 Beginner's Guide
Second Edition

First published: March 2011

Second Edition: April 2013

Production Reference: 1160413

Published by Packt Publishing Ltd.
Livery Place
35 Livery Street
Birmingham B3 2PB, UK.

ISBN 978-1-78216-931-4

www.packtpub.com

Cover Image by Jarek Blaminsky (milak6@wp.pl)

Credits

Author

Remo Laubacher

Reviewers

Ryan Hewitt

Šarūnas Narkevičius

Werner Nindl

John Steele

Acquisition Editor

Mary Nadar

Lead Technical Editor

Savio Jose

Technical Editors

Sharvari Baet

Ankita Meshram

Kirti Pujari

Project Coordinator

Abhishek Kori

Proofreaders

Maria Gould

Aaron Nash

Stephen Copestake

Indexer

Tejal Soni

Graphics

Sheetal Aute

Production Coordinator

Conidon Miranda

Cover Work

Conidon Miranda

About the Author

Remo Laubacher grew up in Central Switzerland in a small village surrounded by mountains and natural beauty. He started working with computers a long time ago and then, after various computer-related projects, focused on ERP and Oracle development. After completing his BSc in Business Administration, Remo became a partner at Ortic, his ERP and Oracle business, as well as a partner at Mesch web consulting and design GmbH. At Mesch—where he's responsible for all development-related topics—he discovered concrete5 as the perfect tool for their web-related projects and has since become a key member of the concrete5 community. You can find his latest publications on `http://www.codeblog.ch/`.

He has also authored *concrete5 Beginner's Guide* and *Creating concrete5 Themes*.

About the Reviewers

Ryan Hewitt has been a web developer for over 10 years and has worked extensively with concrete5, with it being his content management system of choice.

Ryan's background includes working for both large and small development companies, wading through oceans of code and fighting SQL beasts, PHP devils, and CSS nasties. He has written numerous custom online systems and scripts—finding solace in the advantages that well written frameworks and libraries such as CakePHP, jQuery, Boostrap Twitter, and concrete5 bring forth.

Ryan started his own web development business in 2011, with his partner Lelita Baldock, called Mesuva Web Development. From the beautiful coastal town of Goolwa, in South Australia, Ryan and Lelita build a wide range of websites and online shops using concrete5, often heavily customizing them with custom-built blocks and packages.

One of concrete5's greatest strengths as a CMS is its active online community, and Ryan takes pride in contributing answers and insights to the online forum, as well as providing free concrete5 packages and support.

The Mesuva website can be found at `https://www.mesuva.com.au` and Ryan can be contacted through it.

Werner Nindl is an Oracle Hyperion consultant by day and a concrete5 web developer by night. As a consultant, he has lived and worked in Europe, China, and the US. During his day job, Werner manages consulting programs for Financial Consolidation and Reporting.

Intrigued by the capabilities of concrete5, he has started to convert his clients' web sites to concrete5. Participating in the review of this book has helped him to plan for future enhancements. He believes that he can implement those enhancements now at a much lower resource cost then previously planned.

> I want to thank the publishers for the opportunity to participate. First and foremost I want to compliment Remo on his tremendous insight into, and knowledge about, concrete5.

John Steele began teaching himself BASIC on a borrowed Atari. He purchased his first computer, the Timex Sinclair 1000, later trading it in on a Commodore 64. He then taught himself 6502 Assembly followed by the C language, creating a 3D wireframe program to design a hang-glider.

He was a Mathematics major, switching to Computer Science as soon as the degree program was available. He worked as a Systems Programmer at the IBM Almaden Research Center using C, Fortran, Pascal, and 8086 Assembly. Next, he worked as Systems Analyst and Lead Programmer for the largest selling POS software for video stores. He was a beta tester for every version of the Microsoft C compiler.

Fascinated by the Internet, he taught himself PHP3 and MySQL programming and started his business Steelesoft Consulting. He's used just about every Unix-based operating system since the DEC PDP-11 and owns the first version of Linux on CD.

He's also been a technical editor for two PHP4 books by *Osborne-McGraw Hill*.

> I'd like to thank Remo and all the fine folks at concrete5.org and the wonderful people who help others on the Forums everyday.

www.PacktPub.com

Support files, eBooks, discount offers and more

You might want to visit www.PacktPub.com for support files and downloads related to your book.

Did you know that Packt offers eBook versions of every book published, with PDF and ePub files available? You can upgrade to the eBook version at www.PacktPub.com and as a print book customer, you are entitled to a discount on the eBook copy. Get in touch with us at service@packtpub.com for more details.

At www.PacktPub.com, you can also read a collection of free technical articles, sign up for a range of free newsletters and receive exclusive discounts and offers on Packt books and eBooks.

http://PacktLib.PacktPub.com

Do you need instant solutions to your IT questions? PacktLib is Packt's online digital book library. Here, you can access, read and search across Packt's entire library of books.

Why Subscribe?

- ◆ Fully searchable across every book published by Packt
- ◆ Copy and paste, print and bookmark content
- ◆ On demand and accessible via web browser

Free Access for Packt account holders

If you have an account with Packt at www.PacktPub.com, you can use this to access PacktLib today and view nine entirely free books. Simply use your login credentials for immediate access.

Table of Contents

Preface

concrete5 Beginner's Guide covers everything you need to build your own website with a number of customizations and add-ons built from scratch, for those who need a pretty site that also offers some slick functionality.

concrete5 is one of many CMS' out there, but it manags to shine with a number of ideas and impressive solutions. For example, there's a very intuitive in-site editing concept where you can manage the content of your site in the actual layout of it and don't have to understand a complicated backend. The book gives you a quick introduction about this concept, but is focused on developers with the intention to build websites and-applications.

You'll therefore need some experience as a web developer, if possible with the technologies used by concrete5: PHP, MySQL, and jQuery. Experience with concrete5 isn't necessary though. The book guides you step-by-step from installation to the customization, and even to the creation of add-ons.

As you'll see towards the end, the packaging system of concrete5 you use to build your add-ons is very powerful and, thanks to the marketplace, you can easily popularize your own work and, if you want, also get some money by selling your add-ons.

What this book covers

Chapter 1, Installing concrete5, helps you to get a test-site running on your local computer, from where we'll continue to work with concrete5.

Chapter 2, Working with concrete5, discusses the basics of concrete5 you need to know to manage the content of a site, basically a compression of an end-user manual.

Chapter 3, Managing Permissions, looks at the powerful permissions of concrete5. You'll learn how to restrict access to a part of your site as well as allowing editors to see parts of the managing interface of concrete5.

Chapter 4, Managing Add-ons, explains what an add-on is and how you can install them from the marketplace.

Chapter 5, Creating Your Own Theme, shows how to convert an existing HTML layout into a concrete5 theme.

Chapter 6, Customizing Block Layouts, looks at ways to customize block layouts—blocks are layout elements in concrete5—making them look well in your own theme.

Chapter 7, Adding Site Navigation, teaches you how to add a dynamic navigation to your website.

Chapter 8, Creating Your Own Add-on Block, teaches you to create your own block, and the content elements of concrete5 from scratch.

Chapter 9, Everything in a Package, discusses how packages make it easier to work with add-ons that contains different things. We'll wrap a few things we've created in the previous chapters into a package.

Chapter 10, Dashboard Extensions, teaches you how to extend the dashboard, which is the place in concrete5 where you manage users, settings, and a lot more.

Chapter 11, Deployment and Configuration, explains how to copy the site from the local computer to a live server and also explains a few configurations.

What you need for this book

You're almost free to use any kind of tool you want. The screenshots in this book were taken on a Windows computer but Mac OSX as well as Linux works fine as well. A text editor such as Notepad++, a web server such as Apache with PHP and MySQL, and an FTP client such as FileZilla are all you need.

Who this book is for

This book is aimed at developers, knowing the basic web technologies such as HTML, CSS, JavaScript, and PHP required to master the content of this book. Experience with concrete5 isn't necessary but it's helpful to have some experience with PHP and possibly other PHP CMS.

Conventions

In this book, you will find several headings appearing frequently.

To give clear instructions of how to complete a procedure or task, we use:

Time for action – heading

1. Action 1
2. Action 2
3. Action 3

Instructions often need some extra explanation so that they make sense, so they are followed with:

What just happened?

This heading explains the working of tasks or instructions that you have just completed.

You will also find some other learning aids in the book, including:

Pop quiz – heading

These are short multiple-choice questions intended to help you test your own understanding.

Have a go hero – heading

These are practical challenges and give you ideas for experimenting with what you have learned.

You will also find a number of styles of text that distinguish between different kinds of information. Here are some examples of these styles, and an explanation of their meaning.

Code words in text are shown as follows: "You may notice that we used the Unix command `rm` to remove the `Drush` directory rather than the DOS `del` command."

A block of code is set as follows:

```
# * Fine Tuning
#
key_buffer = 16M
key_buffer_size = 32M
max_allowed_packet = 16M
thread_stack = 512K
thread_cache_size = 8
max_connections = 300
```

When we wish to draw your attention to a particular part of a code block, the relevant lines or items are set in bold:

```
# * Fine Tuning
#
key_buffer = 16M
key_buffer_size = 32M
max_allowed_packet = 16M
thread_stack = 512K
thread_cache_size = 8
max_connections = 300
```

Any command-line input or output is written as follows:

```
cd /ProgramData/Propeople
rm -r Drush
git clone --branch master http://git.drupal.org/project/drush.git
```

New terms and **important words** are shown in bold. Words that you see on the screen, in menus or dialog boxes for example, appear in the text like this: "On the **Select Destination Location** screen, click on **Next** to accept the default destination.".

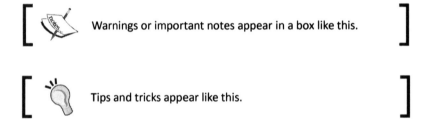

Warnings or important notes appear in a box like this.

Tips and tricks appear like this.

Reader feedback

Feedback from our readers is always welcome. Let us know what you think about this book—what you liked or may have disliked. Reader feedback is important for us to develop titles that you really get the most out of.

To send us general feedback, simply send an e-mail to feedback@packtpub.com, and mention the book title through the subject of your message.

If there is a topic that you have expertise in and you are interested in either writing or contributing to a book, see our author guide on www.packtpub.com/authors.

Customer support

Now that you are the proud owner of a Packt book, we have a number of things to help you to get the most from your purchase.

Downloading the example code

You can download the example code files for all Packt books you have purchased from your account at `http://www.packtpub.com`. If you purchased this book elsewhere, you can visit `http://www.packtpub.com/support` and register to have the files e-mailed directly to you.

Errata

Although we have taken every care to ensure the accuracy of our content, mistakes do happen. If you find a mistake in one of our books—maybe a mistake in the text or the code—we would be grateful if you would report this to us. By doing so, you can save other readers from frustration and help us improve subsequent versions of this book. If you find any errata, please report them by visiting `http://www.packtpub.com/submit-errata`, selecting your book, clicking on the **errata submission form** link, and entering the details of your errata. Once your errata are verified, your submission will be accepted and the errata will be uploaded to our website, or added to any list of existing errata, under the Errata section of that title.

Piracy

Piracy of copyright material on the Internet is an ongoing problem across all media. At Packt, we take the protection of our copyright and licenses very seriously. If you come across any illegal copies of our works, in any form, on the Internet, please provide us with the location address or website name immediately so that we can pursue a remedy.

Please contact us at `copyright@packtpub.com` with a link to the suspected pirated material.

We appreciate your help in protecting our authors, and our ability to bring you valuable content.

Questions

You can contact us at `questions@packtpub.com` if you are having a problem with any aspect of the book, and we will do our best to address it.

1

Installing concrete5

In this chapter, you'll learn what you need to get your own concrete5 site up and running on your local computer. You don't need to have a lot of experience with Apache, PHP, and MySQL configuration as we're going to use Bitnami, which will install all necessary components in almost no time.

Before you can start working with concrete5, you have to set up an environment, where you can test and play around with concrete5 to get used to it. If you have a web hosting account, you can install concrete5 there, but since that isn't always the case, we'll install everything concrete5 needs to work smoothly on your local Windows computer. We're assuming that you're working with Windows but instructions are available for those running Mac OS or Linux; most instructions work the same for all operating systems.

Bitnami installs a local web server, which we'll use to build and test the add-ons we're going to create. In the last chapter of this book, we're going to move the site from your local computer to a live web server.

Preparing for installation

There are a few tools you need, before you can start with the installation process. You probably already work with similar tools, but let's still make sure you've got everything before continuing.

Web browser

concrete5 supports all major browsers as long as you're working with an up-to-date version. Please note: you can create a website which is viewable with an outdated browser, but the in-context editing system won't work correctly, unless you're using a modern browser.

Whether you use Firefox, Chrome, Safari, or Internet Explorer doesn't really matter. concrete5 works with any recent browser with JavaScript capability, but it's recommended to use the latest browser version since most concrete5 community members test new releases with the newest browsers.

Text editor

Since we're going to edit PHP files you'll need a text editor. The requirements are quite small; you can pick almost any text editor you want. Just make sure it does support PHP syntax highlighting. Here are some possible editors:

- **PSPad** (Windows only, free), `http://www.pspad.com`. A simple text editor with in-built FTP support. This can make a quick fix on your website even quicker.
- **TextWrangler** (Mac OS only, free), `http://www.barebones.com/products/textwrangler/`. A very slick and clean text editor with extensive FTP support.
- **Notepad++** (Windows only, free), `http://notepad-plus-plus.org/`. A small and fast replacement for Windows notepad.

There are a lot more text editors, as mentioned previously; you can use almost any editor you want. If you're familiar with another product, just go with it. You won't find anything in this book where you need a special text editor feature.

Archive utility

The same with the file archive utility, there are plenty of tools out there and if you want, you can use the in-built extraction utility of Windows or Mac OS. If you're looking for something more advanced, you can go with **7-Zip** at `http://www.7-zip.org/` or **IZArc** at `http://www.izarc.org/`; both are free and do a good job.

FTP client

Once more, there are lots of choices. You'll have to change file permissions later, so make sure your FTP client includes this option. A powerful and well known client is **FileZilla**, `http://filezilla-project.org/`. It's free as well and has a lot more features than we need.

Installing Bitnami

If you think you've found all the tools you'd like to use to create your website, you're ready to install Bitnami. Bitnami is a WAMP stack which provides a lot of different tools needed to run your favorite open source web application on your computer. WAMP is the short form for: Windows, Apache, MySQL, and PHP. The more common term is LAMP and describes the same, but for Linux. It's basically a combination of different applications.

There's a stack for concrete5 that installs everything including concrete5 in no time, but since we want to have a look at the process of installing concrete5 as well, we're going to use the WAMP stack. If you're working with Mac OS or Linux, check Bitnami MAMP, or LAMP; the process is pretty much the same for all the operating systems.

Time for action – installing Bitnami WAMP stack

concrete5 is a PHP application which uses PHP as its programming language in combination with a MySQL database. There are lots of possibilities to meet the requirements of concrete5. The preferred web server is Apache but IIS like any web server supporting PHP works as well, but only Apache is supported by the core team.

If you already have a server or a local Apache, PHP, and MySQL set up, you can skip this step and continue with the *Downloading concrete5* section a few pages ahead. Otherwise, we are going to need to install Bitnami WAMP stack on your local computer by following these simple steps:

1. Go to `http://bitnami.org/stacks/` and select the MAMP stack for Mac OS, WAMP for Windows, and LAMP for Linux. On the next page, click on **Installer** and double-click the `EXE` as soon as it has been downloaded. You should see the following window or a dialog you have to confirm if files downloaded from the Internet aren't executed directly on your computer:

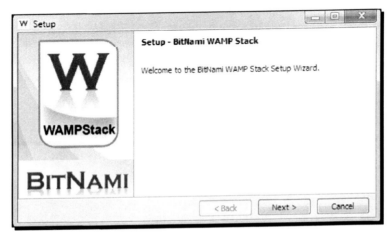

2. Click on **Next** to get to the next installation screen. Here you'll see a screen with a number of preselected components. We don't need them, as we're going to install concrete5 as our Content Management System (CMS) and framework. phpMyAdmin can't be unselected, but that's okay.

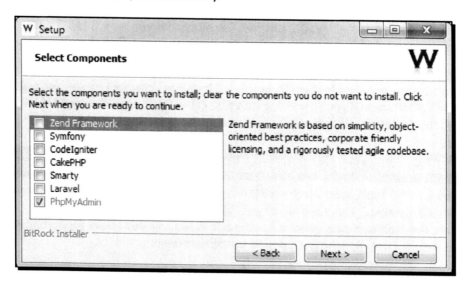

3. Click on **Next** once more and you'll be asked to specify the installation folder. You can keep the suggested value but feel free to change it if you prefer a different location. For this book, we used Version 5.4.10. Your version might be higher. Cause the WAMP folder will have the version number in the name, all follow-up.

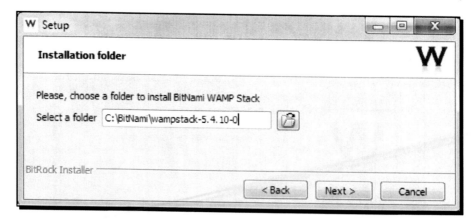

4. Click on **Next** again and you'll be asked to enter the MySQL password for the user `root`. It's important to keep it saved as this is the main user to access your database. You'll need this password later when we install concrete5.

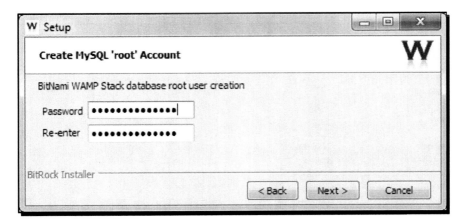

5. There are a few more screens; click on **Next** and you'll have to enter the port number for Apache as well as MySQL in the following screen. You can keep the port number `80` for Apache and `3306` for MySQL. However, it might be possible that another application is already using one or both of these ports, in which case you have to disable the existing application or use a different port number. It's not a problem if you change these numbers; just make sure that you remember the port numbers as you'll need them later when we install concrete5.

After you've clicked your way through all the screens and confirmed the launch process at the end, you should have a running MySQL server as well as a working Apache web server with all necessary components to run a concrete5 site on your local computer. Before we install concrete5, let's make a small change to the MySQL configuration. MySQL table names are not case sensitive on Windows. This will cause some problems if you want to move your site to a Linux server where MySQL is by default set up with case sensitive table names. If you don't feel comfortable with this change, it's not necessary, but recommended if you move your site to another server at some point.

To change this, if you work with concrete5, do the following:

1. Go to the directory where you've installed Bitnami and open the folder `mysql`; it should look as follows:

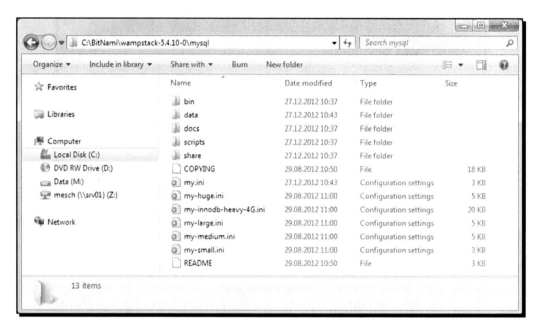

2. The `my.ini` file contains several settings related to MySQL. Open the file and insert the following line immediately after the `mysqld` section:

```
lower_case_table_names = 0
```

The `mysql` section should look like as follows:

```
# The MySQL server
[mysqld]

lower_case_table_names = 0

# Example MySQL config file for medium systems.
#
# This is for a system with little memory (32M - 64M) where MySQL plays
# an important part, or systems up to 128M where MySQL is used together with
# other programs (such as a web server)

# Replication Master Server (default)
# binary logging is required for replication
##log-bin=mysql-bin

# required unique id between 1 and 2^32 - 1
# defaults to 1 if master-host is not set
# but will not function as a master if omitted
server-id   = 1
```

3. Now that MySQL is properly configured, locate the manager tool in your start menu. You should be able to find it in **All Programs | Bitnami WAMP Stack | Manager tool** and open it. You should see the following dialog:

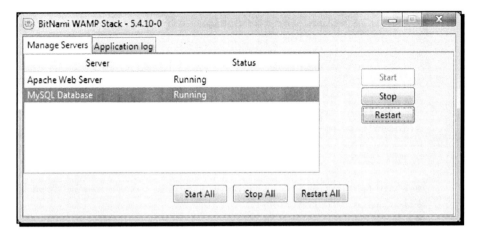

4. Select **MySQL Database** and click on the **Restart** button in the right pane. The buttons go gray. When the buttons return to their regular state the restart of MySQL is complete.

5. If everything worked you should be able to open your browser and enter `http://localhost/`.

> If you had to change the port of your Apache service, make sure you append it to the hostname. Port number 80 is the default port to access websites and can be omitted. However, if you had to change to a different number like 8000, you have to use an address like this: `http://localhost:8000/`.

There's also one small change we have to make to the Apache configuration in order to make sure we can use a file called `.htaccess`, which allows concrete5 to change certain Apache configurations. Follow these steps:

1. Go to the directory where you've installed Bitnami and open the folder `apache2` and then `conf`.

2. Within that directory, open the file called `httpd.conf`.

3. Look for a section which starts with `<Directory "C:/BitNami/wampstack-5.4.10-0/apache2/htdocs">` and then look after a property called `AllowOverride`. You'll have to change its value from `None` to `All`.

4. The relevant part should look like as follows afterwards:

```
DocumentRoot "C:/BitNami/wampstack-5.4.10-0/apache2/htdocs"
<Directory "C:/BitNami/wampstack-5.4.10-0/apache2/htdocs">
    #
    # Possible values for the Options directive are "None", "All",
    # or any combination of:
    #    Indexes Includes FollowSymLinks SymLinksifOwnerMatch
       ExecCGI MultiViews
    #
    # Note that "MultiViews" must be named *explicitly* ---
       "Options All"
    # doesn't give it to you.
    #
    # The Options directive is both complicated and important.
       Please see
    # http://httpd.apache.org/docs/2.4/mod/core.html#options
    # for more information.
    #
    Options Indexes FollowSymLinks

    #
    # AllowOverride controls what directives may be placed in
       .htaccess files.
    # It can be "All", "None", or any combination of the keywords:
    #    Options FileInfo AuthConfig Limit
    #
    AllowOverride All

    #
    # Controls who can get stuff from this server.
    #
    Require all granted
</Directory>
```

5. After you've saved the change, go to the Bitnami Manager tool, select the `Apache Web Server` process, and restart it.

What just happened?

The Bitnami WAMP Stack setup package installed a working web server, including PHP with the most commonly used modules and a MySQL database. This is what a lot of web applications need, and you can use this environment for other CMSs as well.

You've also had a quick look at one MySQL configuration file to avoid problems when moving your data to a Linux server. If you want to know more about this setting, the MySQL documentation is going to answer almost any question about table names: `http://dev.mysql.com/doc/refman/5.5/en/identifier-case-sensitivity.html`.

We also enabled support for `.htaccess` files in Apache. We'll need it later in this chapter when we enable pretty URLs.

Pop quiz – requirements for concrete5

Like any other software, concrete5 needs certain things to run. Try to answer the following questions.

Q1. Which of the following server-side programming language(s) has been used to build concrete5?

1. PHP
2. Microsoft ASP
3. Java
4. All of the above

Q2. Which of the following database(s) can you use with concrete5?

1. PostgreSQL
2. MySQL
3. Oracle
4. All of the above

Q3. Which of the following operating system(s) can you use to run concrete5?

1. Microsoft Windows
2. Mac OS X
3. Linux
4. All of the above

Q4. Name the web server(s) you can use to run concrete5:

1. Microsoft IIS
2. Nginx
3. Apache
4. lighttpd

Downloading concrete5

Your local web server is running, there's nothing else to prepare, and you are now ready to install concrete5. There are just a few more steps till you can log in to concrete5.

Time for action – downloading the latest version

Before we can install anything we have to get the latest concrete5 version from this URL: `http://www.concrete5.org/developers/downloads/`. After downloading the zip archive for concrete5, follow these steps:

1. Remove all the files and directories from Bitnami in the directory at `C:\BitNami\wampstack-5.4.10-0\apache2\htdocs`.

2. Open the ZIP archive, open the first directory in it, and extract all the files to `C:\BitNami\wampstack-5.4.10-0\apache2\htdocs`.

3. After you've extracted the ZIP file you should see a structure like that shown in the following screenshot:

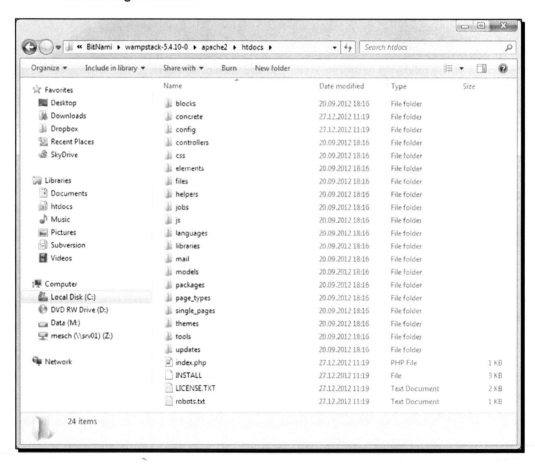

At the time of writing, concrete5 5.6.1 was the latest version. You can download a newer version if available; changes in the installation process should be minor if there are any at all.

What just happened?

You've downloaded and extracted the concrete5 CMS files. Depending on your archive utility it might have happened that empty folders like updates, files, and others haven't been created. Make sure your structure looks like the one shown in the preceding screenshot.

Before we continue, a few words about the file structure you've just created. It's important that you understand the structure of concrete5 before you start working with it. It's helpful to have a clear understanding about the structure so you can find your files easily. You'll later see that all add-ons in the marketplace follow this structure. Using the suggested structure helps to keep the structure clean, no matter who builds the concrete5 site or add-on.

It might look a bit bulky to have so many folders in the root of your website, but you'll realize that it makes perfect sense to have this structure the more you work with concrete5. We'll have a closer look at some of the directories later in this chapter.

Creating an empty MySQL database

You must create an empty SQL database before you can install concrete5.

Time for action – creating a MySQL database

Use phpMyAdmin, which is included in the Bitnami stack, to create the database:

1. Open http://localhost/phpmyadmin/ in your web server and you should see the following page:

2. Log in with the user `root` and the password you've entered during the installation process of Bitnami.

3. Click on the **Users** tab and then on **Add user** and enter the following values:

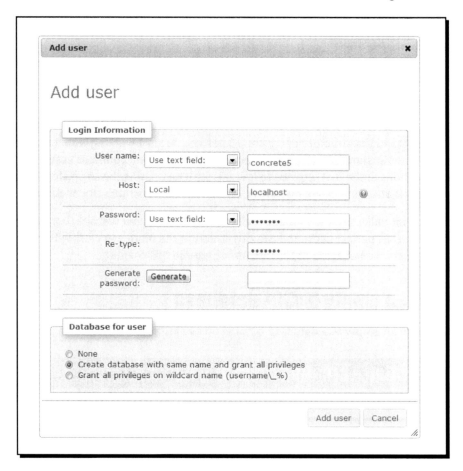

4. Make sure you remember the password as you'll need it later when we install concrete5. Also make sure you select the radio button **Create database with same name and grant all privileges**. Click on **Add user** to confirm all values and continue creating the users and database.

5. We just created a new user called **concrete5** as well as a database with the same name. There's one more change we have to make before we can use the new database for concrete5. In the left-hand column, select the new database and then click on **Operations**:

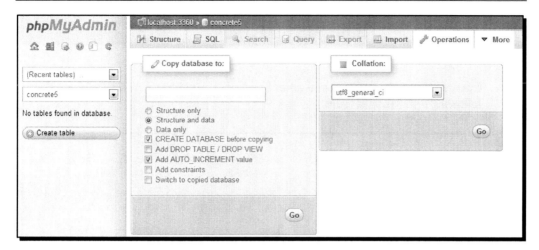

6. Change the value for **Collation** to `utf8_general_ci` and confirm the change by clicking on **Go**. With this step, we made sure that our database and therefore concrete5 can work with non-Latin characters such as umlauts and even Japanese or Chinese characters.

What just happened?

All the components are ready; Apache, including PHP, should be running and there's an empty MySQL database to host your concrete5 site.

 Please note: concrete5 can't be installed in a database which isn't empty!

Installing concrete5

We're finally ready to get to the installation of concrete5. Let's install it!

Time for action – installing concrete5

To install concrete5 follow these steps:

1. Open your favorite browser and enter `http://localhost/`. You should see the
following installation screen:

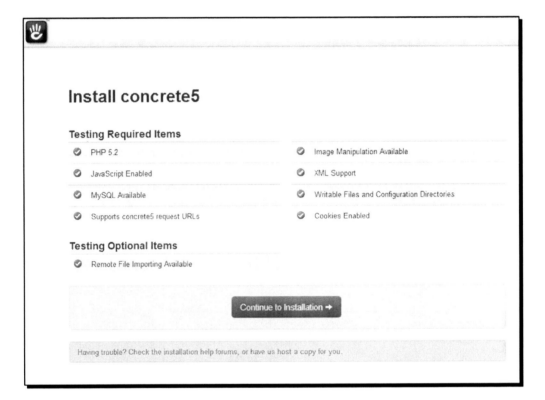

2. There are a number of checks that make sure your environment supports all the
necessary functions needed for concrete5 before installing it. Our Bitnami stack
contains everything and therefore only shows you green icons. A few words
about the required items:

- **PHP**: Whenever possible, try to use the latest PHP version but make
  sure you run at least 5.2.4.

- **JavaScript enabled**: The concrete5 interface uses a lot of JavaScript
  to make things easy and smooth to use. It won't be possible to edit
  any content if you disable JavaScript in your browser.

- **MySQL available**: concrete5 needs a MySQL database; no other
  databases are supported.

- **Supports concrete5 request URLs**: By default you'll see `index.php` in each concrete5 URL you open. To get rid of this, you need to have the Apache module `mod_rewrite`, which we're going to deal with later in this chapter.

- **Image manipulation available**: There are a number of functions such as the creating of thumbnails, which need image libraries in PHP.

- **XML support**: In concrete5 you'll have some XML files to describe data structures, which is why XML support is mandatory.

- **Writable files and configuration directories**: Usually not a problem if you work with a WAMP stack on Windows. The web server must be able to write some files in your website's installation directory. We'll discuss this issue later, when we move the site to the production server.

- **Cookies enabled**: Cookies are used in the log in process and must be enabled in your browser.

3. Once you've managed to get every icon to be green, click on **Continue to Installation** to get to this screen:

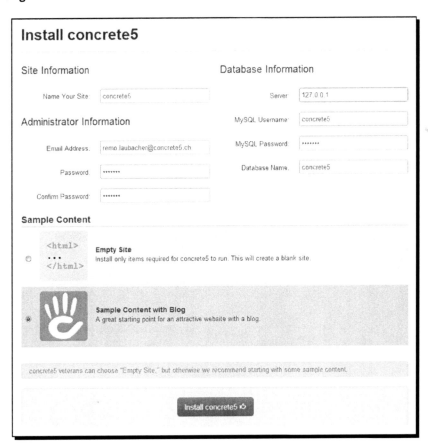

4. To install concrete5 you have to enter the following information:

- ❑ **Name Your Site**: You can enter any name you want, which can be changed in the dashboard later.

- ❑ **Email Address**: This is the admin mail address. Make sure it exists; this is where you'll receive a link to change the eventually forgotten admin password.

- ❑ **Password**: This is the password for the user admin; make sure it's not too easy since admin is the main user with access to everything in concrete5.

5. You will also have to enter the following database information:

- ❑ **Server**: Since the database is running on the same machine as the web server, just enter 127.0.0.1. If you changed the default MySQL port from 3306 to something else like 3307, use 127.0.0.1:3307.

- ❑ **MySQL Username**, **MySQL Password**, and **Database Name**: concrete5 or whatever you used when you created the user in phpMyAdmin.

6. Next is the **Sample Content** section. If you select **Sample Content with Blog**, concrete5 will create a few pages to play around with. Enable this; if you're new to concrete5, it will create some nice pages where you can see the different blocks you can use to build your website. You can remove those pages later.

7. If you've entered all the necessary information, click on **Install concrete5**!

What just happened?

A few seconds after you've clicked on **Install concrete5** you should see a screen with a confirmation that your site is up and running. Navigate to the actual site available at http://localhost/ and you should see the following screen:

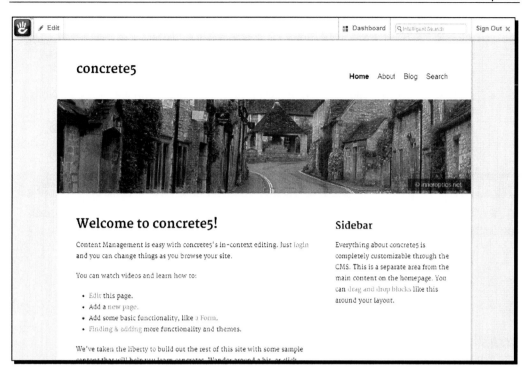

You might wonder why we've used `127.0.0.1` and not `localhost` when connecting to the MySQL database. Both values would work, but it can happen that `localhost` is much slower because it resolves to an IPv6 address on Windows, in which case you'd run into a timeout first because MySQL doesn't support IPv6.

The configuration file

After you've successfully installed concrete5 you'll find a file called `site.php` in the `config` directory. This is where the installation process has saved the information you've entered during the process. Here's how it looks:

```php
<?php
define('DB_SERVER', '127.0.0.1');
define('DB_USERNAME', 'concrete5');
define('DB_PASSWORD', 'concrete5');
define('DB_DATABASE', 'concrete5');
define('PASSWORD_SALT', 'C8MKVa6UZveKlYxFGvmFFqspBAOR5hLjMf9Xsz');
```

- ◆ DB_SERVER, DB_USERNAME, DB_PASSWORD, and DB_DATABASE are obviously just database related. If the credentials to access your MySQL database have changed, this is where you have to modify them to make sure concrete5 can access your database.

- ◆ PASSWORD_SALT: This is a random string used in combination with the password to generate the password hashes found in the user table. Salts are used to complicate dictionary attacks and even if they are useless without a password, you should still not publish a real password salt to keep your site safe.

Pop quiz – the configuration file

Q1. You'll often have to check or modify a few lines in the configuration file, so where can you find it?

1. `<concrete5 installation directory>\config.php`
2. `<concrete5 installation directory>\config\config.php`
3. `<concrete5 installation directory>\config\site.php`

Disabling caching

There are a few different caching functions in concrete5 which can improve the performance of your site but also make things difficult if you keep changing the files. If you change a file without telling concrete5 anything about it, it will keep using the old values in the cache and not reflect the changes you've made. It's therefore recommended to disable all caches while working on a new site.

Time for action – disabling caching

Follow these steps to disable all caches in concrete5:

1. Log in to concrete5 and type `cache settings` in the intelligent search box and select the first entry in the result.

2. In the screen you can see now, select all the radio buttons labeled as **Off** and confirm the change by clicking on **Save**.

What just happened?

We just disabled the cache in concrete5 to avoid some potential problems with outdated results. In the last chapter when we upload the site, we'll enable the cache again!

Enabling pretty URLs

When you browse to a subpage in your concrete5 site you'll notice an odd thing in every URL; there's `index.php` in it like in `http://localhost/index.php/about/`. Every request to a page in concrete5 is processed by `index.php`, this has several advantages. It's easier to check the permissions because there's a single point where the page rendering happens.

But even with these advantages you probably don't like to see `index.php` in every URL. Luckily it's rather easy to change it if your web server supports rewrite rules. Our Bitnami stack does, but only because we previously changed `AllowOverride` to `All` in the relevant section before. Now that we have everything needed for pretty URLs, here's what we have to do to get rid of `index.php`.

Time for action – enabling pretty URLs

Follow these steps to get rid of the `index.php` from your URLs:

1. Log in to concrete5.

2. Click on the **Intelligent Search** box in the top-right corner.

3. Type `pretty`, and while you type, concrete5 searches for the correct entry. Once found, click on **Pretty URLs**.

4. Check **Enable Pretty URLs** and hit on **Save**; you should see the following screen:

5. concrete5 should have created a file called `.htaccess` in the root of your website (`C:\BitNami\wampstack-5.4.10-0\apache2\htdocs\.htaccess`). This is the file where the rewrite rules are stored that remove `index.php` from the URLs.

What just happened?

Congratulations, you're done! concrete5 is running and you've also activated some options to improve the behavior of concrete5.

You've enabled pretty URLs, which uses the Apache `mod_rewrite` module to rewrite URLs. You can now open a subpage by entering `http://localhost/about/` without having `index.php` in the address. In case you'd like to know more about this Apache feature, this is the official documentation:

`http://httpd.apache.org/docs/2.2/mod/mod_rewrite.html`

`.htaccess` is a configuration file most commonly used by Apache to configure Apache modules on a directory level. It's a simple text file you can open with any text editor of your choice. If you haven't worked with Apache before, the content might be a bit confusing but concrete5 took care of it. You shouldn't have to modify anything on your own in this file.

> Pretty URLs can also be used with Microsoft IIS but you need to install a rewrite filter first.
>
> If you want to try it on your own, you can find a solid and free rewrite filter at this address: `http://iirf.codeplex.com/`.

File and directory structure of concrete5

As mentioned previously, there are a lot of folders in concrete5. Most of these top level folders are empty—resist the temptation to delete these as they are required for customizations. To give you a head start, here's a short list of the most important folders:

Folder	Explanation
blocks	You can find custom blocks and block templates in this folder. You'll learn more about blocks in the next few chapters.
concrete	Probably the most important part, this is where all core files, the actual CMS is located. Never update anything in this folder.
config	The folder where concrete5 puts the configuration files.
files	The file manager stores your files in this directory.
packages	This is where you have to put add-ons if you install them manually.
updates	The concrete5 auto update feature puts the new core in this directory. Never update anything in this folder.

There are a few more folders but you probably won't need them unless you dive deep into concrete5. There's one important thing to remember when working with concrete5: The directory `concrete` looks a lot like the `root` directory, but never change anything in the `concrete` directory. You'll find several directories in both places. That's because you can override a single file by placing it in the same structure in the top level.

Here's one example without going into too much detail. Later in this book, we're going to work with a block called content block, a few times. This block basically adds a formatted text to your page. The actual output is printed from this file: `/concrete/blocks/content/view.php`. How can we change that file without causing any problems with updates? Simply copy the file and place it here: `/blocks/content/view.php`. The structure is the same; there's just no `concrete` in the path. You'll have to create some directories first, but at the end, you just copy and paste a file and can then change its content.

Dispatcher process

As we've mentioned previously, every request to a page in concrete5 is forwarded to `index.php`. You might be able to see this by looking at the URL which starts with `index.php`, but if you enabled pretty URLs, this is hidden by some Apache `mod_rewrite` instructions. No matter which option you're using, `index.php` is always involved.

The actual logic is located in a file included by `index.php`, which you can find in `concrete/dispatcher.php`. Every time you request a page, the code of the dispatcher is executed. If you want to dig deeper into concrete5, you'll want to have a closer look at this file at some point. For now, let's just have a look at this quick summary of what happens in the dispatcher:

- Initializing the error handling
- Fetching all constants and configurations necessary for the site
- Loading the database classes and establishing a connection
- Creation of a session necessary to remember things such as login information
- Loading all settings related to localization
- Checking events that have to be run at some point
- Parsing of the URL and fetching the correct object from the database related to the current URL
- Rendering of the page object as well as all its blocks

You can find more information about the dispatcher flow on this page: `http://www.concrete5.org/documentation/introduction/dispatcher-and-application-flow/`.

Summary

You've reached the end of the first chapter!

♦ You should now have a working concrete5 installation from where you'll learn how to work with concrete5

♦ In case you have to check or modify your concrete5 configuration, you should know where to find the files

♦ We've looked at the requirements to run concrete5

♦ All the tools you'll need to go through this book should be installed on your computer

♦ We're going to use this test site to build our own demo site including some block customization

2

Working with concrete5

In this chapter you'll learn how to use concrete5 to manage the content of your site. If you build websites for customers, this is the part your customers have to learn and understand. More precisely, you'll learn to add, edit, and remove content and you'll also learn how to insert columns and various text styles.

We're going to look at the following topics:

- Installing new blocks
- The dashboard—the place where you manage users, settings, and more
- Using page defaults to add content that appears in new pages
- Working with the sitemap
- A feature that allows you to split a content into two columns
- Using a stack to share the same content across different pages
- Using the design menu to add custom CSS rules without coding

Getting familiar with concrete5

Before you start customizing and extending concrete5, you have to get familiar with the tools you'll need when you want to update your site's content. Since you don't want to let everyone update your site, you have to log in using the account, which has been created during the installation. Let's go through this step-by-step.

Time for action – logging in to concrete5

Perform the following steps to log in to concrete5:

1. If you followed the first chapter step-by-step, you can enter `http://localhost/` and get to the default concrete5 home page.

2. At the bottom of the page you'll find a link, **Sign In to Edit this Site**. Click on this link. If you changed the theme, you might not find that link at the bottom. In such a case simply append `/login/` or `/index.php/login/`; for example, `http://www.your-site.com/login/`.

3. You can now log in with the user admin and the password generated during the installation process.

What just happened?

When you're logged in, you'll see the exact same page with one major difference. There's a toolbar on the top to execute certain actions on the current page:

The following table explains the different elements of the toolbar:

Button	Explanation
Edit	Before you can edit the content, you have to activate the edit mode. You can click on this button to start editing a page or just hover it to see more options related to the current page.

Button	Explanation
Dashboard	This brings up the administration panel, where you can create users, install add-ons, and a lot more.
Intelligent Search	This textbox allows you to quickly search for a page in the dashboard. Enter a keyword such as *permissions*, *files*, *attributes*, or anything you're looking for and concrete5 will search through all available dashboard pages and list the result right underneath the search field.
Sign Out	Click on this button to log out of concrete5.

Let's have a quick look at the options available in the edit menu:

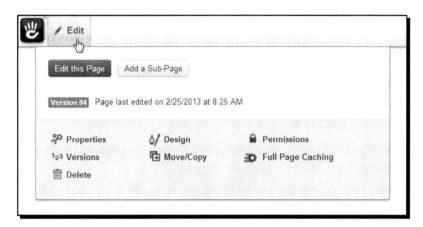

The following table explains the available options in this menu:

Button	Explanation
Edit this Page	This button switches the page into the edit mode just like the **Edit** button does.
Add a Sub-Page	This button adds a new page underneath the current page.
Properties	Each page has properties such as a name, description, meta title, and usually attributes you can define on your own. Think about a background color, which is different for each page.
Versions	concrete5 keeps a copy of every change you make. This button allows you to view, copy, and bring back a previous version in case you want to undo a certain change.
Delete	Click on this button if you don't need the current page anymore.
Design	A page has a theme and a page type, which might have a different structure; one has a single column and another one two. This button shows a dialog where you can change this.

Button	Explanation
Full Page Caching	concrete5 caches several things to improve performance. It's usually not needed, but check this function if you need more aggressive caching.
Permissions	As you'd expect, you can hide a page from certain users and groups. This button shows you a dialog where you can change permission-related options.
Move/Copy	This buttons shows you a dialog where you can select the new parent of the current page if you want to move it around.

Adding new blocks

Now that we are in edit mode, we can start editing our site. This works by adding blocks to predefined areas. You'll see the different elements and standard blocks of concrete5 as we go through the next *Time for action* section step-by-step.

Time for action – adding new blocks

Perform the following steps to add a new block to your concrete5 page:

1. First, we would like to change some of the content on the home page. Click on **Edit** to activate the edit mode on the page.

2. The look of the page changes a bit when you're in edit mode, but you're still able to see the actual page:

3. At the bottom of each area you can find a link called **Add To <Area-Name>**. If you click on it, it will display a small menu with different actions, shown as follows:

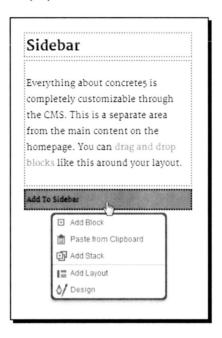

4. Right now, we only need **Add Block**. We're going to use the other items later in this chapter. If you click on **Add Block**, you'll see a dialog with all available blocks:

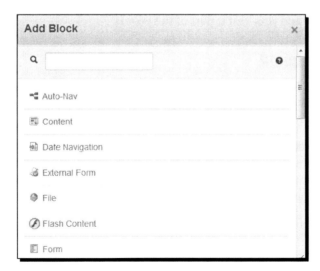

5. Let's start by selecting **Content** to insert a new formatted text block. Another dialog will pop up and display a WYSIWYG editor, where you can enter text, including images and links to other pages. It mostly works like any other text editing application. You've got text formatting, and some paragraph formats that you'll probably know if you've worked with the Internet technology before.

It should be pretty intuitive, but please have a quick look at the toolbar on the top of the text area. If you want to insert a link to a concrete5 page or a file from the file manager, you have to use the toolbar above the text area:

6. Click on **Add** and your text is part of the page!

What just happened?

You should now understand how concrete5 changes the way a page looks when you enter edit mode. This is also one feature that makes concrete5 different from most CMSs; you can edit the content in a view, which looks a lot like the actual page.

A page in concrete5 consists of sections called areas, such as Main or Sidebar. An **area** is basically a place where you can insert content. Unlike other CMSs, editable areas in concrete5 themes aren't specific to a content type. An area can be the main part, where you place the content or a column on the left-hand or right-hand side, as well as a header or footer area.

The content elements are called **blocks** and can be put in any area several times. If you're in the edit mode, you can easily spot a block by looking for the red striped lines.

By default, concrete5 ships with the following blocks:

- **Auto-Nav**: This block is necessary to build a dynamic navigation. We'll cover this block at full length later in this book.
- **Content**: This block inserts formatted text using a WYSIWYG editor.
- **Date Navigation**: This block create a list of pages grouped by the month in which they were created.
- **External Form**: This block lets you build a form using an **Model-View-Controller (MVC)** approach. Programming experience is required for this, but don't worry, you can probably build a lot of sites without using this block.
- **File**: This block inserts a download link to a file you've uploaded to the file manager.
- **Flash Content**: Use this block to insert a flash banner or animation.
- **Form**: This block offers a nice and easy way to build forms. Not as flexible as an external form, but it doesn't require any HTML or PHP coding!
- **Google Map**: This block uses a Google map to show your visitors where they can find your company.
- **Guestbook / Comments**: If you want your visitors to leave comments on your page, use this block.
- **HTML**: For those who know HTML, this lets you insert plain HTML code.
- **Image**: This block places content, including a hover effect in the page.
- **Next & Previous Nav**: This block inserts links to navigate to the previous or next page in the site map order.
- **Page List**: This block displays a set of pages; it can be used to build a simple news list, or blog.
- **RSS Displayer**: This block pulls news articles from another page by including an RSS news feed.
- **Search**: This block displays a form to let visitors search for pages on your website.
- **Slideshow**: This block creates an image slideshow with a smooth transition in just a few clicks.
- **Survey**: This block creates a simple survey and displays the result using a pie chart.
- **Tags**: This block is useful for blogs where you assign tags to posts.
- **Video Player**: This block plays videos in different formats.
- **YouTube Video**: This block puts a YouTube video on your website.
- **Blog Date Archive**: As the name suggests, this block is useful for blogs where you want to group posts by months and years.

Your playground site should also contain some words you've entered using the **Content** block.

Now that you've added a new block, you should also try to edit an existing block.

Time for action – editing existing blocks

Perform the following steps to edit an existing block on your site:

1. Once a block has been added, you can simply edit it again by clicking on it. The following menu appears with different options:

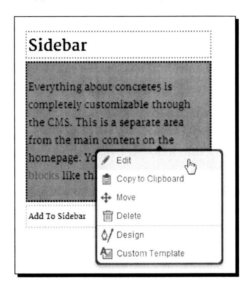

The different options are as follows:

- **Edit:** This option opens the block editing dialog, which you've seen when you added a new instance of the block. In the case of the **Content** block, you'll see the same WYSIWYG editor you saw when you added a new block, but depending on the block type, the dialog will look different.

- **Copy to Clipboard:** This option copies the block into a clipboard from where you can paste it into different areas of the same or other pages.

- **Move:** If you click on this option, you switch into a different mode, where you can drag blocks around to reorder them.

- **Delete:** You don't need the block anymore? Click on this option and it's removed from the page.

- **Design:** This option lets you style the blocks by using some CSS rules. There's another *Time for action* section about this later in this chapter.

- **Custom Template:** Some blocks ship with different templates to change the look of the output. We're going to have a detailed look at this feature in *Chapter 6, Customizing Block Layouts*.

2. Once you've clicked on **Edit**, you can change the content like you did when you added a new block. Change the content and once you're done, confirm your changes by clicking on **Save** at the bottom right-hand corner of the dialog.

What just happened?

We had a quick look at editing an existing block. There's not much; once you know how to add a block, editing it usually is pretty much the same. You click on the block, select **Edit**, and update the values you've previously entered.

Have a go hero – adding more blocks

As you've seen in the previous chapter, concrete5 ships with a lot more blocks than just the content block we've discussed. Try to add and edit all the blocks you can use to get familiar with concrete5. It's going to be routine when updating page content!

Time for action – exiting edit mode

When you changed into the edit mode, the toolbar on the top changed a bit. The **Edit** button looks different and when you hover or click on it, you'll see a slightly different menu too as shown in the following screenshot. You'll need one of the new items to confirm and publish your changes:

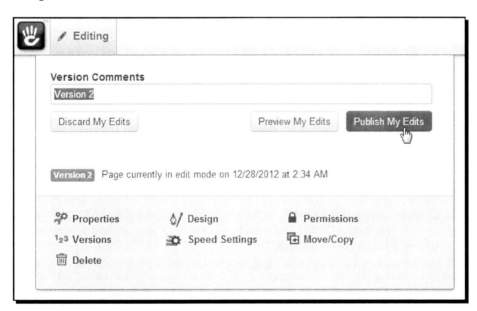

1. The obvious first choice is **Publish My Edits**. It's what you'll need when you're done editing the page and want to confirm all changes and make them visible to the public.

2. If you don't want to keep the changes, click on **Discard My Edits** and you're back, where you've been before.

3. If you want to keep a draft of the changes, click on **Preview My Edits**. This will keep the changes, but not approve them, thus making them invisible to the public. You can see unapproved versions by clicking on **Versions**, where you can also manually approve it.

Pop quiz – concrete5 inside the editing mode

Try to remember the things you can do while you're inside editing mode.

Q1. What kind of blocks, without installing an add-on, can you add to a concrete5 page?

1. Formatted text using the content block
2. A YouTube video
3. A simple form
4. Pictures combined into a slideshow
5. A Google map
6. All of the above

Q2. How do you publish changes made to a page?

1. By closing the browser window
2. By clicking on the **Edit** button
3. By clicking on the **Publish My Edits** button in the menu you see when you hover the **Edit** button

Working with the dashboard

Even with the really slick editing system, there are still some tasks you can't do while you're browsing the site. This is why there's still a dashboard, where you can find several options and forms to modify your concrete5 site.

While you're browsing the site while logged in, there's always a button called **Dashboard** in the top right-hand corner. Click on it and you should get to the dashboard:

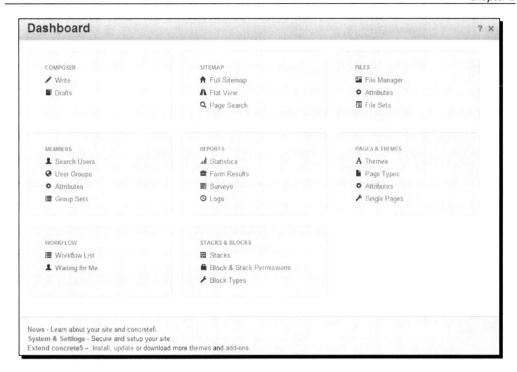

We'll quickly go through the groups of items. Most parts on the dashboard are easy to understand—with some time and patience you'll probably be able to figure out most of the options on the dashboard pretty easily.

When you open the dashboard, you'll see the following boxes:

Item	Explanation
COMPOSER	The composer allows you to create and manage pages in a more database-like interface. This can be helpful if you have a lot of similar items such as blog posts, news entries, and others.
SITEMAP	This is the place where you can find all the pages you've created. Either by looking at a hierarchical tree or by a flat view or a search dialog.
FILES	Most websites contain files in the form of pictures or downloads. This is where you can manage them.
MEMBERS	By default, you'll only have one user, the super admin, but if you want, you can create as many users as you want, assign them to groups, grant them the right to edit pages, and even build a community site on top of them.
REPORTS	Some blocks, such as the survey or form block, report data which you can find under this section at any time you want. There's also an option to export the data to Excel.

Item	Explanation
PAGES & THEMES	This allows you to: ◆ Install and activate themes ◆ Create and edit page types ◆ Add new page attributes ◆ Create single pages
WORKFLOW	This is something you'll probably only need if you have a big site or company with lots of users involved. There's an extensible API in concrete5, which you can use to build custom workflows. You can also use the basic workflow, which is included by default.
STACKS & BLOCKS	A **stack** is basically a collection of blocks grouped together. We'll have a look at them later in this chapter. You can also see a list of installed blocks and manage the permissions to add blocks and stacks.
News, System & Settings, Extend concrete5	At the bottom you can find more links. News will of course display news about concrete5, Settings will show you a long list of different concrete5 settings, and Extend concrete5 allows you to install new add-ons. We'll cover the installation of add-ons later in this book though.

Time for action – changing the site's name

1. Click on the **Dashboard** button and then **System & Settings** in the bottom left-hand corner.

2. In the top left-hand corner click on **Site Name**.

3. Change the name of the site and click on **Update** to confirm the change.

What just happened?

We've used one of the many options in the dashboard to change a setting of your site. The site name is used in the title of every page and therefore, also found by search engines.

Adding more pages

concrete5 uses a site map to build a hierarchical tree of pages. This means that every page has one root page. The top level is home and can't be removed.

If you already have a website project going on, you have probably thought about the hierarchical site structure for quite a bit. Use that structure if you have one, otherwise we're just going to add some random pages.

Time for action – adding pages to create a news section

Perform the following steps to add new pages to your site:

1. When you're in the **Dashboard**, click on **Full Sitemap**.

2. Click on the **Home** page and you'll be presented with a menu. Right now, we only need **Add Page**:

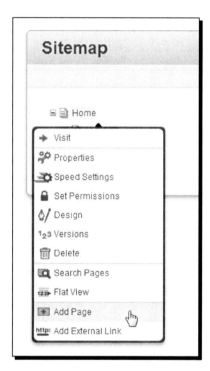

3. Click on **Add Page** to bring the dialog up, where you can select the page type you want, and select **Full**:

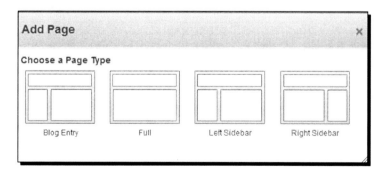

4. In the next screen you have to enter the **Name** of the page. It will automatically suggest the **URL Slug** used to access the page. If you want, you can override the suggested value:

5. Click on the **Add Page** button and you should see the updated site map with the **News** page added as the last page under the home page.

6. The page we just created is going to hold all the news entries together. Let's add one sample entry by clicking on **News** to bring up the menu and select **Add Page** again. Select a page type of your choice and enter a page name. You should have another page underneath news.

What just happened?

After the new pages have been added, you can click on one and select **View** to see the page. There are already a few blocks in the new page, even if you didn't add any of them. concrete5 took all the blocks, which are predefined in the defaults and added them to your new page.

You've also seen that there are different page types, each of which will result in a different page layout. Don't worry if you picked the wrong one; you can always hit the **Design** button in the toolbar while you're in edit mode, to bring up the dialog where you can change the page type at any time.

We're going to add some more blocks to our page in the next *Time for action* section. After that we're going to look at page defaults to help you to understand how some of the blocks automatically appeared in the new page.

When you're logged in, you can always hit **Add Page** in the toolbar on the top. This creates a child page to the current page. To add a top level page, simply visit the home page and add your new page from there. For the purpose of this exercise, we have used the **Sitemap** tool as an alternative way to add a page.

Time for action – adding blocks to a new page

Add new blocks to your page by performing the following steps:

1. Open the **News** page; it already works but we can't see our news entry. How can concrete5 know that we want to have a news list on this page? It can't, so let's help concrete5 and create that list manually.

2. Go into edit mode by clicking on **Edit**.

3. Display the block list by clicking on **Add To Main**.

4. Select **Page List**.

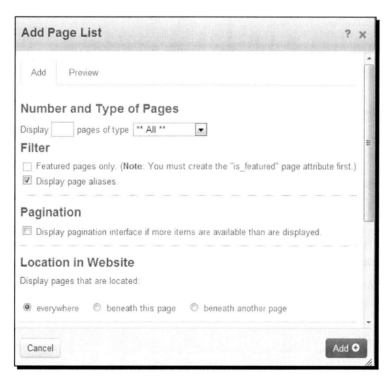

5. Change the option in the **Location in Website** section to **beneath this page**. This makes sure that only pages underneath news will be displayed. All other options can be left the way they are.

6. Click on **Add** to insert the list into your page.

7. Leave the edit mode by clicking on **Editing** and then **Publish My Edits**.

What just happened?

There's a rather simple, but working news section in your site, which we'll improve later by adding some more advanced features.

Even if the website you're creating still looks boring, at least you've got a structure. This makes the design process easier as well, since you can easily add some content to your design and see how it looks in the website:

- If you misspelled a page name, click on it and select **Properties**. You can change the name at any time.

- Selected the wrong page type? No problem, click on a page and hit **Design** and you'll see a dialog where you can select another page type.

Have a go hero – adding more pages

You've seen how pages can be added to represent a news section. The site map should give you a good overview of your site. Try to add all the pages you think you need on your site; whatever you do in the site map it's not going to break anything.

Managing page defaults

There are situations where you might want to put the same block on several pages. This could be a picture or a content block to save you some clicks.

In concrete5 you can manage not only the page content, but also the page type content. What does this mean? Since every page is derived from a page type, they behave like templates. Blocks in the page types are, by default, placed in every new page.

Time for action – adding default blocks to a page type

Perform the following steps to add default blocks to a page type:

1. Go to the dashboard and select **Page Types**:

2. You can see a list with all available page types. Pick the page type **Full** or the one where you'd like to add some default blocks by clicking on the **Defaults** button in the row of the page type of your choice:

3. You'll be redirected to a screen which looks like a normal page, and the alert message on top of the page shows us that we are actually on a page type. Switch to edit mode by clicking on **Edit** in the toolbar:

4. Click on **Add To Main** and select the **Content** block. Enter some content and hit **Add**.
5. Click on **Editing** and then **Publish My Changes**.

What just happened?

By adding a block to the page type defaults, you've created a template-like page, which will be copied to each page you're going to create from the same page type. After this step, you'll have a content block in every new page of that type.

Even if you're using this block in only 90 percent of all cases, you can still benefit from this feature. Removing or modifying a block that has been added by using the page defaults is no problem.

Adding blocks to existing pages

What if you added a block to a page type which is already in use? Blocks that you add to the page type defaults aren't automatically added to existing pages. We'll see how you can add them in the next section.

Time for action – adding blocks to existing pages

1. Go back into edit mode and click on the block you want to copy to the existing pages.
2. Select **Setup on Child Pages**:

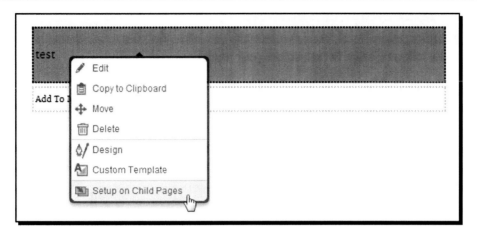

3. Select the pages in the dialog where you want to insert the block. Confirm your selection by clicking on **Update** and all pages you've selected receive a copy of the block.

What just happened?

When we modified our page defaults, we already had some existing pages. We had to execute a few steps to get them to our existing pages.

Please note that if you select a page where the block already exists, it will lead to a duplicate block.

Moving and sorting pages

While you are probably able to create a page structure without making a mistake, I'm not. Luckily it's very easy to move pages around.

Time for action – moving and sorting your pages

Perform the following steps to restructure your pages:

1. Click on **Dashboard** and then **Full Sitemap**.

2. Click on the icon of the page (not the name) you want to move, but don't release the mouse button.

3. You can now drag the item around and change its position by dropping it between two other sitemap items. A line will appear where the page is moved:

4. If you drop the item on top of another page, the following dialog shows up:

5. Instead of just being able to rearrange your page, this dialog allows you to create an alias—a second URL for your page—as well as make copies of pages including its children.

What just happened?

We've discovered some drag-and-drop functionality in concrete5. Whenever you want to restructure your site and the page orders, these tools will help you achieve the task very quickly.

Splitting content into columns

As you've seen, you can use page types to choose between different page layouts. But what if your site looks like a newspaper—has more than 10 different layouts, which are mostly unique, two boxes on the left-hand side of one page, three boxes on the next one, and twice as many on the following page? You could create a page type and template for each of them, but there's a smarter way.

Time for action – creating a multi-column layout

Perform the following steps to give your pages a multi-column layout:

1. Pick a page you've created in the previous section and open it.
2. Activate the edit mode by clicking on **Edit Page**.
3. When you click on **Add To Main**, you should see the already familiar pop-up menu, but this time don't add a new block—select **Add Layout**:

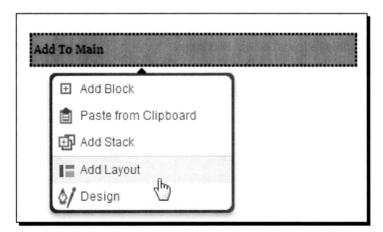

4. After that, the following dialog should pop up:

5. In this pop-up window you've got several fields to enter values:

- ❑ **Columns:** In this field enter the number of columns your layout should have.

- ❑ **Rows:** In this field enter the number of rows you need for your table layout.

- ❑ **Spacing:** If you want to have some space between the columns, enter the value in pixels in this field.

- ❑ **Lock Widths:** Mark this checkbox if you want to avoid accidental changes to the column widths. You can unlock the layout at any time.

- ❑ **Save this style as a new preset:** If you need the same number of columns and rows several times, activate this and you'll be able to reuse it when adding a layout on another page.

6. Click on **Add** when you're done.

7. A layout block has been added to the Main area that contains three subsections:

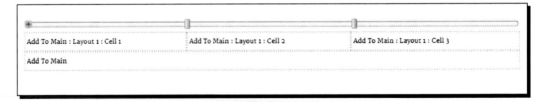

8. The additional areas behave like any other areas, but there are some small differences if you look above the area:

Item	Explanation
	Click on this icon if you want to edit, delete, or unlock/lock a layout.
	Columns in an unlocked layout can be resized by dragging these handles.

What just happened?

You have seen how easily you can split content into several columns. One area has been split into three columns to build a newspaper-like page. There's also a way to save these layouts as presets in case you want several pages to have the same column layout.

Keep in mind that with this feature, you can easily create a rather messy looking site. While it gives you some flexibility, you might want to try to use page types first. They make it easier to keep the layout consistent and offer enough flexibility in most cases.

We have reordered blocks with the move feature. A feature that works not only with split areas, but areas in general.

With everything you've read so far, you can create lots of different page layouts without having to write a single line of HTML code.

What you've learned so far gives you the knowledge to create pages for your site with different layouts and different content by using just a few of the tools of concrete5.

 If there's some real content you want to add to your website, feel free to add it now. We won't remove any of the pages we've created, even when we create a new website layout!

Have a go hero – adding more columns and blocks

Before you continue, try to add some blocks to the split areas. Try to build a newspaper-like page with three columns, some content, and pictures. Since we're not working with real newspaper pages, you can also add some videos and show your grandparents what newspapers are going to look like in the future.

If you click on an existing block, you can select **Move** in the pop-up menu. concrete5 will then change the mode and enable the block's drag-and-drop functionality. You can even move blocks from one split area into another.

Copying blocks using the clipboard

If you want to rearrange content on your site, it might happen that you only need one block from one page and would like to have it on a new page. In concrete5 you have something called **clipboard**, which works a lot like the clipboard you're working with on your computer. Let's have a quick look at how you can copy a block from one place to another.

Time for action – copying the block using the clipboard

Perform the following steps to copy the block using the clipboard:

1. Navigate to the page where you have the block you want to copy. Click on the block and select **Copy to Clipboard**:

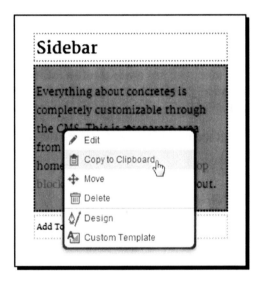

2. Navigate to the page where you want to move the block. Click on the **Add To Area** link where you want to paste the block and select **Paste from Clipboard**:

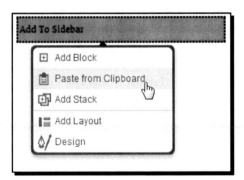

3. A dialog pops up with a list of all blocks in your clipboard. Click on the one you want to insert and you'll immediately see the block in its new place.

What just happened?

We've had a quick look at the way you can copy a block in concrete5. The clipboard in concrete5 isn't integrated into your operating system; it works only in concrete5, but since all the data is stored in the database, you can log out, shut down your computer, and will still find all the blocks in the clipboard. They stay there until you click on the little trash icon next to it to remove them.

Working with stacks

A **stack** is basically a collection of blocks you can use in multiple places on your site. Any kind of block can be part of a stack. Let's create a new stack and add it to a page.

Time for action – working with stacks

Perform the following steps to add stacks to your page:

1. Click on **Dashboard** and then on **Stacks**:

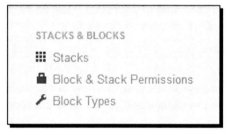

2. You should see a screen like the following, where you create a new stack. Enter a name like shown here:

3. After you've entered the name of your stack, click on **Add** and the new stack will be added to the list. Click on your stack to edit it.

4. Click on **Add Block** and you'll see the list of blocks. Select the content block or any other block you want and enter all the data the block interface is asking for.

5. After you've added a new block, there's a new button called **Approve Changes**. Click on it to confirm the change and you're done creating the stack.

6. Head back to the page where you want to insert the stack. Click on the area where you want to add the stack, but don't click on **Add Block** but rather on **Add Stack**:

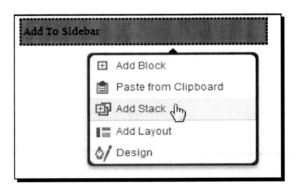

7. Click on **My Stack** and you'll see a new dialog. Here, you can add a single block from the stack or add the whole collection of blocks. We'll simply add all of them.

8. Confirm all the changes by clicking on **Editing** and then on the **Publish My Changes** button.

What just happened?

We've created a stack, which you can use to combine several blocks into one object. A stack can then be placed on several pages, but it always links to its original content. This means that if you change the stack in one place, you'll change it on all pages where you've added it.

Styling with design and CSS

Some blocks already contain options to personalize the look or behavior of it, some blocks don't. However, concrete5 has a feature that uses CSS to customize the look of a block, even if the block developer didn't add any options to support CSS properties—custom colors, fonts, and so on. It's mostly meant as a backup plan for small tweaks to styling, rather than a tool for styling up a site.

You can see the following dialog to edit these CSS properties, when you click on a block you've already added:

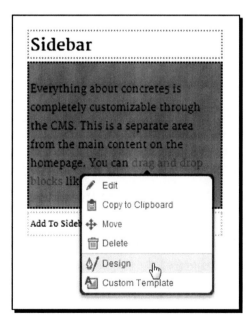

There are several options, which apply different CSS rules to the selected block:

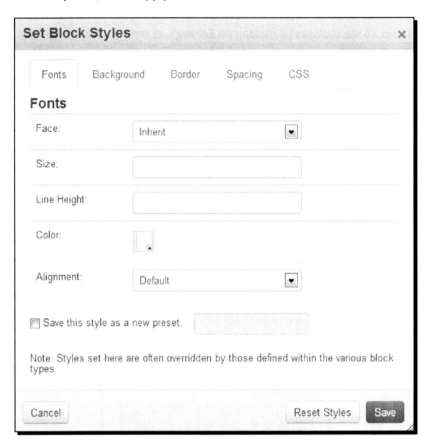

Time for action – styling your blocks

We would like to add an image to a page, but one that looks a bit emphasized, centered, and with a border around it. Perform the following steps to style your blocks:

1. Navigate to the page where you want to add the picture.

2. Go into edit mode.

3. Click on **Add To Main** and select **Add Block**. From the list, pick the **Image** block.

4. Select **Choose Image** to bring up the file manager pictures.

5. In the top right-hand corner you can select a picture from your local hard disk by clicking on **Choose File**. Hit **Upload** if you've selected the file you want to upload.

6. A small dialog appears, where you can perform different actions on the new file:

- **Properties**: A file can have any kinds of properties. This action can be used to add meta information or a simple description to a file. It's not needed in our case.

- **Set**: In concrete5 you have a concept similar to folders but also slightly different. Files are assigned to sets, but unlike folders, one file can be assigned to several sets or even no sets. It's not needed in our case though.

7. Close the dialog by clicking on **Continue** and you should see a new file in the manager.

8. Click on the thumbnail of the new file and select **Choose** to pick the file as the one you want to display in the image block.

9. Hit **Add** to insert the image block.

10. Click on the block after you've added it and select **Design**. You'll see some fields to add predefined CSS rules but also a text field in the CSS tab, where more experienced CSS writers can add their own styles manually.

11. Go to the **Border** tab, set the border style to `solid`, and width to `2px`. In the **Spacing** tab enter `2px` in each padding field and hit **Update**:

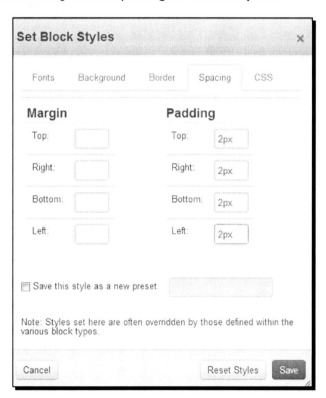

12. Our picture now has a black border, a simple design element you can add without any line of code. You can probably make it look even better:

What just happened?

We've added a picture block, where we uploaded a new picture to the concrete5 file manager from our local hard disk.

We then added some CSS rules by using the concrete5 design feature to add a border around the picture. While this might seem like a nice feature, keep in mind that you'll quickly lose the overview of styles you've applied. As a general rule, try to manage the CSS rules in the theme if you want to change the look of your site and not misuse this feature.

The **Design** dialog is not only available on blocks but also on areas. If you click on **Add Area <Name>**, you can find the **Design** item as well. This allows you to change all blocks within an area, for example, you can change the font face for a whole area.

Have a go hero – customizing more styles

There's a lot more you can do with the **Design** dialog; here are some ideas:

◆ Add font styles, face, size, line height, and change the text color

◆ Insert a background color or picture

◆ Add different border styles to the block

◆ Put some space between the blocks by adding padding and margin

◆ Insert custom CSS rules or add an existing class to a block for more advanced CSS styling

Have a go hero – play around

We've covered a bunch of different things to manage your website's content. We didn't look at all the different tools, screens, or buttons, but you will soon realize that what you've seen should be enough for most situations.

But before we continue, try to make sure you're familiar with the following tools. Try to achieve these tasks:

◆ Add a page and edit some of its properties such as the title, the URL, and so on.

◆ Each page can have a description, which will be picked up by search engines. You can find it in the properties as well. You can find this in the properties of each page, add a meta title or description and save the changes, and search engines will pick them up. Here's a little hint:

- Move and delete pages by using the **Sitemap** option of **Dashboard**.
- Add, remove, and reorder blocks.
- Upload, delete, and set properties for your files in the file manager.
- Try to use these files in file, download, and videos blocks.
- Add a form with various controls and submit data that you'll later find in the **Dashboard** under the **Reports** section.
- Put blocks in the clipboard or a stack.

Once you've successfully managed to execute these tasks, you should be familiar with managing concrete5 page content.

Summary

We've already looked at everything you need to manage the content of your website. Using the features in this chapter you can create almost any page content you want.

In this chapter we've learned how to add and edit blocks, and the basics you need to know to update content on your site. We've also worked with the site map to manage pages in case you need more subpages or want to remove some of them.

We also had a quick look at two features that can be handy but shouldn't be used too much since they also help you to create a mess. The layout features allow you to split content into columns and the design features allows you to add custom CSS properties without modifying any files.

We've also created a new stack, a collection of blocks that you can place on different pages, but update on one. A nice feature that makes it possible to share content across several pages.

3

Managing Permissions

In this chapter, we're going to look at the most important permissions you can manage to restrict the access to your site.

These are the topics that we'll cover:

◆ Creating new groups and users

◆ Granting access to parts of the dashboard to a group and to a number of users

◆ Allowing users of a group to edit the content of your site

◆ Creating a protected area on your site that is not available to the public

◆ Reducing the number of blocks available to a certain group

◆ A quick look at the advanced permission mode where you can lock down a single area or block and more

Managing basic permissions

When you run a website, you might want to have some personalized users with access to edit the page content, but without the rights to update all site settings. In this chapter, we're going to create a group that you can assign to any number of users, if you want to give them edit access.

We're also going to create a section in your website that is only visible to registered users. A first step towards an extranet!

Adding users and groups

Users usually come and go; to keep the handling as easy as possible, we're going to create a group for everything, even if there's just one user in it.

Time for action – adding groups

Carry out the following steps to add a group:

1. Log in to concrete5 and click on the **Dashboard** button.
2. Select **User Groups** in the member function box on the left-hand side.
3. Click on **Add Group** to bring up the dialog to create a new group.
4. The screen to create new groups is straightforward, as follows:

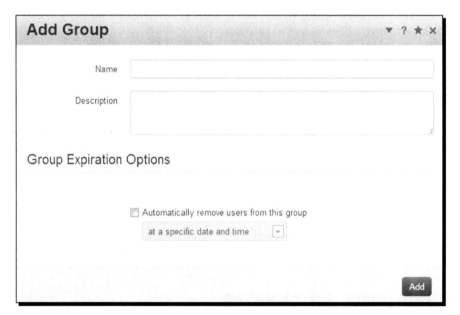

5. Enter Editors in the **Name** field and a description if you want. Click on **Add** to create the group.

6. Create another group named `Members`, which we'll use to manage the users with access to our secret website section. The final result should look similar to the following:

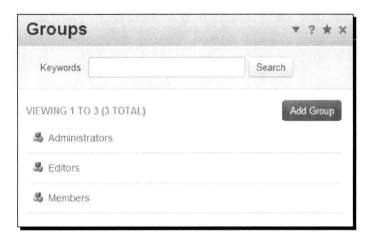

What just happened?

We created two new groups, which we'll use during the process of building a small community website. One for the users with access to manage the website content and another one for members who only get access to the normal website view without any access to the dashboard or in-site editing toolbar.

Group expiration options

You might have noticed the expiration settings at the bottom (see the preceding **Add Group** screenshot) when you created the groups. We don't need them at this point, but they can be quite handy. Imagine you want to build a website where you sell subscriptions. How do you make sure people have to pay after a certain period has passed by? You just set an expiration option and you're done! There are two different ways to do this, which are as follows:

- **Automatically remove users from this group at a specific date and time**: Enter a fixed date on which the members should be removed or deactivated from the group.

- **Automatically remove users from this group once a certain amount of time has passed**: Set a period after which the members of the group have to be removed or deactivated.

Time for action – adding users

1. Go to the **Dashboard** and select **Search Users**.

2. Click on **Add User** and you see a screen similar to the following screenshot:

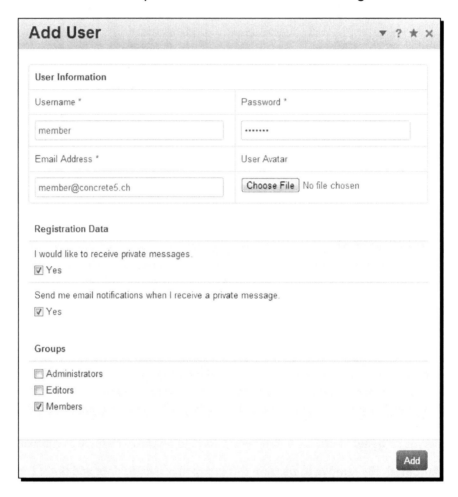

3. The first three fields are mandatory. Enter your user credentials for the account you want to use as a member of your site in **Username**, **Password** and **Email Address**. Tick **Members** in the **Groups** section to assign the user the necessary group.

4. Click on **Add** to confirm everything.

5. Create another user who you want to use as an **editor** for your site. You should now have three users at the end, as shown in the following screenshot:

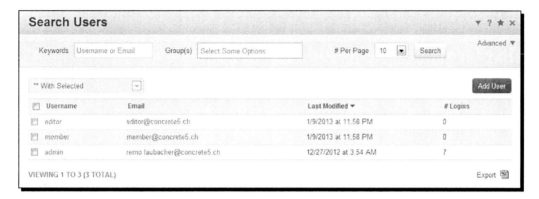

What just happened?

We've created two new users and assigned them to groups, which we'll use to allow them to edit the page and view a protected section that we're going to create. They are now visible when you have a look at the user section in the dashboard. In case the list gets bigger, concrete5 offers several tools, including the following:

♦ A search box to find a username or e-mail address

♦ Filters to display users belonging to one or more groups

♦ An Excel export if you want to process the user data manually

Working with user attributes

When you created the new account, you've probably seen the box named **Registration Data**. Almost every website has different needs, while you need a username, password and a unique e-mail address for all of them, you probably don't need the same user attributes on every site.

concrete5 has a flexible and extendable attribute system that allows you to create and assign attributes not just to users but also pages and files.

During account creation, you will have seen the two default attributes about message processing created during the installation process. We don't need them at this point, but in case you want to keep track of more data about your users, create attributes and you'll have a flexible system to manage your user data. We're going to add page attributes, which work the same way as user attributes, in *Chapter 5*, *Creating Your Own Theme*. If you can't wait, go to the **Dashboard** and click on **Attributes** in the members box, where you'll see everything you need to delete, edit, and add attributes.

Granting sitemap and file manager permissions

By default, a group has no rights. To give a group access to edit your website's pages, we have to grant them more rights. First, let's make sure that they get access to the sitemap.

Time for action – assigning sitemap permissions

Carry out the following steps to grant sitemap permissions:

1. Focus on the **Intelligent Search** box in the toolbar on top and type `Task Permissions`.

2. Click on the first entry in the list called **Task Permissions**.

3. Our new groups don't have any rights yet; click on **Access Sitemap** to display the dialog where you can manage the permissions for this task.

4. In this dialog you can either include or exclude a group from a certain task. Click on the plus icon on the right-hand side in the first box, **Included** and you'll see the following dialog:

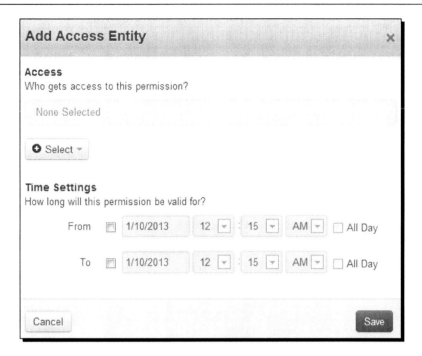

5.   Click on **Select** and then **Group**. You'll see a list of available groups; select **Editors** and then confirm the change by clicking on **Save**. Click on **Save** again to update the permission list and click on **Save** once more to confirm the change. Editors should now be listed in **Access Sitemap**.

What just happened?

We've granted our editors the right to access the sitemap. This allows them to move and delete pages using the in-site editing toolbar. They don't have access to the dashboard sitemap yet though. You'll find an explanation about granting partial access to the dashboard later in this chapter.

When we've allowed our editors to access the sitemap, we've only selected the first task in the list. If you have another look at the task permissions, you can see that there are a lot more tasks you can work with. You can grant the right to install packages, perform backups, empty the trash, and more. Most of them don't need to be changed, but if you have to, feel free to make any change you want.

Now that you've allowed your editors to access the sitemap, you have to grant them access to the file manager. They need to be able to add pictures and files to the pages they create, don't they?

Time for action – granting file manager permissions

1. Focus the Intelligent Search box in the toolbar, type File Manager Permissions, and select **File Manager Permissions**.

2. You can see a list of tasks related to file management. The dialog works the same way as the dialog where you just granted the right to access the sitemap. Click on **Search Files** in **File Manager**, then click on the **Add** link in the first box **Included**. Select the **Editors** group again by clicking on **Select** and then **Group**.

3. As you can see, there are a number of tasks and most of them are useful for an editor. Adding the group manually to each task needs a few clicks, but there's an easier way. Hover the groups next to **Search Files in File Manager** and drag them down to the next task, as shown in the following screenshot:

4. Assign the groups **Administrators** and **Editors** to every task except **View Files,** since **Guest** is already assigned to this task which includes everyone.

5. Once you've assigned all the groups, don't forget to click on **Save** to confirm the changes.

What just happened?

You granted all members of **Editors** access to the file manager. This allows them to upload, delete, and use the files within the pages.

As you've seen when you granted the group the right to access a task, you can also assign a single user and more to a task. concrete5 offers a lot of possibilities when working with permissions but try to avoid having too many different concepts. Avoiding groups might look nice but keep in mind that if you remove and add new users, you'll have to set the permissions again. If you try to work with groups, you can make sure that changing personnel isn't going to cause more work than necessary.

Have a go hero – time restriction for permissions

When we allowed a group to access a task, we saw some options where you can specify a date range. Have a quick look at the following screenshot to see some time related options available when working with permissions by clicking on the clock icon next to a group:

You probably won't need such advanced permissions very often, but try to have a look at them to understand what's possible; you might convince one more customer to work with you because of one little feature which is available out of the box.

Granting page editing permissions

We've seen how we can work with different tasks and allow users and groups to access them. However, the most important right you'll have to grant is the right to edit pages. This will make sure that not only the admin can update content, but also a limited number of users.

Time for action – granting edit access

1. Type permissions & access in the **Intelligent Search** box and select the first entry in the list.
2. Enable the checkbox next to **Editors**.
3. Confirm the change by clicking on **Save**.

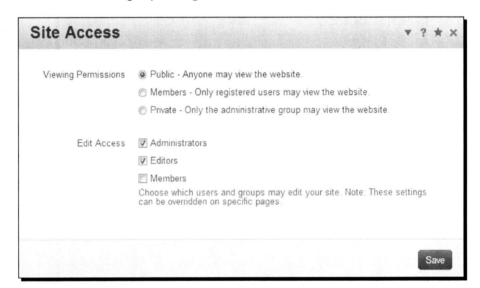

What just happened?

We've now allowed every user who is a part of the group **Editors** to manage the content of your site. Together with the previously changed permissions to access the sitemap and the file manager, you have the basics you'll need to allow a non-administrator to edit content.

If you log in using the user editor, you'll see the editing toolbar on top, but without any access to the dashboard. We'll look at how you can grant partial access to the dashboard later in this chapter.

Managing edit access on a page by page basis

By activating edit access for all members of **Editors**, we allowed them to edit every page in our website. Internally, concrete5 assigns permissions to each page, even with the global setting that we just enabled.

Due to this detailed execution, we can manage permissions on a more precise level, if necessary. You can find the actual permissions concrete5 assigned if you navigate to the sitemap and click on a page in the tree and select **Set Permissions** as shown in the following screenshot:

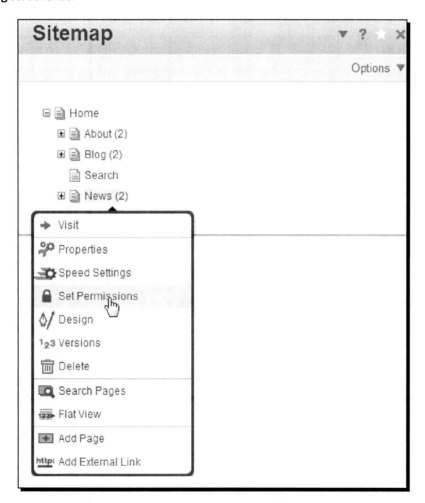

The dialog is split into two different parts; on the bottom, you can see all the groups allowed to edit the page, and on top there's a list of groups able to view this page.

As we globally activated edit access to the group **Editors**, the checkbox for the **Editors** group is ticked for every page by default. However, if you want to revoke the edit right for one page, go ahead and uncheck the checkbox in this dialog, as shown in the following screenshot:

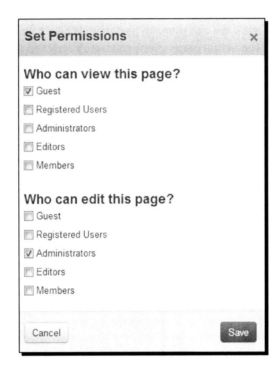

Creating a protected website section

You may have some secret information that you would like to put on the website that only certain members should see. This can be handled with a password protected section.

Time for action – creating a protected website

Carry out the following steps:

1. Navigate to **Dashboard** and then **Full Sitemap**.
2. Create a new page named VIP.
3. Click on the new page and select **Set Permissions**.
4. Uncheck the checkbox next to **Guest** in **Who can view this page**.
5. Tick the checkbox next to **Members** in **Who can view this page**.
6. Click on **Save**.

What just happened?

The sitemap should look similar to the following screenshot:

We removed the guests' right to access our VIP page but allowed members to access it. When you log out, you won't see the VIP page anymore:

You can send users belonging to the members group to the same login page you're using when you want to edit your website: `http://localhost/login/`. Use the member account you've created earlier to log in and a new page will be visible:

That's everything you need to do if you want to protect a page. Every block you place in such a page won't be accessible to users who aren't logged in. A secret guestbook or a personal poem—you decide who gets access to it!

Granting partial dashboard access

The permissions we've set should work for most situations; but as always, there might be an exception where an editor would like to see the hierarchical page tree in the dashboard to get a better overview or access the file manager.

It would be nice if we could allow editors to access the dashboard, but only certain parts of it. We don't want them to delete our users or change the site-wide settings. It takes a few clicks, but we can allow our users to access only a few items in the dashboard.

Time for action – granting partial dashboard access

1. Go to the **Dashboard** and click on **Full Sitemap**.
2. In the sitemap, click on **Options** and then tick the checkbox **Show System Pages** to display the dashboard pages in the sitemap.
3. Click on the **Dashboard** page and click on **Set Permissions**.
4. Tick the checkbox for **Editors** in the upper part, **Who can view this page.**
5. Click on **Save**.

    Notice that the Dashboard page has a complex structure of subpages. When setting permissions for the Dashboard page, every subpage inherits those permissions. This means that we granted access to every item in the dashboard, exactly what we didn't want to do. While the inheritance is usually quite handy if you want to change permissions, in this case it leads to a few more clicks. We have to revoke the rights from all the dashboard subpages that we don't want the editors to have access to.

6. Expand the dashboard page by clicking on the small plus icon in front of the page name.
7. Expand the **Sitemap** as well.
8. Click on the subpage **Members** and then click on **Set Permissions**.
9. Uncheck the checkbox for **Editors** in the **Who can view this page?** section.
10. Do the same for the following pages that are under **Dashboard**:
    - **Pages & Themes**
    - **Stacks & Blocks**
    - **Extend concrete5**
    - **System & Settings**

What just happened?

As long as you didn't get a tennis elbow from all the clicks, you should now have a dashboard which is partially accessible by your editors. When you log in to concrete5 with your editor account, you'll only see a part of the dashboard, as shown in the following screenshot:

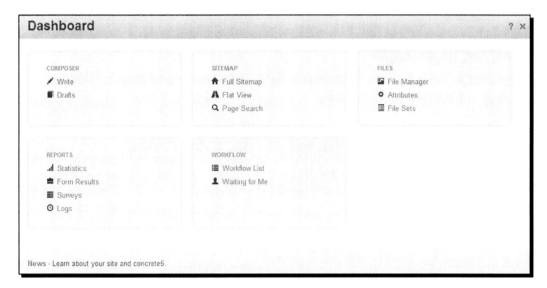

You're of course free to set the dashboard access in a different way. If you want, you can even change the permission on a sub-subpage of the dashboard. The concept of page permissions is always the same, no matter what page or page level you are on.

Restricting block access

By default, every user that has the permission to edit a page can use any installed block. It might happen, that this list gets longer than necessary and confuses someone or it could also be that you want to make sure that not everyone can use any blocks. No matter what intention you have, you can use the following functionality to limit the available blocks for a certain group.

Time for action – restricting access to blocks

1. If you're still logged in with the user `editor`, log out and log in again with `admin`.

2. Focus the **Intelligent Search** box and type `Block & Stack Permissions` and click on the first entry in the list.

3. Click on **Add Blocks** to display the groups allowed to add new blocks.

4. Switch to the second tab **Details**.

5. Next to **Editors**, change the value to **Custom**.

6. Select the blocks you want the editors to use and confirm the change by clicking on **Save**.

What just happened?

We've used the block permissions to restrict the available blocks. A few simple clicks and the list of available blocks is a lot clearer.

Working with the advanced permission mode

The permissions you've seen in the previous section should be enough for most websites. However, sometimes you want to restrict access even more. What if you wanted to achieve the following restrictions?

- Restrict the blocks that a user can use
- Hide a single block or area from a user
- Make sure an editor can change content but not publish it

You haven't seen all of it, but anything is possible; you just have to activate the advanced permission mode.

Time for action – activating the advanced permission mode

Carry out the following steps:

1. Navigate to the dashboard.

2. Type advanced permissions in the **Intelligent Search** box and click on the first entry in the list. You'll get to the following screen:

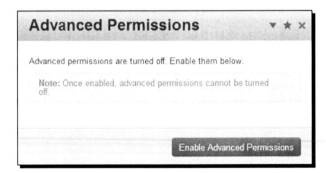

3. Click on the **Enable Advanced Permissions** button to active the advanced mode.

What just happened?

We've enabled the advanced permission mode with a single click and now have the full permission power of concrete5 available. But keep in mind that once the advanced permission mode is active, there's no way back. The advanced permission mode is fine and works well but if you realize that you won't need it, you cannot simply undo the change. It might be wise to test the advanced permission mode on a playground site first and once you know that you really need it, enable it in production.

Managing advanced page permissions

When you open the permissions dialog for a page, you'll see a completely different dialog with a lot more options:

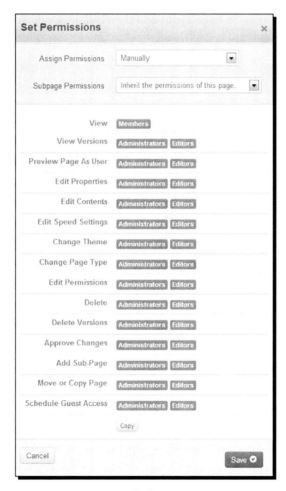

In the preceding screen, you can specify the source of the permissions. You have the following options:

- Use **Manually** in the **Assign Permissions** drop down to set page specific permissions
- You can use **By Area of Site (Hierarchy)** to use the permission from the parent page
- Select **From Page Type Defaults** if you want to use the permissions specified on the page type defaults, the template page

You can also specify the permissions a new subpage gets by using the second drop down. There are two different options:

- Select **Inherit the permissions of this page** if you want to use the permissions from the current page on all new subpages.
- Use **Inherit page type default permissions** to use the permissions specified in the page type defaults. You can manage the page type default permissions if you go to the **Dashboard**, click on **Page Types** and then **Defaults**, which is next to the page type you're using.

Time for action – removing permissions to change permissions

We previously allowed all editors to edit pages. Now that we are using the advanced permissions, our editor has received full permission to edit all page related options. However, we don't want to let editors play around with permissions and therefore want to revoke this right. Carry out the following steps to make sure the editor can't mess around with permissions:

1. Go to the **Dashboard** by clicking on the button in the toolbar on top.
2. Click on **Full Sitemap** to open the sitemap.
3. Click on the **Home** page and then **Set Permissions**.
4. In the permissions dialog, click on **Edit Permissions**.
5. Click on the trash bin next to the **Editors** group.
6. Click on **Save** to confirm the change and close the dialog.
7. Click on **Save** once more to confirm and close the dialog.

What just happened?

We revoked the right to edit permission from the editors group. We did this on the home page, the top-level page of concrete5. By default, every subpage inherits the permissions from this home page; our change has therefore been applied to every page in our site.

Managing area permissions

By default, an area gets its permissions from the page it belongs to. If you need to, you can also set more specific permissions per area. If you navigate to a page in the switch into the edit mode and then click on **Add To Main**, you'll see a menu entry called **Set Permissions**:

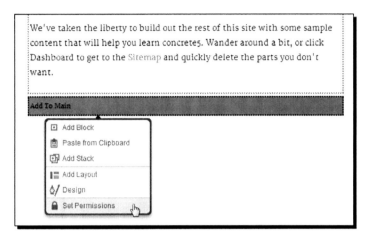

Click on it and you'll see the following dialog:

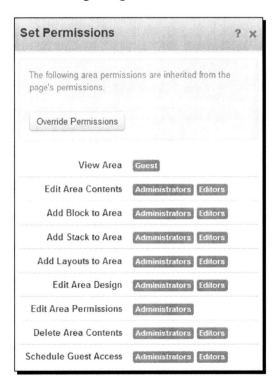

As you can see, all the permissions we've made to the page are displayed as well. This includes the change we've made to the edit permissions entry. As stated in the box at the beginning of the dialog, the permissions are inherited from the page. Click on the button if you're sure you want to override these permissions. As you can see in the preceding screenshot, the granularity of these permissions is rather high; you can restrict a group from seeing an area, or give schedule access to it and restrict the ability to add new blocks, stacks, and more.

Managing block permissions

Just like you can manage permissions per area, there's an option to manage permissions for a single block. While you're in the edit mode, click on a block of your choice and you'll see a menu entry called **Set Permissions** as shown in the following screenshot:

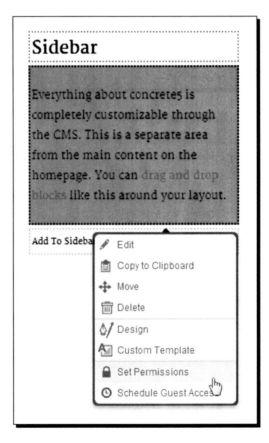

If you click on it, you'll see the following dialog:

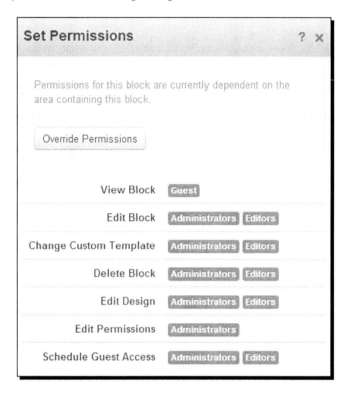

As you can see in the information box, the permissions are inherited from the area by default and just like we did in the area, we can override them and manage our permissions for the block manually.

Managing subpage permissions

concrete5 also allows you to restrict the page types a user is allowed to use for a new subpage.

Time for action – setting subpage permissions

Carry out the following steps:

1. Navigate to the **Dashboard** and click on **Full Sitemap**.
2. Click on the **Home** page and then **Set Permissions**.

3. Click on **Add Sub-Page** and select the second tab, **Details**:

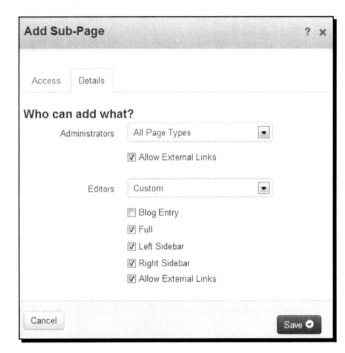

4. In this dialog, select **Custom** next to **Editors** and select all page types you want the editors to use for new subpages.

5. Confirm the new setting by clicking on **Save**.

What just happened?

If you have a person who's only responsible for managing press releases, they only need one page type. By using the advanced permission mode, you can make sure that they don't see and have to be concerned about the other page types.

This is useful if your website gets bigger and has lots of page types. However, keep in mind that it might help your end users, but it also increases the effort necessary to manage the website.

Pop quiz – permissions in concrete5

Q1. Which features are only available when you activate the advanced permission mode?

1. Area permissions to restrict the blocks which can be added to an area.
2. Grant rights to the file manager.
3. Block permissions to specify who can read, write, and delete a specific block.
4. Page permissions to hide a certain page from a user group.
5. Time based page visibility to hide a page for a specified time.

Q2. Can you turn off the advanced permission mode?

1. No, once the permission mode is active, there's no way back.
2. Yes, you can switch back to the basic permission mode.

Summary

In this chapter you've learnt how to configure your concrete5 website.

We've created new groups and users which we then granted a few permissions. These permissions made sure that an editor has access to certain parts of concrete5 such as the editing system as well as the file manager and the sitemap, but doesn't have the right to change system settings.

We've used the built in permission system to add a protected page which is only visible to a user part of a specific group.

We then looked at permissions and created users without global administration rights to edit the website.

4
Managing Add-ons

concrete5 ships with a bunch of built-in blocks to build a basic site without adding any additional components. However, the deeper you get into concrete5 the more you'll realize that you want more features.

Thankfully, there's a marketplace with some free and some commercial add-ons to extend concrete5 without having any development skills.

We are going to look at the structure of add-ons to learn about their parts in order to get a first impression about how an add-on looks under the hood. Even if you don't intend to build your own blocks or packages, this helps you to understand the basics of concrete5 and makes it easier to help and support your customers.

In this chapter we're going to look at the following topics:

- ◆ A few words about what an add-on actually is
- ◆ The installation of a new add-on from the marketplace
- ◆ The manual installation process of an add-on
- ◆ A quick look at the basic structure of a theme and block

Introduction to add-ons

A concrete5 add-on is basically a directory with a bunch of files. Everything you need is located within a single directory. For most add-ons, you only have to click on one button to install it.

There are two main kinds of packages in the marketplace; one that installs a theme and maybe a few block templates, and the rest which will install a block, a single page, a job, or anything else you can extend in concrete5. We're going to have a quick look at themes and block packages in this chapter.

Installing add-ons from the marketplace

If everything works fine, you can use the dashboard to install new add-ons without ever leaving your site.

Time for action – installing an add-on

Carry out the following steps for installing an add-on:

1.   Go to your dashboard and click on **Extend concrete5** in the bottom-left corner.

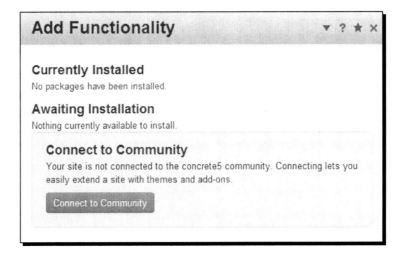

2.   Before you can access the marketplace, you have to connect your site to the `concrete5.org` community. Click on **Connect to Community**. You're redirected to a screen where you can log in using your `concrete5.org` account.

3.   In case you don't have an account on `concrete5.org` yet, click on the **Register** button shown here:

 This has nothing to do with the user accounts you've already created within your site. This is an account for concrete5.org. You can use one account to connect all your sites to the marketplace; you can also use it to access the support forums on concrete5.org.

4. Enter your username, e-mail, and a password which you have to confirm, and select the checkbox to confirm that you've read the terms of use and then click on **Sign In**. Here's an example:

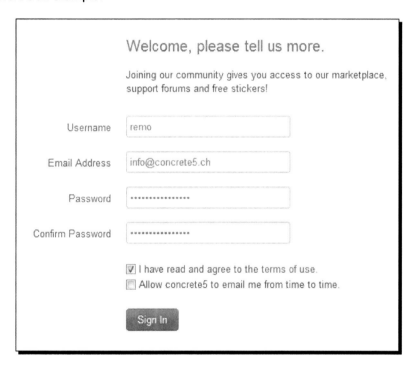

5. You should get a confirmation that your site is connected to the concrete5.org community. There's a link called **add-ons** at the bottom of the screen. Click on it and you'll see a screen called **Browse Add-Ons**.

6. Search for an add-on you want, such as, for example `Gallery Block`, click on it, and confirm it by clicking on **Download & Install**. The new add-on will be installed shortly afterwards.

Time for action – uninstalling an add-on

Carry out the following steps if you want to remove an add-on:

1. You don't like the add-on you just installed? Go to **Extend concrete5** again and locate the previously installed add-on. Click on the **Edit** button next to the add-on.

2. At the bottom, you can find a button **Uninstall Package**, click on it, and you'll see a new screen where you have to confirm the action. If you enable the checkbox **Yes, remove the package's directory from the installation directory**, concrete5 will remove the directory and files of the package as well. Most add-ons are pretty small; it usually doesn't hurt to keep the package files.

What just happened?

By connecting your site to the `concrete5.org` marketplace, you gained direct access to all add-ons uploaded to the marketplace. We've installed an add-on and also uninstalled it. The process to install a theme works the same way; click on **themes** at the bottom in the dashboard and you'll get a list of available themes.

Have a go hero – installing more add-ons

There are plenty of add-ons in the marketplace. It might help you to know some of them in case you run into a requirement in the future. Why not have a closer look at the marketplace and install a few more add-ons?

Manually installing an add-on

The automatic installation process depends on a few PHP modules, such as cURL which if missing, will make it impossible to install an add-on using the preceding procedure. In case you aren't sure if cURL is enabled on your server, go to *Chapter 11, Deployment and Configuration* and look at the *Time for action – getting PHP information* section. Once you've created the file described in that section, you can see some information about cURL if it's installed. In case it isn't, contact your host and ask if they can install it. But don't worry if you can't use cURL, we can always install an add-on manually.

Time for action – installing an add-on manually

Carry out the following steps to install an add-on manually:

1. Go to `http://www.concrete5.org` and click on **Marketplace** at the top.

2. Find the add-on that you want to install. You can search for `AddThis` for example, and click on the **Details** button.

3. Scroll to the bottom of the details page for the selected add-on and click on the **Download Archive** link. Pay attention to the **Work With** reference as not every add-on works with every version.

4. On the next screen, click on **Download Now**. If there are multiple versions available, you'll see a list where you can pick them right now. If you work with an up-to-date version of concrete5, you can usually go with the latest version.

5. Extract the downloaded ZIP file into the packages folder of your concrete5 site. If you're working with a default Bitnami setup, the folder is `C:\BitNami\wampstack-5.4.10-0\apache2\htdocs\packages`.

6. Go back to your site's dashboard.

7. Click on **Extend concrete5**.

8. At the bottom, there's a list named **Awaiting Installation**. In that list, you can find all add-ons you've placed in the packages directory. Simply click on the **Install** button next to it and it will be installed.

What just happened?

We have found an add-on on the marketplace, downloaded the add-on, and manually installed the add-on through the extend functionality. By manually downloading and extracting the add-on, you've avoided the need for a few PHP modules which aren't installed on every host.

If you manually install an add-on, you're also less likely to run into file system permission problems because you're moving the files on your own. There are a few hints about moving your site to a Linux server in *Chapter 11, Deployment and Configuration,* where we also quickly look at the file permissions. The user account the web server uses has usually only very few rights to reduce the potential security risk. However, this can also make it more difficult for web applications to execute certain commands on the server, such as downloading and extracting files.

Neither file system problems nor missing PHP modules are very common issues though. It might help you to understand how the installation process works, but if the integrated marketplace works for you, there's no reason not to use it.

Working with theme add-ons

A theme is responsible for the look of your website. concrete5 ships with four default themes. We can choose between those themes. You can see them when you navigate to **Dashboard** and then click on **Themes**. You can see all the default themes on the following screenshot:

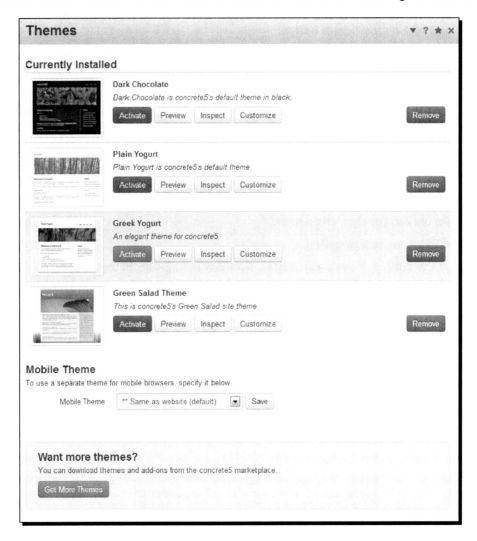

A theme isn't restricted to a certain layout structure such as a blog. concrete5 themes can be built using any HTML and CSS code you want. You can even create your JavaScript files on the fly. You therefore find lots of different layouts in the marketplace and there are pretty much no limits, so you can build whatever you like.

You can activate one of the default themes by clicking on **Activate**. Confirm the activation on the next screen and your website changes its layout immediately. If you're working on an active site, you might want to hit **Preview** first to see how your page is going to look with the new theme.

Parts of a theme

We're going to create a theme in the next chapter, but before we start creating our own layout, a few words about the way pages and their page types are organized in concrete5.

When you click on **Inspect**, you'll see a dialog like the following screenshot where some elements of the theme will be displayed:

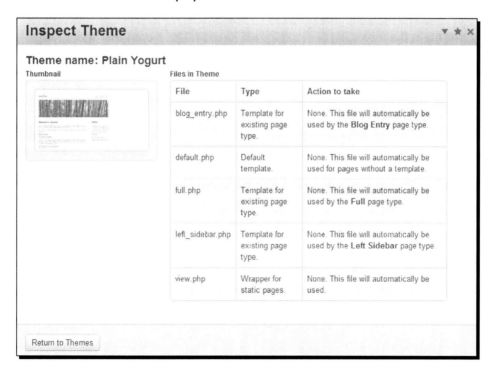

Each theme contains at least one template, the `default.php` file which will be used for a page type without a template. The following illustration shows you the difference between a page type and template:

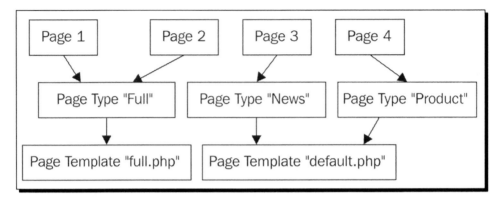

Each page has one page type. If there's a file in the theme with the same name as the page type, it will be used and therefore has its own layout. For every page type without a matching file in the theme, `default.php` will be used. This means that several page types can share one layout. In the preceding illustration, **News** and **Product** both have the same layout.

Theme file structure

Not every theme contains the same files but there are some files which you'll find in most of the themes. We're going to create a complete theme in the next chapter but just to give you a first impression about the basic structure of a theme without going into all the details. This can be helpful to understand concrete5 a little bit better, even if you don't intend to create your own theme.

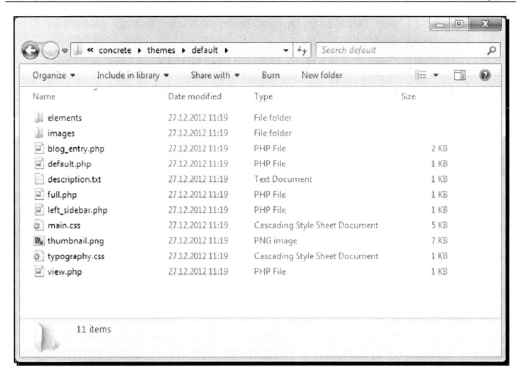

Most themes contain more or less the same files; the preceding screenshot shows you the most common files. Here's a list explaining the directories and files shown in the preceding screenshot:

- `elements`: This directory usually contains two files, which are `header.php` and `footer.php`. They are used to make sure you don't have to add a header and footer to every template you create. They are optional though.

- `images`: Most themes use a few pictures, and put them in this directory.

- `blog_entry.php`: This is the default template file used for blog posts.

- `default.php`: This is the default file used by concrete5 to render your page.

- `description.txt`: This file is used when you install a theme; it contains the name and a short description.

- `full.php`: This is like `default.php` a template, but only used by full pages.

- `left_sidebar.php`: This is another template for the this lacks clarity.

- `main.css`: The CSS file in concrete5 themes is usually called `main.css`. You aren't forced to call your CSS file `main.css` though.

- `thumbnail.png`: This is only displayed in the dashboard to make it easier to identify your theme.

- `typography.css`: This is a second CSS file used by the page but also by the content block for a proper preview of your text.

- `view.php`: This is a special template used for single pages which you have to create programmatically.

Working with block add-ons

We've already seen a few blocks in the previous chapters. In case you forgot, a block is basically an element you can place in an area. Thanks to the really extensible architecture of concrete5, it's quite easy to create a new block and add new functionality to your website.

Blocks are just like anything in concrete5 built using the **Model-View-Controller (MVC)** pattern. This makes sure that every element in concrete5 follows the same structure. A developer who builds add-ons for concrete5 should have experience with object-oriented programming and the MVC pattern.

Understanding the MVC pattern isn't very difficult but helps pretty much any developer. It basically makes sure that the layout (view) is in a file, split apart from the logic (controller) and the data (model). You can find more information about the pattern on Wikipedia: `http://en.wikipedia.org/wiki/Model_View_Controller`.

Block structure

What files does a block need?

This goes a bit deeper but might still be handy for a non-developer to know. Just by knowing where the files are located can help you to make some minor modifications to blocks but remember one thing: never modify anything in the `/concrete` directory. We'll look at the correct way of making changes to the core blocks in *Chapter 6, Customizing Block Layouts*.

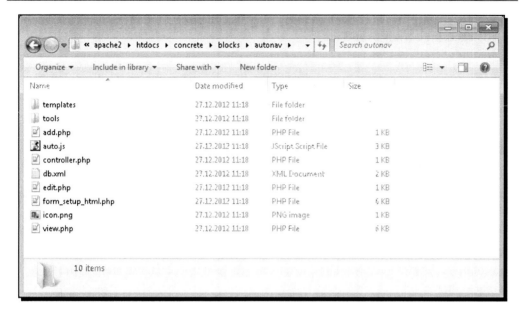

The preceding screenshot shows you the files a basic block has, and the following are their purposes:

- `templates`: A block can have different layouts. A picture gallery might use a pop-up to display the picture or some JavaScript for a more dynamic design. You'd find these block layouts here.

- `tools`: Some blocks use AJAX in their interface. These AJAX scripts are usually located in this directory.

- `add.php`: This is the file used for the block dialog when you add a new instance of a block.

- `auto.js`: This is an automatically added JavaScript file when you add or edit a block.

- `controller.php`: This is where all the magic happens; processing your data, converting your input, saving it to the database, and so on.

- `db.xml`: Most blocks have their own tables; you can find the table definition in this file.

- `edit.php`: When you edit an existing block, this is the file used for the interface.

- `form_setup_html.php`: As most blocks work almost the same way, whether you add or edit them, they share parts of their interface by moving it into this file.

- ◆ `icon.png`: This is a little icon measuring 16 x 16 pixels used in the block list when choosing a block to add.

- ◆ `view.php`: This file renders the block output.

- ◆ `view.css`: This file is not needed in the `autonav` block but IS often present. It contains CSS instructions used by the block output file `view.php`.

Packages

A package is basically a container for elements such as blocks, themes, attribute types, jobs, and so on. You can use it to wrap a theme, resources, and blocks into a single package. This is mostly useful if you intend to build a big add-on where all the elements are connected together.

By using a package, you make add-ons easier to handle and install. You can also make the installation process a bit more solid by extending the package's installer method to check the requirements.

You can easily recognize a package by looking at its structure, which is shown in the following screenshot:

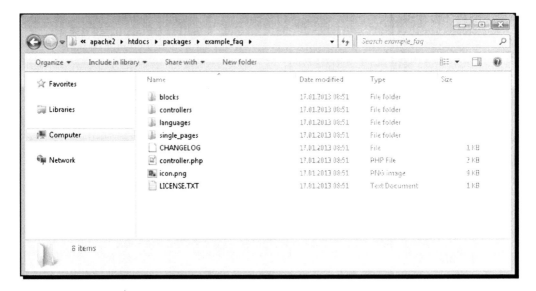

There are several indications telling you that you're looking at a package and not just a block or theme:

- There's a subdirectory called `blocks` or `themes` or many of the directory names you can find in the root of your site.
- The controller is the only PHP file you can find in the root. A block would at least need a file called `view.php`.

 Every add-on in the marketplace is built as a package to make the handling as easy as possible. No matter if there's just a single block in it or a complex structure of blocks, single pages, jobs, and more, it's called a package.

Pop quiz – what's a package?

Q 1. concrete5 allows you to use packages; what's their purpose?

1. Wrapping different elements such as themes and blocks into a single element for easy handling and deployment.
2. Preparing your concrete5 site for deployment to another server.
3. Creating an installer for your add-on where you can check the requirements and create concrete5 objects that your extension needs to work.
4. Preparing a concrete5 extension to be published in the official concrete5 marketplace.

Summary

While there's a lot more you can extend in concrete5 by using a package, blocks and themes are the ones you'll most likely need on a daily basis when you work with concrete5. A package could contain controllers, single pages, events, and a lot more to extend almost anything you want without touching the core. You haven't reached the end after you've gone through themes and blocks!

We've had a quick look at the marketplace; you should know how to install add-ons automatically and also manually if necessary.

You should have a basic understanding about the structure of themes, blocks, and packages. We're going to cover all of them in the next few chapters, but make sure you know what an add-on directory looks like. Following the same pattern as every concrete5 developer keeps the process simple and clean for everybody.

5
Creating Your Own Theme

In this chapter, we're going to change the layout of the site we've created. To achieve this, we will convert an HTML file into a concrete5 theme. This means that we have to replace and insert a few lines of PHP code to make things a bit more dynamic. However, you'll see that the basic conversion process is rather easy and quick; creating a concrete5 theme does only require very little PHP skill and almost no time.

Some code snippets are just modifications to other snippets in this chapter. If you want to re-create the theme code on your own, you have to follow each step and follow the instructions precisely. If you're in a hurry, at the end of the chapter you'll find a link from where you can download the final code used in this chapter.

In this chapter, you'll learn how to create concrete5 themes by going through the follow topics:

- A simple example showing you how to convert an existing HTML to a concrete5 theme

- An explanation and more examples about page types

- A number of snippets that can help you to get more out of your theme

- An example that shows you the use of attributes to add a page-specific background picture

- How to use customizable styles to allow certain CSS properties to be changed in the dashboard

Starting with a new layout

Before we start creating a concrete5 theme we need a layout. In this book, we're going to use a simple layout without any pictures to keep the code as short as possible—it's about concrete5, not about HTML and CSS.

If you don't have the time for an exercise, you can use your own layout. With good knowledge about the basic technologies of concrete5, you should be able to amend the instructions in this chapter to match your own layout. If you don't feel very comfortable working with PHP you should probably use the printed HTML code in this chapter.

Here's a screenshot of what our site is going to look like once we've finished our theme:

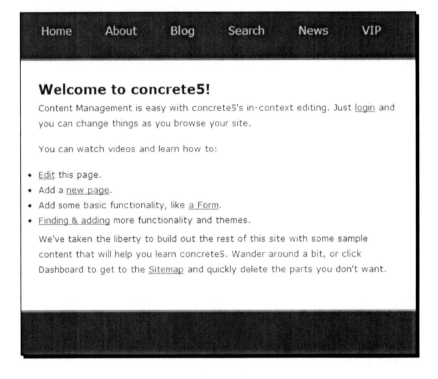

While this layout isn't very pretty, it has an easy structure; navigation on top and a big content area where we can insert any kind of block we want. In case you're using your own layout, try to use one with a simple structure; navigation on top or on the left with one big place for the content, and try to avoid Flash.

Downloading the example code

You can download the example code files for all Packt books you have purchased from your account at http://www.packtpub.com. If you purchased this book elsewhere, you can visit http://www.packtpub. com/support and register to have the files e-mailed directly to you.

The HTML code

Let's have a look at the HTML code:

```
<!DOCTYPE html>
<html lang="en">
    <head>
        <title>concrete5 Theme</title>
        <meta http-equiv="Content-Type" content="text/
html;charset=utf-8" />
        <style type="text/css" media="screen">@import "main.css";</
style>
    </head>
    <body>

        <div id="wrapper">
            <div id="page">
                <div id="header_line_top"></div>
                <div id="header">
                    <ul class="nav-dropdown">
                        <li><a href="#">Home</a></li>
                        <li><a href="#">Test</a></li>
                        <li><a href="#">About</a></li>
                    </ul>
                </div>
                <div id="header_line_bottom"></div>
                <div id="content">
                    <p>Paragraph 1</p>
                    <p>Paragraph 2</p>
                    <p>Paragraph 3</p>
                </div>
                <div id="footer_line_top"></div>
                <div id="footer"></div>
                <div id="footer_line_bottom"></div>
            </div>
        </div>

    </body>
</html>
```

There are three highlighted lines in the preceding code:

- ◆ The CSS import: This is to keep the layout instructions separated from the HTML elements; we've got all the CSS rules in a different file named `main.css`. This is also how almost all concrete5 themes are built.

- ◆ The header block contains the navigation. As we're going to apply some styles to it, make sure it has its own ID. Using an ID also improves the performance when using CSS and JavaScript to access an element, as an ID is unique.

- ◆ The same applies to the content block. Make sure it has a unique ID.

> Most web technologies we use nowadays are standardized in one way or another. Currently, the most important organization is W3C. They also offer tools to validate your code.
>
> Checking your code is never a bad idea. Navigate to `http://validator.w3.org/` and enter the address of the website you want to check or in this case, as your website isn't accessible by the public, click on **Validate by Direct Input** and paste the HTML code to see if there are any mistakes. While it should be fairly easy to produce valid HTML code, things are a bit tricky with CSS. Due to some old browser bugs, you're often forced to use invalid CSS rules. There's often a way to rebuild the layout to avoid some invalid rules but often this isn't the case—you won't be doomed if something isn't 100 percent valid but you're on the safer side if it is.

CSS rules

As mentioned earlier, all CSS rules are placed in a file named `main.css`. Let's have a look at all CSS rules you have to put in our CSS file:

```
/* global HTML tag rules */
html, body, div, pre, form, fieldset, input, h1, h2, h3, h4, h5, h6,
p, textarea, ul, ol, li, dl, dt, dd, blockquote, th, td {
    margin: 0;
    padding: 0;
}
p {
    margin: 5px 0px 15px 0px;
}
html {
    height: 100%;
}
body {
    background-color: #989898;
    height: 100%;
```

```
}

/* layout rules */
#wrapper {
    margin: 0 auto;
    width: 980px;
    text-align: left;
    padding-top: 35px;
}

#page {
    background: #FFFFFF;
    float: left;
    width: 960px;
    padding: 5px;
    -moz-box-shadow: 0 0 15px black;
    -webkit-box-shadow: 0 0 15px black;
    box-shadow: 0 0 15pxblack;
    border-radius: 10px;
}
/* header */
#header {
    background: #262626;
    border-radius: 10px 10px 0px 0px;
    height: 75px;
}
#header_line_top {
    background: #262626;
    height: 0px;
}
#header_line_bottom {
    background: #e64116;
    height: 3px;
}
/* content */
#content {
    min-height: 300px;
    padding: 30px;
    color: #1E1E1E;

    font-family: verdana, helvetica, arial;
    font-size: 13px;
    line-height: 22px;
}
```

```
/* footer */
#footer {
    background: #262626;
    height: 75px;
    border-radius: 0px 0px 10px 10px;
}
#footer_line_top {
    background: #e64116;
    height: 3px;
}
#footer_line_bottom {
    background: #262626;
    height: 0px;
}
/* header navigation */
#header ul{
    margin: 0px;
    padding: 20px;
}
#header ul li {
    float: left;
    list-style-type: none;
}
#header ul li a {
    margin-right: 20px;
    display: block;
    padding: 6px 15px 6px 15px;
    color: #ccc;
    text-decoration: none;
    font-family: verdana, helvetica, arial;
}
#header ul li a:hover {
    color: white;
}
```

Converting HTML and CSS to a concrete5 theme

We've got our HTML and CSS files, and now we want them to be part of a new concrete5 theme with two editable areas, one for the content and one for the header. We will ignore the footer for now.

Time for action – creating the concrete5 theme header

Carry out the following steps:

1. Directly in the root of your site, in the `themes` directory, and in case of bitnami in the `htdocs` directory, create a new directory named `c5book`, but any other name is fine as long as you're using letters and underscores, and avoid the special characters available on your keyboard.

2. Create a thumbnail of your site measuring 120 x 90 pixels and save it as `thumbnail.png` within your theme directory.

3. Create a file named `description.txt` in the new directory by using a text editor, such as Notepad.

4. Open the file and enter the name of the theme in the first line and the description on the second line. Its content should look like the following:

   ```
   c5book Theme
   Concrete5 Theme by Remo Laubacher
   ```

5. Save and close the file. You should have a structure like the one shown in the following screenshot:

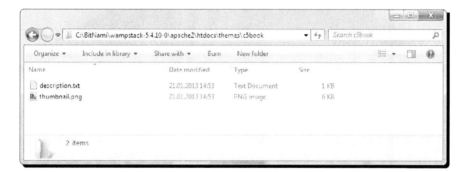

6. As we're going to create several page layouts sharing the same header and footer, let's create a directory named `elements` for these common files.

7. We are going to split a part of the HTML code into a file called `header.php`. To do this, create a file named `header.php` in a new subdirectory called `elements` and insert the preceding HTML code, including the `DIV` element with the ID `header_line_bottom`, but look closely as we had to change a few lines.

   ```php
   <?php
   defined('C5_EXECUTE') or die('Access Denied.');
   ?>
   ```

```
<!DOCTYPE html>
<html lang="<?php echo LANGUAGE?>">
    <head>
        <meta http-equiv="Content-Type" content="text/
html;charset=<?php echo APP_CHARSET ?>" />
        <link rel="stylesheet" media="screen" type="text/css"
href="<?php echo $this->getStyleSheet('main.css') ?>" />

        <?php  Loader::element('header_required'); ?>
    </head>
    <body>

        <div id="wrapper">
            <div id="page">
                <div id="header_line_top"></div>
                <div id="header">
                    <?php
                    $a = new GlobalArea('Header Nav');
                    $a->display($c);
                    ?>
                </div>
                <div id="header_line_bottom"></div>
```

What just happened?

There are a few highlighted lines in the preceding code, which we modified in order to use our HTML code in concrete5:

- The first line makes sure you can't directly call our file to ensure that everything is running in the concrete5 context.

- The next line specifies the content type and uses the constant APP_CHARSET to get the correct encoding, which by default is utf8.

- The next highlighted line includes our CSS files the proper concrete5 way. You can avoid the PHP function if you want to but you'll get access to a nice concrete5 feature if you use $this->getStyleSheet(); thanks to which you can easily change the properties of your CSS file in a nice interface without touching a single line of code. More information on this is available in the *Creating customizable themes* recipe.

- Loader::element makes sure the concrete5 in-site editing toolbar is included. This is necessary to display the in-site editing toolbar, once you're logged in to your site.

◆ The last highlighted line defines the area where blocks can be placed. The string `Header Nav` is what the user will see while editing the page. Please note that we've used `GlobalArea` and not `Area`. Using `GlobalArea` adds an area of which the content is identical on all pages using this area. If you use `Area`, you'll get an editable area which has a different content on each page.

We've split a part of our HTML code into a new file named `header.php`. While this isn't mandatory, most themes follow this procedure and you probably should too, as long as you don't have any good reason not to.

Even if you just have one page layout, you never know what will happen next and keeping your files clean and short makes them easier to read as well.

Let's create the next element, the footer!

Time for action – creating the concrete5 theme footer

Carry out the following steps:

1. In the `elements` directory, create a new file named `footer.php`.

2. From the original HTML file, copy everything starting at `footer_line_top` to the end of the file and insert it in the new file.

```php
<?php defined('C5_EXECUTE') or die('Access Denied.'); ?>

        <div id="footer_line_top"></div>
        <div id="footer"></div>
        <div id="footer_line_bottom"></div>
    </div>
</div>

<?php Loader::element('footer_required'); ?>

</body>
</html>
```

3. There are only two lines we have to insert. The first one is again just a protection to disallow direct calls to our file. The second one is a placeholder for a snippet you can specify in the concrete5 dashboard. This is often used for a JavaScript statistics tracking code as well as code files you want to load after the content is rendered. It's also used to load the editing toolbar and therefore mandatory.

4. Save and close the file; there's nothing else to do there.

What just happened?

We created another shared element which holds the code for our footer. There's not much code in it as we're trying to keep things simple and therefore we are not putting any content in the footer.

In case you create more theme templates, you can use this footer for all of them, which makes sure that if you want a login link at the bottom you can do it once and it will appear on all page types and therefore all pages as well.

Time for action – creating a page template

Carry out the following steps:

1. Go back to the directory where you've created `description.txt` and create another file named `default.php`.

2. Insert the content `DIV` along with some PHP code:

```php
<?php
defined('C5_EXECUTE') or die('Access Denied.');
$this->inc('elements/header.php');
?>

<div id="content">
    <?php
    $b = new Area('Main');
    $b->display($c);
    ?>
</div>

<?php $this->inc('elements/footer.php'); ?>
```

What just happened?

Just like we did in the header, there's a line at the top to avoid direct calls and a few more lines of code to insert another editable area named `Main`. In all the themes you can find in the marketplace there's an area called `Main`. By following this rule, concrete5 makes it possible to switch between themes without losing the content.

As you can see, the creation of the last file was also quite easy. There isn't a lot left from the original HTML code. However, having a small `default.php` file is also quite helpful, as you sometimes copy this file in case you need more page templates.

Time for action – creating more page templates

Carry out the following steps:

1. concrete5 themes usually ship with a few default templates, one of them usually being `left_sidebar`. Let's create it by copying `default.php` in a new file named `left_sidebar.php`.

2. We're going to add two sub `DIV` elements to hold our left and main column:

```php
<?php
defined('C5_EXECUTE') or die('Access Denied.');
$this->inc('elements/header.php');
?>

<div id="content">
    <div id="left-sidebar">
        <?php
        $as = new Area('Sidebar');
        $as->display($c);
        ?>
    </div>

    <div id="main">
        <?php
        $b = new Area('Main');
        $b->display($c);
        ?>
    </div>

    <div class="clear"></div>
</div>
<?php $this->inc('elements/footer.php'); ?>
```

3. As we've added new HTML elements, we also have to insert a few more CSS rules in a new file called `main.css` right in the root of your theme where you've created `description.txt` before. These are the rules you need:

```css
#left-sidebar {
  float: left;
  width: 250px;
  margin-right: 30px;
}
#main {
```

```
    float: left;
    width: 600px;
  }
  .clear {
    clear: both;
  }
```

4. Let's create another file named `right_sidebar.php`. Call the sidebar container `right-sidebar` and switch the two `DIV` elements. Some more CSS rules are necessary as well:

```
#right-sidebar {
    float: left;
    width: 250px;
    margin-left: 30px;
}
```

What just happened?

We've created two more page templates for our site. If you move your mouse cursor on the **Edit** button, you can click on **Design** in the popup menu and then select the left or right sidebar template to change the location of the sidebar.

While you probably remember the layouts you can use to split an area into columns, it might be beneficial to create page types as it is easier for the user to specify the layout when creating a new page. However, you're of course free to avoid additional templates by splitting an area into several columns. It's up to you; whatever you like!

Pop quiz – what are page templates and page types?

Q1. Which of the following statements is true about page templates and page types?

1. A page template is a physical file in your theme where you build your HTML structure to implement your site's layout(s).

2. A page type always has its own page template.

3. A page type can have its own page templates but doesn't need to have one.

4. Unlike page templates, pages types can be used in the concrete5 interface as a logical element to filter and search for pages.

Installing your theme

Once you've created all the files, you probably want to see how it looks on your site.

Time for action – installing theme

Carry out the following steps:

1. Type **Themes** into the intelligent search box and select the first entry in the search result.

2. Your new theme should appear at the end of the installed themes in the section **Themes Available to Install**. Click on **Install**, as shown in the following screenshot:

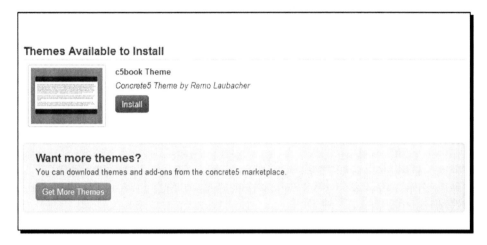

3. After you've installed the theme, you'll see a screen with all page types available in your theme. Click on **Return to Themes** to get back to the previous screen.

4. Your new theme is installed now, but it's not activated yet. Click on **Preview** if you want to look at it before activating it or just click on **Activate** to use it right away. You'll have to confirm this action.

What just happened?

We've installed our new theme which has been converted from a static HTML page. A theme is nothing but a bunch of files in a single directory, but it won't be available in concrete5 unless you follow the preceding steps.

PHP constants and functions

The following subchapter isn't one you have to go through step by step, it's rather a collection of small snippets that you can use to improve your concrete5 theme or block. The code snippets won't have any purpose in the upcoming chapters—you can implement them if you like, but you don't have to.

By default, concrete5 sets a bunch of constants that you can use when you create a theme but also a block or any other type of add-on. A lot of these constants are used internally and don't have any use for you when building themes or add-ons, but some are helpful and the rest give you at least an impression about a few internal workings of concrete5. There are also lots of functions to check the state of the current page, get information about the user, and much more.

While the basic template we've created works well for most situations, there are several things you can do within a template and not only in the user interface. The code lines aren't real life examples; they just give you a hint about things you can do once you run into a problem.

Again, instead of publishing a complete list of constants you might need, we're going to look at a simple way to get a list which will always show you all constants, no matter what version of concrete5 you're using.

Time for action – getting a list of available constants

Carry out the following steps to get a list of the available constants:

1. Open `default.php` from your theme in a text editor.

2. Look for the following PHP block:

```php
<?php
$b = new Area('Main');
$b->display($c);
?>
```

3. Before the closing PHP tags `?>`, insert a few more lines so it looks like the following:

```php
<?php
$b = new Area('Main');
$b->display($c);

echo '<pre>';
print_r(get_defined_constants(true));
echo '</pre>';
?>
```

4. Open a page of a type without a page template. Remember, we've created a template for the left and right sidebar. Pick the full width for example, otherwise the inserted code won't be executed.

5. The output will contain a huge list of constants categorized by modules. At the end there's a category named user; these are the constants which are not coming from PHP itself but rather from concrete5. Look at them and you'll find a lot of constants related to directories, URLs, locales, and more. You don't need all of them but they could be useful some day and give you some insights about the internals of concrete5.

What just happened?

Even if you've built software for a long time you'll still find methods, properties, and a lot more you haven't used before. You can try to remember all of them, but you'll probably have a hard time doing so. The preceding code can help you to get some information about the constants used in a PHP project.

Time for action – listing all available functions

As with most classes, you often have to call a method to get a value and not directly access a property as the method might do some additional checks you'd lose if you'd access the property directly. Let's start with what we have got to do to get a list of all available functions:

1. To get a list of all available methods without looking into the code, just add the following code where you'd like to get more information. Let's put it in default. php again like we did with the constants:

```php
<?php
$b = new Area('Main');
$b->display($c);

echo '<xmp>';
$reflection = new ReflectionClass($this);
print_r($reflection->getMethods());
echo '</xmp>';
?>
```

2. This will print a long list where you can find all available methods next to the property named `name`:

```
Array
(
    [0] =>ReflectionMethod Object
        (
            [name] =>getInstance
            [class] => View
        )

    [1] =>ReflectionMethod Object
        (
            [name] =>getThemeFromPath
            [class] => View
        )
```

What just happened?

The *Time for action – listing all available functions* section illustrated all the available methods in the current context, helping you to get a first impression about the available methods. The following two *Time for action* sections can be used in other PHP-based projects.

You won't get a nice explanation about the constants or methods, but you'll still know if something is available, helping you to be sure that you're on the right track. However, once you have found the correct class, you can open the following page to get more information about the methods and properties of it: `http://www.concrete5.org/api/`.

Time for action – checking for edit mode

There are situations where you have to know if the user is currently editing the page. For example, the in-site editing toolbar sometimes causes problems because it shifts down a few elements. If your layout has been built using absolutely positioned layers, you probably have to move down the layers a bit in case the toolbar is visible.

The current page object can be accessed by using the global variable $c, which contains a method that returns `true` if the page is currently in edit mode.

1. Open `default.php` of your theme or any other page type template.
2. Look for the code `new Area` and right before it, insert the highlighted lines as shown here:

```php
<?php
if ($c->isEditMode()) {
   echo 'You are editing this page at the moment!';
}

$b = new Area('Main');
$b->display($c);
?>
```

What just happened?

By calling the isEditMode() method on the current page, which you can access by $c, you can check if the user is currently editing the page. This offers you some flexibility in case a layout or block causes problems in edit mode. This simple check makes it easy to change, hide, or disable certain functions on your site in case it's necessary.

Time for action – hiding content from anonymous visitors

Carry out the following steps:

1. We've already seen how we can hide a page or even a block from a user by using the concrete5 user interface in combination with the advanced permission mode.

2. Let's hide content by using some code. Put the following lines in default.php:

```php
<?php
$u = new User();
if ($u->isLoggedIn()) {
   echo '<a href="/secret/">Secret key to world domination</a>';
}

$b = new Area('Main');
$b->display($c);
?>
```

What just happened?

The preceding two *Time for action* sections can both be used to change the content by adding some logic to the template.

While we've put both of them in a theme template, they are not only restricted to this location. You can use the command new User() almost anywhere in concrete5. The method $c->isEditMode() also works in several places: theme templates, page list templates, or autonav templates.

Time for action – restricting numbers of blocks per area

By default, you can place as many blocks in an area as you want. However, there are situations where a restriction to a single block might have some advantages.

In an absolute positioned layout, it can happen that the Add To Main link overlaps with another area or you simply want to make sure that there's just a single image block in the header area. Have a look at the following two steps to add this restriction:

1. Open the theme template where you'd like to add a restriction to the number of blocks. default.php does the job again.

2. Look for the PHP part where you specify the area and insert the highlighted line shown here:

```php
<?php
$b = new Area('Main');
$b->setBlockLimit(1);
$b->display($c);
?>
```

What just happened?

By simply adding one more line to our area, we made sure that only one block can be inserted. This nifty little method makes sure that the interface stays clean and consistent. In case you've made a wrong decision, no worries—the line can be removed without any problems at any time.

Time for action – inserting a block wrapper in an area

While you can do a lot with the CSS layout feature in concrete5, it might happen that you have to surround your block with some HTML code to style your site the way you want it to look. There's a simple way to add some wrapping code around each block in an area, as follows:

1. Once more, open a theme template like default.php and look for the place where you create the area.

2. Replace the PHP block using the following snippet:

```php
<?php
$b = new Area('Main');
$b->setBlockWrapperStart('<div class="mainBlock">');
$b->setBlockWrapperEnd('</div>');
$b->display($c);
?>
```

What just happened?

The two lines of PHP code we've inserted in the preceding snippet simply surround each block in the `Main` area with a `DIV` element.

When you now create your CSS files, you can access them using `.mainBlock`. A few lines in your CSS file like the following will add a line at the bottom of each block:

```
.mainBlock {
  border-bottom: 1px solid black;
}
```

Working with page attributes

concrete5 ships with a few default attributes for pages, users, and files. You can easily add new attributes to these objects to attach different kinds of metadata to them. You can use attributes to create dynamic elements in your theme without creating your own block.

A few things you can do with the default attributes:

◆ Exclude a page from the navigation

◆ Specify metadata for search engines

◆ Exclude a page from the search index

These are just a few of the things you can do by default, without adding a new attribute. However, what can we do if we create our own attributes?

Imagine we'd like to have a different background picture on each page. We could create a block for this, but we can also use an attribute and a little modification to our theme.

Time for action – using attributes to set background picture

Carry out the following steps:

1. Go to the dashboard and click on **Attributes** in the **Pages and Themes** section.

2. At the bottom, click on the **Add Attribute** drop-down box and select **Image/File**, then click on the **Add** button.

3. In the next screen, enter `background` for **Handle** and `Background Picture` in **Name**. The handle is what you'll need to access your attribute from the code. You can see this on the following screenshot:

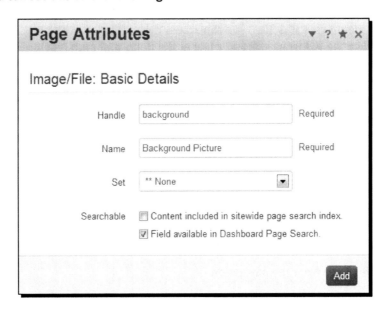

4. Click on **Add**. The **Background Picture** attribute has been added to the available attributes.

5. Go back to the **Dashboard** and click on **Page Types**.

6. Click on **Settings** next to the first page type.

7. In the list of attributes, check the checkbox next to **Background Picture**. This ensures the attribute is displayed by default for each page of this type.

8. Click on **Save**.

9. Do the same for all page types where you'd like to use this attribute.

10. Go to the home page by clicking on the **Return to Website** button on top.

11. Move your mouse cursor over the **Edit** button and click on **Properties** and select the second tab, **Custom Attributes**. This is where you can find all the attributes on a page. Our attribute is already in the list of selected attributes because we've added it to our page type before.

12. Use the file selector next to our new attribute to select a new background picture for the current page.

13. Click on **Save** and the selected picture will be assigned to our page.

What just happened?

We've created a new image attribute, which we've used to assign a background picture to a page of our choice.

This procedure works with every attribute, text, number, dates, and so on. You can use them in the same way if you want to manage page-specific metadata.

It's now possible to assign pictures to a page, but nothing happens with this data at the moment. We've got to add a few lines of code to display the new background picture.

Time for action – accessing attribute data from a template

Carry out the following steps:

1. Open `header.php` of your theme in your editor. You can find it in `/themes/ c5book/elements`.

2. Remove the `<body>` tag; we're going to replace it with some code, which includes the background picture.

3. Insert the following code right where you've removed the `<body>` tag:

```php
<?php
$backgroundAttribute = $c->getAttribute('background');
if ($backgroundAttribute) {
    $backgroundFile = $backgroundAttribute->getRelativePath();
    echo "<body style=\"background:url('{$backgroundFile}')\">";
} else {
    echo "<body>";
}
?>
```

4. Reload your page and you'll see the new background picture instead of the color gray.

What just happened?

We removed the static body tag and inserted some PHP code to fetch the attribute value. This works by using `$c->getAttribute()`. `$c` is a global variable referring to the current page. You can use `$c = Page::getCurrentPage();` if you prefer to use a method to get the current page object.

The parameter of `getAttribute()` is the handle of the attribute you created. You can use it to access any page attribute you want.

Pop quiz – what are attributes?

Q1. What are concrete5 attributes?

1. Attributes are settings you can apply to the HTML code of your concrete5 theme.
2. Attributes are flexible add-ons you can assign to all objects in concrete5 such as pages, page types, groups, maintenance jobs.
3. Attributes can have different types such as numbers, checkboxes, files. You can create and assign them to users, pages, and files.
4. concrete5 uses attributes to classify all pages of a site making it easier to keep an overview of them.

Inserting blocks in templates

Putting blocks in areas is a rather simple task, but if your users aren't experienced computer users, it might be even too easy. What if they accidentally delete or modify the autonav, the navigation block? It would break the site very quickly.

You can enable the advanced permission mode, which allows you to specify permissions on blocks and areas. However, enabling this mode can give you too much power and makes managing the site more complicated. While this shouldn't be a problem once you're more familiar with concrete5, there's another way you might want to check out—put blocks in your templates!

Time for action – replacing the header area with a template block

Carry out the following steps:

1. Open `elements/header.php` from your theme in your text editor.

2. Look for the following highlighted lines and remove all of them:

```php
<div id="wrapper">
<div id="page">
<div id="header_line_top"></div>
<div id="header">
        <?php
          $a = new GlobalArea('Header Nav');
          $a->display($c);
        ?>
</div>
```

3. Next, insert the following PHP code instead:

```php
<?php
$autonav = BlockType::getByHandle('autonav');
$autonav->controller->orderBy = 'display_asc';
$autonav->controller->displayPages = 'top';
$autonav->render('templates/header_menu');
?>
```

4. Save the file and reload your page, the header navigation is still there, but if you switch into edit mode, there's nothing you can edit in the header navigation.

What just happened?

By replacing the area with the preceding small code, we've put the autonav block directly into the template, disallowing any modification in the user interface.

We've set a few properties to specify the intended autonav behavior and called render with the argument `templates/header_menu`. This makes sure we're using the header menu template which you can find in `concrete/blocks/autonav/templates`. Please note, there's no `.php` extension when calling the render method.

If you wanted to use the default template of a block, just specify `view`:

```
$autonav->render('view');
```

Putting blocks in a template using this procedure works for almost any block, but how do you know what kind of properties they have?

Time for action – finding autonav block properties

There are several tools doing a similar job, the developer console of Chrome or Safari, Firebug for Firefox, or the built-in inspector of Firefox. Open Chrome or Safari and follow these steps to find the block properties:

1. After the installation procedure has succeeded, log in to your concrete5 test site `http://localhost/login/`.

2. Navigate to the home page and switch to the edit mode. Click on **Add to Main** and **Add Block**.

3. Pick the block you want to find the properties for. Autonav is a good choice as it has a few properties you might not find very intuitive.

4. When the block edit dialog is visible, right click on the first drop-down list, as shown in the following screenshot:

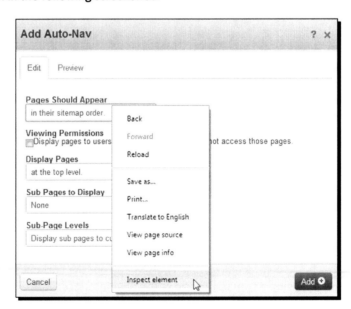

5. After you've clicked on **Inspect element**, the console will show up and automatically select the element named **orderBy**.

6. Click on the arrow on the left of the selected element and you'll see the following:

```
▼<select name="orderBy">
    <option value="display_asc">in their sitemap order.</option>
    <option value="chrono_desc">with the most recent first.</option>
    <option value="chrono_asc">with the earliest first.</option>
    <option value="alpha_asc">in alphabetical order.</option>
    <option value="alpha_desc">in reverse alphabetical order.</option>
    <option value="display_desc">in reverse sitemap order.</option>
</select>
```

What just happened?

Using the Chrome developer console, we discovered where we can quickly find block properties. In our case, the sort order in an autonav block is defined using a property called `orderBy` and values such as `display_asc` and `chrono_desc`.

concrete5 block edit dialogs work like a common HTML form and therefore use tags such as `input` and `select` to update the block properties.

While this might be an uncommon kind of documentation, it will work with blocks which have been released a minute ago, even if the developer didn't take the time to write the documentation.

In the case of autonav, a complete example with all available properties would look like the following:

```
$autonav = BlockType::getByHandle('autonav');
$autonav->controller->orderBy = 'display_asc';
$autonav->controller->displayUnavailablePages = 1;
$autonav->controller->displayPages = 'top';
$autonav->controller->displaySubPages = 'relevant';
$autonav->controller->displaySubPageLevels = 'enough_plus1';
$autonav->render('view');
```

Time for action – specifying block templates in an area

Sometimes you might want to set a default block template for an area. This might happen if the default template doesn't work at all and the customer would have to select a custom template for each block he/she adds. Let's save his/her time and specify a block template in our template.

1. Open a theme template like `default.php`.

2. Look for the PHP block which defines an area and insert the highlighted line from the following snippet:

```php
<?php
$b = new Area('Main');
$b->setCustomTemplate('autonav', 'templates/header_menu');
$b->display($c);
?>
```

What just happened?

The single line of code that we've added to our theme templates makes sure that for every autonav block where no template has manually been specified in the user interface, the `header_menu` template is used.

While setting `header_menu` for all autonav blocks is probably a bit useless, you'll learn how to build your own block templates in the next chapter. Once you've created your own templates, it's just a matter of time till you'll realize that overriding the default block template can be quite handy.

Applying a theme to a single page

There are a few pages in concrete5 that you don't have to create on your own. They exist whether you like it or not but luckily the chances are you'll like them.

Assume you're using the existing login page you can find at `http://localhost/login/` to grant some visitors access to the VIP section on your page. This works out of the box but it doesn't look like it should, as it still has the classic concrete5 look and doesn't look like our site at all.

To apply the look of our site, we have to do two things. Create a special file in our theme to handle these pages and activate the theme for these pages. The next two *Time for action* sections are going to do these steps.

What's a single page?

A single page is a page which is likely to exist just once in your site. This is usually due to a certain functionality or layout such as the dashboard pages. A second screen to create users is quite useless which is why the dashboard has been built using single pages.

For those familiar with other MVC frameworks, single pages are usually called **views** or **layouts**.

Time for action – creating a single page layout

Carry out the following steps:

1. Create a file named `view.php` in your theme.

2. Put the following code in it:

```php
<?php
defined('C5_EXECUTE') or die('Access Denied.');
$this->inc('elements/header.php');
?>

<div id="content">
<?php
echo $innerContent;
?>
</div>

<?php $this->inc('elements/footer.php'); ?>
```

What just happened?

We've created another file in our theme which looks a lot like `default.php`. However, there's one major difference; `view.php` must always output the variable `$innerContent`. The content of single pages is generated by program code and saved in `$innerContent`.

Some controllers use more variables which you'll have to process as well in order to replace the concrete5 core layout. The login page, for example, has another variable in order to make sure errors are printed too.

Time for action – adding variables to handle login errors

Carry out the following steps:

1. Before you put any code in `view.php`, open `concrete\themes\core\ concrete.php` and have a look at the content of the file. Right before `$innerContent` is printed, there are a few lines about printing any existing errors. This is what we're going to need in our `view.php` file too. Copy and insert it in the new file, and it should look like the following:

```php
<?php
defined('C5_EXECUTE') or die('Access Denied.');
$this->inc('elements/header.php');
?>


<div id="content">

<?php
Loader::element('system_errors', array('error'  => $error));
?>

<?php
echo $innerContent;
?>
</div>

<?php $this->inc('elements/footer.php'); ?>
```

2. Now that we handle errors as well, we can use our `view.php` file to style the login page. Open `config/site_theme_paths.php` in your editor.

3. There are already a few examples we can use as a template, or alternatively simply remove everything and insert the following lines instead:

```php
<?php
defined('C5_EXECUTE') or die('Access Denied. ');
$v = View::getInstance();
$v->setThemeByPath('/login', 'c5book');
```

4. Save the file and log out of concrete5 and go to `http://localhost/login/`.

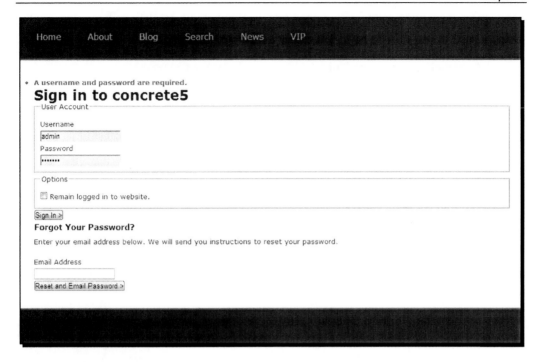

What just happened?

We've added `view.php` to our theme which can be used to apply a theme layout to single pages. The login page has now been embedded into our page with a small modification to `config/site_theme_paths.php`.

We're going to create our own single pages later in this book as well, but if you just want to style existing single pages, this is everything you'll need.

Pop quiz – what's a single page?

Q1. A page like the one available at `http://localhost/login/` is called a single page in concrete5, but what are they?

1. Single pages behave exactly like a normal page, it's just a synonym.
2. They are used for pages with a unique functionality not needed in other places of the site.
3. Single pages are built using custom code following the MVC pattern.
4. Dashboard pages, as well as extensions to the dashboard by add-ons, are built using single pages.

Q2. In which situation would you consider using a single page? Please note that it's not always a must to use a single page, but rather a recommendation.

1. A configuration page part of an add-on visible in the dashboard.
2. As a contact form to let your website visitors send you a message through a form.
3. A custom 404 page to handle requests to pages not available anymore.
4. The member profile of your community with lots of custom functionality.

Creating customizable themes

Creating a concrete5 theme does require some programming skill; it's a tool for programmers and not just designers and end-users after all. However, there's a nice way to allow end users to change some colors in a theme without any programming skill.

This feature allows you to change colors, fonts and insert custom CSS rules using the concrete5 interface without touching any files at all.

Time for action – creating a customizable theme

Carry out the following steps:

1. Open `main.css` from your theme.

2. Look for `body` and replace it using the following code:

```css
body {
    /* customize_background */ background-color: #989898; /*
    customize_background */
    height: 100%;
}
```

3. Search for `#header_line_bottom` and replace it with these lines:

```css
#header_line_bottom {
    /* customize_header_line */ background-color: #e64116; /*
    customize_header_line */
    height: 3px;
}
```

4. Search for `#footer_line_top` and replace it with the following lines:

```css
#footer_line_top {
    /* customize_footer_line */ background-color: #e64116; /*
    customize_footer_line */
    height: 3px;
}
```

5. At the end of the file, insert the following line:

```
/* customize_miscellaneous */ /* customize_miscellaneous */
```

What just happened?

We've added some comments to our CSS file. They don't generate any errors if you validate the file but concrete5 parses them and generates an interface on top of it where you can change the values surrounded by these comments.

After you've saved the modified CSS file, you can go back to the **Dashboard** and select **Themes**. Next, click on **Customize** next to the active theme. All the comments are transferred into a simple interface where you can change the values by clicking on the icon on the left of each property. Change them and you'll immediately see a preview of how the page is going to look with the new values. If you're satisfied with your choice, click on **Save** and your site will go green in no time, as shown in the following screenshot:

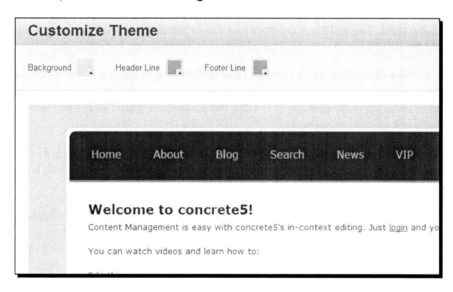

It often happens that a new theme ignores the custom values. This is usually due to a problem in the way the CSS file is included. If it has been directly linked using a relative path, concrete5 won't be able to replace the values. Make sure you use the following code to include your CSS file in case you want to use customizable style sheets:

```
<link rel="stylesheet" media="screen" type="text/css" href="<?php echo
$this->getStyleSheet('main.css')?>" />
```

Have a go hero – adding more customizable styles

You've seen how you can add your own customizable styles, why not try to add more to make it possible to customize more aspects of your theme without the need to touch a file?

Summary

In this chapter, we looked at the process to transform a static HTML site into a concrete5 theme by adding a few PHP calls in our files. We split our theme into three parts; a header, the actual content file, and a footer, to make it easier to create different page templates to allow a quick change of the page structure.

After we finished our theme, we installed it and had a look at different functions you might be able to use in case you want to get a little bit more out of concrete5.

Afterwards, we created a new page attribute where we can assign a page specific background picture. The attribute example was rather simple, but once you've got into it, you should be able to come up with a lot of different applications for attributes.

Next, we added a navigation block right into our template to avoid the need to use page defaults or manually add the navigation on each page. This also made it impossible for the end user to accidentally remove or modify the navigation, a part of the site which is quite likely not to change every day.

We also looked at a way to assign our page theme to existing single pages such as the login page. This allows us to use built-in concrete5 functionality for a community without having to write lots of code.

If you followed each step of this chapter, you should have created a bunch of files for your concrete5 site. For those who were in a rush or accidentally skipped a step, you can download the complete theme in the `9314_05_c5book_theme.zip` **folder on** the Packt Publishing website.

Extract the file to `/themes` and you can install it in your **Dashboard** when you go to **Themes** in the dashboard of your site.

In the next chapter we're going to look at how you can customize the block output by creating custom block templates. Block templates help you to turn the slideshow block into a gallery, add a thumbnail to a page list, and a lot more, so head over to the next chapter to get more knowledge about this exciting topic!

6

Customizing Block Layouts

In the previous chapter, we looked at themes to customize the site's layout. While this has probably been the more important part, concrete5 does not limit you to page layout customization. You can also adapt every block layout to suit your needs, without touching its actual logic, the inner working of it.

You can use PHP as well as JavaScript and CSS to change the output of a block with this feature. We'll cover this topic with the following steps:

- An example showing you how to add a thumbnail to the page list block output
- A bit of theory with an example to explain how you can add CSS and JavaScript files to block templates
- Another example that extends the content block to make it possible to insert pictures that open in a lightbox
- An example that turns the core slideshow block into a picture gallery
- An example that shows you how to inject a JavaScript in every page of your concrete5 site

Custom templates to modify a block layout

In *Chapter 4*, *Managing Add-ons*, we've had a quick, first look at the structure of a block. We're going to take a deeper look at the two elements of that structure:

- `view.php`: We're going to refer to it as the **default block template**. It's the file responsible for the output of the block.
- `templates`: This directory contains more (optional) block templates. Some blocks already ship with several templates, some only with the default block template.

What does this mean in more detail?

- A core custom template can be found in `/concrete/blocks/<block-name>/templates`. Custom templates are optional though; you won't find a lot of templates by default.

- A custom template could also be placed in `/blocks/<block-name>/templates`. What's the difference to the location mentioned previously? You should never make any modification to a file in the `concrete` directory. This is why it's possible to override templates by using the same path without concrete at the beginning, which will make it possible to update concrete5 without losing your modifications.

- If there's no custom template, the block will either use `view.php` from the location `/concrete/blocks/<block-name>` or `/blocks/<block-name>`. Again, the latter path would be chosen if `view.php` existed in both the locations.

When you click on a block you've added, there's a menu item called **Custom Template**:

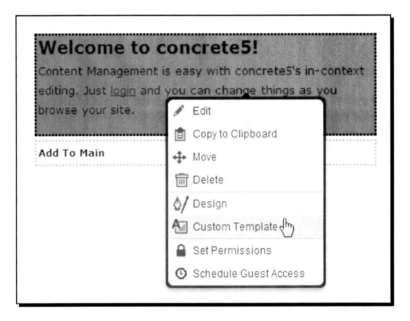

After you've clicked on it, a small dialog appears with a list of available templates:

If you pick **(None selected)** the block will use the default block template `view.php`. In the current version of concrete5, only the `autonav`, `page_list`, and `rss_displayer` block ship with additional templates. A lot of add-ons from the marketplace contain several templates though.

Thumbnails in a page list

Earlier in this book, we added a page list block to the news page to display all child pages. If that's not the case anymore, go to the **News** page and add a page list block and select **beneath this page** to display the child pages.

This block makes it easy to create a list of pages, whether we're using it to display news, archive, or products, it works quickly and easily. Unfortunately it also looks pretty plain, there's just a title and if you want a description, no preview picture or anything else that looks appealing. (set in the page properties).

Like most news pages, we're going to use a thumbnail to give the visitor a better impression of the article.

Time for action – adding thumbnails to a page list

You can add thumbnails to your page list by following these steps:

1. In the dashboard, click on **Attributes** in the **Pages & Themes** section. Choose **Image/File** and click on **Add** to add the new attribute.

2. Enter `thumbnail` in the **Handle** field and `Thumbnail` for the **Name** field, and click on **Add**.

3. Go to the sitemap and open the properties for the child page of **News**:

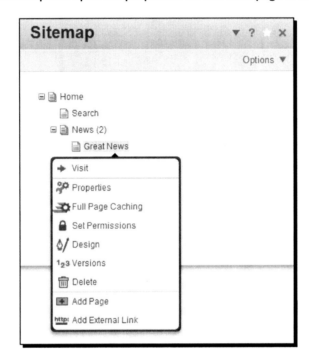

4. Activate the **Custom Attribute** tab.

5. Select our new attribute **Thumbnail** from the list in the left-hand side column.

6. Scroll back to the top and click on **Choose File** and pick a picture you'd like to use for this page.

7. Hit **Save** to confirm the modification to the page.

8. We've entered all the data, so let's create the new template. You can start by copying the file `concrete\blocks\page_list\view.php` to a new file at the location `blocks\page_list\templates\news.php`, but since we need very little functionality, you could also start with an empty file if you want. You have to create both directories, `page_list` and `templates`, first.

9. In the previous chapter, we used $c in a theme template to access our page. In the page list, we've got several pages in a loop. With each iteration, $page gets updated with the next page in the list. While the variable has a different name, it still refers to the same class which means that all methods we've used before work on $page as well.

We're going to use getAttribute again to get our thumbnail and print it before the description:

```php
<?php
defined('C5_EXECUTE') or die('Access Denied.');
$th = Loader::helper('text');
?>

<div class="ccm-page-list">

    <?php
    foreach ($pages as $page):

        // Prepare data for each page being listed...
        $title = $th->entities($page->getCollectionName());
        $url = $nh->getLinkToCollection($page);
        $target = ($page->getCollectionPointerExternalLink() !=
            '' && $page->openCollectionPointerExternalLinkInNewWind
            ow()) ? '_blank' : $page->getAttribute('nav_target');
        $target = empty($target) ? '_self' : $target;
        $description = $page->getCollectionDescription();
        $description = $controller->truncateSummaries ?
          $th->shorten($description, $controller->truncateChars) :
        $description;
        $description = $th->entities($description);

        // get value from thumbnail attribute
        $img = $page->getAttribute('thumbnail');
        ?>

        <h3 class="ccm-page-list-title">
            <a href="<?php echo $url ?>" target="<?php echo
            $target ?>"><?php echo $title ?></a>
        </h3>
        <div class="ccm-page-list-thumbnail">
            <img src="<?php echo $img->getRelativePath() ?>"
            width="<?php echo $img->getAttribute('width') ?>"
            height="<?php echo $img->getAttribute('height') ?>"
            alt=""/>
        </div>
        <div class="ccm-page-list-description">
            <?php echo $description ?>
        </div>

    <?php endforeach; ?>

</div>
```

10. Once you've saved our new template `news.php`, go back to the news page and activate the edit mode.

11. Click on the page list block and select **Custom Template**. In the dialog, pick our template **News** and click on **Save**.

What just happened?

If you created the template and changed the block template, your list will look like this:

We've made a copy of the default page list template and created a new one which prints the picture selected in the `thumbnail` attribute.

By adding a new block template outside of the `concrete` directory, we made sure that a future update to a newer concrete5 version doesn't affect our template.

You might have noticed it; the template name in the user interface started with a capital letter and didn't have a PHP extension at the end. concrete5 tries to keep the user interface as easy as possible and hides some of the cryptic programmer stuff. There's some convention for template names:

◆ Template names in the interface start with a capital letter

◆ There's no PHP at the end

◆ The letter after an underscore is uppercase

This means that the file name `packt_publishing.php` would be displayed as `Packt Publishing`.

While the template we've created should work quite well, you might get a huge picture in the page list because we output the image with the same dimensions as when you uploaded it. Wouldn't it be nice if concrete5 could restrict the maximum dimensions of the thumbnail?

Time for action – restricting thumbnails to a custom dimension

Sometimes you might have to specify an exact dimension to suit your needs. concrete5 has several helper classes, one called image which offers several functions, including a function which generates and caches a thumbnail.

```php
<?php
defined('C5_EXECUTE') or die('Access Denied.');
$th = Loader::helper('text');
$ih = Loader::helper('image');
?>

<div class="ccm-page-list">

    <?php
    foreach ($pages as $page):

        // Prepare data for each page being listed...
        $title = $th->entities($page->getCollectionName());
        $url = $nh->getLinkToCollection($page);
        $target = ($page->getCollectionPointerExternalLink() != ''
          && $page->openCollectionPointerExternalLinkInNewWindow()) ?
          '_blank' : $page->getAttribute('nav_target');
        $target = empty($target) ? '_self' : $target;
        $description = $page->getCollectionDescription();
        $description = $controller->truncateSummaries ?
          $th->shorten($description, $controller->truncateChars) :
        $description;
        $description = $th->entities($description);

        // get value from thumbnail attribute
        $img = $page->getAttribute('thumbnail');

        // create thumbnail with maximum size 170 x 140
        $thumb = $ih->getThumbnail($img, 170, 140);
        ?>

        <h3 class="ccm-page-list-title">
            <a href="<?php echo $url ?>" target="<?php echo $target
            ?>"><?php echo $title ?></a>
        </h3>
        <div class="ccm-page-list-thumbnail">
            <img src="<?php echo $thumb->src ?>" width="<?php echo
            $thumb->width ?>" height="<?php echo $thumb->height ?>"
            alt=""/>
        </div>
        <div class="ccm-page-list-description">
            <?php echo $description ?>
        </div>

    <?php endforeach; ?>

</div>
```

What just happened?

We extended the first template to assure the thumbnails don't exceed a certain dimension. The image we used in the last example works not only within templates, but also in a controller, theme template, or any other file which is part of the concrete5 framework.

The image helper function we used makes sure that the thumbnail gets cached in order to avoid unnecessary CPU time for further page views.

 Having some knowledge about methods of classes available in concrete5 usually helps you a lot, no matter what kind of add-on you're working on. While it might be a bit overwhelming at the beginning, at least try to remember the methods mentioned in this book. Once you get more used to the concrete5 framework you'll quickly be able to learn new methods.

Have a go hero – improving the thumbnail page list

Page types can be assigned attributes which will be displayed automatically, without selecting them in the drop-down list. Try to create a new page type called News. You can then add a new page list block and restrict it to displaying pages of that type only.

The page list has a thumbnail but still looks rather simple and not very stylish. Since we've assigned our new element a CSS class called `ccm-page-list-thumbnail` you can easily access the element and change its layout. Try to use it in your theme to improve the layout; make the thumbnail appear on the left of the description, add a line at the end of each list, and other such improvements.

Have a go hero – exploring concrete5 helpers

We did take a quick look at the image helper to generate a thumbnail, but concrete5 helpers not only help you to generate thumbnail but also e-mails, HTML forms, JSON strings, and a lot more.

You can find them by opening the directory `concrete\helpers`. You'll need a few of them later in this book, but we can't cover all of them. It still helps if you know what's actually there, so why not try to use a few of them and see what they do?

Block template folder

In the previous example, we've created a single file used as a custom template. Instead of having just a single file, a template can also be a folder containing several files. This allows you to put CSS and JavaScript files and your template in a single directory. It also ensures that CSS and JavaScript files are properly included in the header of your page.

Time for action – creating a template folder

Follow these steps to create a folder for your templates:

1. Create a new folder in `blocks\page_list\templates` called `news_2`.

2. Copy the previously created `news.php` file into this directory and rename it `view.php`.

3. Create a new file called `view.css` with the following content:

```css
.ccm-page-list {
    border-bottom: 1px solid gray;
    padding-bottom: 20px;
    margin-bottom: 20px;
}
.ccm-page-list a {
    color: #262626;
    text-decoration: none;
}
```

What just happened?

We've created a folder instead of a single file for our template. While `view.php` is mandatory, there are lots of optional files you can use. Within a template in the `templates` folder, the following are the files included by concrete5 in the header:

◆ `view.js`

◆ `view.css`

◆ `js/<anything>.js`

◆ `css/<anything>.css`

The following screenshot shows you an example of this structure:

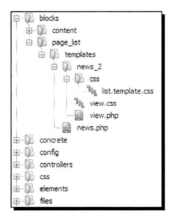

Pop quiz – how to include CSS and JavaScript files

Q1. If you created a template for the content block found at the following location: `blocks\content\templates\my_template`, how can you include the CSS and JavaScript files without touching any line of code in the core?

1. All files with the extension `.js` located in the directory called `js`.

2. All files with the extension `.css` or `.js`.

3. All files with the extension `.css` located in the directory called `css`.

4. Files in the root of the template directory called `view.css` or `view.js`.

Picture pop-ups in a content block

concrete5 contains a bunch of add-ons by default and a lot more can be downloaded or bought at the marketplace. While you can definitely find a lot of really nice add-ons, sometimes you can easily rebuild things with just a few small tricks.

Assume you've got a blog style page where you have some pictures in the text. It would be nice if you could click on them like a gallery, wouldn't it?

jQuery is the preferred JavaScript library of concrete5 and is included by default. It usually makes sense to use jQuery based libraries to avoid any conflicts between JavaScript libraries. Using jQuery, MooTools, and YUI at the same time works, but you have to make some modifications which can be time consuming and annoying. To keep this easy, we're going to use jQuery lightbox, written by Leandro Vieira.

jQuery, MooTools, YUI

jQuery, MooTools, and YUI are JavaScript libraries with the intention to make the development of websites and applications with JavaScript easier. You can find out more about jQuery at `http://jquery.com/`, about MooTools at `http://mootools.net/`, and about YUI at `http://yuilibrary.com/`. It doesn't hurt to know something about MooTools and YUI, but we'll focus on jQuery as it's the most used JavaScript library in concrete5.

Time for action – building a lightbox gallery

To build a lightbox gallery follow these steps:

1. Create the following directory: `blocks/content/templates/lightbox`.

2. Copy `concrete/blocks/content/view.php` into the new directory, and keep the filename `view.php`.

3. Download the jQuery lightbox plugin from this site `http://leandrovieira.com/projects/jquery/lightbox/`.

4. From the downloaded jQuery ZIP file, extract the folders `images`, `css`, and `js` into the directory `blocks/content/templates/lightbox`, but make sure `jquery.lightbox-0.5.min.js` is the only JavaScript—you have to remove all other files ending with `.js`.

5. Add another file called `view.js` in the same directory as `view.php`. We need it to initialize the lightbox script. Its content has to look like this:

```
$(document).ready(function() {
    $("a.lightbox").lightBox({
        imageBtnPrev: CCM_REL + "/blocks/content/templates/lightbox/
        images/lightbox-btn-prev.gif",
        imageBtnNext: CCM_REL + "/blocks/content/templates/lightbox/
        images/lightbox-btn-next.gif",
        imageLoading: CCM_REL + "/blocks/content/templates/lightbox/
        images/lightbox-ico-loading.gif",
        imageBtnClose: CCM_REL + "/blocks/content/templates/
        lightbox/images/lightbox-btn-close.gif",
        imageBlank: CCM_REL + "/blocks/content/templates/lightbox/
        images/lightbox-blank.gif"
    });
});
```

6. Go to the page where you'd like to insert a lightbox gallery and add a new content block.

7. Enter a text such as `Skyline` and select it. This text will serve as a link to a picture.

8. Click on **Add File** in the toolbar on top of the text editor. Select the picture you want to see when clicking on the link.

9. Select the link again and click on the anchor icon. Switch to the **Advanced** tab and enter `lightbox` in the **Classes** field and then click on **Update**.

10. Click on **Add** once back on the content block and you should see a link called `Skyline` in it.

11. Click on the block and click on **Custom Template**, then select our template called **Lightbox**.

12. Exit the edit mode and publish the changes immediately.

What just happened?

After you've changed the template, you can click on the link and you will see something like this:

We've created another block template along with several folders and files to include the jQuery lightbox files. The only file we had to create was `view.js` where we initialized the jQuery plugin; everything else was created by copy and paste action. If you're used to working with blocks and templates, this process takes very little time.

Have a go hero – creating another JavaScript gallery

While lightbox seems to be an obvious choice for a picture gallery nowadays, there are a lot more different galleries. You'll find lots of examples when you search for **jQuery galleries** on Google.

Look for the one you like and try to convert it into a concrete5 template. At the end of the chapter you can find another gallery template based on a script called `ADGallery`.

Adding a Gravatar picture in the guestbook

Gravatar is a widely used service for creating a thumbnail of a person. It is a feature often used in blogs to display a face next to a comment. Internet users upload their picture at `http://en.gravatar.com/` and assign it to their e-mail address.

The application can then generate an **md5** hash by using this e-mail address and can display an image of them, without exposing the actual mail address.

This procedure works with PHP like it does with any language where you can generate an md5 hash:

```php
$gravatarHash = md5(strtolower(trim('your.mail@address.com')));
echo "<img src=\"http://www.gravatar.com/avatar/{$gravatarHash}\" />";
```

Let's add that feature to the guestbook block.

Time for action – adding a Gravatar picture to the guestbook

Follow these steps to easily add a Gravatar to the guestbook:

1. You will now need to create the following directory structure: `blocks/guestbook/templates`. Next, copy `view.php` from `concrete/blocks/guestbook/view.php` and place it in `blocks/guestbook/templates` and then rename it to `gravatar.php` to make it clear what the template is going to be used for.

2. The default block template contains quite a lot of code as it contains some functions to manage the comments. We won't have to bother with it, but we have to find our way around it. There are only a few lines we have to insert; open `gravatar.php` and search for `<div class="contentByLine">` and insert the highlighted lines before the `div` element.

```php
<div class="guestBook-entry<?php if ($c->getVersionObject()-
>getVersionAuthorUserName() == $u->getUserName()) { ?> authorPost
<?php } ?>">
    <?php if ($bp->canWrite()) { ?>
        <div class="guestBook-manage-links">
            <a href="<?php echo $this->action('loadEntry')
            . "&entryID=" . $p['entryID']; ?>#guestBookForm"><?php
            echo t('Edit') ?></a> |
            <a href="<?php echo $this->action('removeEntry') .
            "&entryID=" . $p['entryID']; ?>" onclick="return
            confirm('<?php echo t("Are you sure you would like to
            remove this comment?") ?>');"><?php echo t('Remove')
            ?></a> |
            <?php if ($p['approved']) { ?>
                <a href="<?php
                echo $this->action('unApproveEntry') . "&entryID="
                . $p['entryID']; ?>"><?php echo t('Un-Approve') ?>
                </a>
            <?php } else { ?>
                <a href="<?php echo $this->action('approveEntry')
                . "&entryID=" . $p['entryID']; ?>"><?php echo
                t('Approve') ?></a>
```

```
        <?php } ?>
    </div>
<?php } ?>

<?php
$gravatarHash = md5(strtolower(trim($p['user_email'])));
echo "<img src=\"http://www.gravatar.com/avatar/
{$gravatarHash}\" alt=\"\"/>";
?>
<div class="contentByLine">

    <?php echo t('Posted by') ?>
    <span class="userName">
        <?php
        if (intval($p['uID'])) {
            $ui = UserInfo::getByID(intval($p['uID']));
            if (is_object($ui)) {
                echo $ui->getUserName();
            }
        }else
            echo $p['user_name'];
        ?>
    </span>
    <?php echo t('on') ?>
    <span class="contentDate">
        <?php echo date($dateFormat,
        strtotime($p['entryDate'])); ?>
    </span>
</div>

    <?php echo nl2br($p['commentText']) ?>
</div>
```

3. Save the file and go back to your site and navigate to a page where you'd like the new guestbook to appear.

4. In edit mode, add a new guestbook block to your page.

5. When added, click on it again and select **Custom Template** and find our new **Gravatar** template in the list.

6. Post a new comment and check what happens.

What just happened?

The new template we created adds a Gravatar thumbnail to the guestbook by extending the default block template with a few lines of additional code. In case a person hasn't uploaded a picture, you'll see the default Gravatar picture, but the script still works.

If you use this template and post a new comment, it will automatically try to get a picture from Gravatar and display it like this:

Avoiding duplicate code in a custom template

You might have noticed that we copied the `view.php` from the concrete/blocks directory to our top level blocks directory to create a template. This makes sure we don't have to touch the core but also generates some redundancy, especially if the original `view.php` was huge. However, there's a solution that includes the original template without copying any of its content.

This works nicely if you just want to wrap an existing template. Assume you want to add some CSS rules to a content block. You'll quickly realize that there's no wrapping `DIV` in it which makes it hard to apply styles for the content block. You can override any paragraph but if that's not what you want to do you have to create a new template and add a surrounding `DIV` element.

Time for action – including an existing template

You can include an existing template to your concrete5 site by following these steps:

1. Create a new file at the following location:

```
blocks/content/templates/wrapper.php
```

2. Enter the following code in the new file:

```
<div class="content-wrapper">
<?php
$bvt = new BlockViewTemplate($this->getBlockObject());
$bvt->setBlockCustomTemplate(false);

include($bvt->getTemplate());
?>
</div>
```

3. Save the file and go back to your concrete5 site.

4. Add a new content block and click on it after you've hit **Add** and select **Custom Template**.

5. Select **Wrapper** and update again.

What just happened?

When you look at the HTML code generated by concrete5 you'll find an additional DIV in the output with a class called `content-wrapper`.

You can use this class in your CSS file called `main.css`. Add a rule like this to change the background color:

```
.content-wrapper {
    background-color: silver;
}
```

We've created a new template which basically includes the existing content block default block template. There's just an additional HTML tag we've added to make it easier to access the content block output by CSS rules.

How did this work? We've used the function `$this->getBlockObject()` to get the instance of the block for which we're creating a template.

We call `setBlockCustomTemplate` with `false` as its parameter to avoid rendering the custom template (our file). It temporarily disables the custom template and allows us to get the filename of the default block template by calling `getTemplate`. We include it and we're done.

This procedure is especially useful if you just want to add code to the beginning or end of an existing template. You can then be sure that once the default block template gets updated, it will be included in your own custom template.

You'll find a more useful example in the next section!

Transforming a slideshow into a gallery

By default, concrete5 ships with a slideshow block you can use to quickly add a few pictures with a smooth fading effect. But sooner or later you will quite likely want to create a more classical picture gallery.

We've already created a template for the content block which you can use to embed a picture gallery within your content. This can be nice because it allows you to wrap text around your pictures to tell you a bit more about the pictures.

But what if you just wanted to show some pictures? Maybe the 500 pictures you took from your last trip to the moon? Adding every picture and link manually would be rather annoying and looking at 500 pictures in a slideshow without seeing a thumbnail is also quite time consuming, but adding pictures to the slideshow block is rather easy. Let's turn the slideshow block into a gallery!

Time for action – creating a gallery template for a slideshow

Create a gallery slideshow template by following these steps:

1. We're going to use the same JavaScript as we used with the picture pop-up template for the content block. You can use the file you've previously downloaded or go to jQuery lightbox at `http://leandrovieira.com/projects/jquery/lightbox/` and download the jQuery lightbox ZIP file again.

2. Create a new directory named `blocks/slideshow/templates/gallery`.

3. From the downloaded jQuery ZIP file, extract the folders `images`, `css`, and `js` but make sure there's only `jquery.lightbox-0.5.min.js` in it—you have to remove the other JavaScript files.

4. Create a new file called `view.php` in the `gallery` directory. We're not going to copy the original `view.php` as we have to rewrite most of the code anyway. The following code block shows you the complete content of our `view.php`; it's a lot smaller than the default slideshow template:

```
<div class="ccm-slideshow-gallery">
<?php
defined('C5_EXECUTE') or die('Access Denied.');

foreach($images as $imgInfo) {
  $f = File::getByID($imgInfo['fID']);
  $fp = new Permissions($f);
  if ($fp->canViewFile()) {
```

```
        $fileName = $f->getFileName();
        $picturePath = $f->getRelativePath();
        $thumbnail = $f->getThumbnail(2);

        echo "<a title=\"{$fileName}\"
          href=\"{$picturePath}\">{$thumbnail}</a>";
    }
}
?>
</div>
```

5. Create another file called `view.js` in the same directory. We need it to load the lightbox script:

```
$(document).ready(function() {
    $(".ccm-slideshow-gallery a").lightBox({
        imageBtnPrev: CCM_REL + "/blocks/slideshow/templates/
          gallery/images/lightbox-btn-prev.gif",
        imageBtnNext: CCM_REL + "/blocks/slideshow/templates/
          gallery/images/lightbox-btn-next.gif",
        imageLoading: CCM_REL + "/blocks/slideshow/templates/
          gallery/images/lightbox-ico-loading.gif",
        imageBtnClose: CCM_REL + "/blocks/slideshow/templates/
          gallery/images/lightbox-btn-close.gif",
        imageBlank: CCM_REL + "/blocks/slideshow/templates/
          gallery/images/lightbox-blank.gif"
    });
});
```

What just happened?

The process we went through is again quite simple and very similar to the picture pop-up template we created before.

We put all the files related to the jQuery lightbox right into our template directory. This makes it easier to install the template as all the files are located in a single folder. Copy and paste is enough to install this template in a new site.

Next, we created a completely new `view.php` which basically uses a variable called $image generated by the controller of the slideshow block. Depending on the settings you can make when adding a slideshow block, the controller puts a sequence of pictures in the image variable and forwards it to the template. We simply used this array to print a thumbnail and a link to the picture in the original size of the picture.

Our last file, `view.js`, is again similar to the file we created for the picture pop-up content template. We only changed the jQuery selector to access all links within our DIV element and not just link with the `lightbox` attribute.

Time for action – adding a slideshow gallery

Follow these steps to add the slideshow gallery we created:

1. In the dashboard, go to the file manager and select all files you'd like to appear in the gallery by ticking the checkbox next to the picture:

2. As shown, click on **Sets** in the drop-down box above the files. We're going to use a new set of files to access our files from the slideshow block. In the dialog which appears, enter the name of the new set and tick both the checkboxes. Click on **Update** and all selected files will now belong to the new set:

3. Go to the page where you'd like the gallery to appear.

4. Enable the edit mode and bring up the block list by clicking on **Add To Main**. From the list, select **Slideshow**.

5. In the **Type** box, select **Pictures from File Set**. The interface changes and concrete5 automatically selects the first available set. Since we only have one, you don't have to change it. If you're using the original slideshow template, you can specify the display duration and fading time, but since our template is going to turn the slideshow into a gallery, these values won't be used.

6. Click on **Add** to insert the slideshow to our page. Click on the block again and select **Custom Template**, select our new template called **Gallery,** and hit **Save**.

7. Leave edit mode and publish all changes.

What just happened?

We added a bunch of files to a new set which we then used in our slideshow block. So far we did what we'd have to do when we'd like to add a slideshow. But since we created a new template for the block, we changed the template to our new custom template.

After we've finished editing the page, you should be able to use the new lightbox gallery immediately.

Slideshow using file attributes

In the previous chapter, we worked with attributes assigned to pages. As already mentioned, attributes can also be connected to files. Assume you've got a nice collection of photos which are really important to you, and you would therefore like to add a note to each picture, telling a little bit about its story. Having this kind of information assigned to files makes it easy for you to pull them into any part of concrete5 you want.

In this section, we're going to add a new attribute to our files where we can save a little description about the file. We then create another template for the slideshow block which uses this attribute to display the additional information about the picture right in the slideshow.

Time for action – adding file attributes to our slideshow

Include the file attributes in the gallery by following these steps:

1. In the intelligent search box, type **Attributes** and select the entry next to **Files**. You should see the two default attributes, **width** and **height**. We are going to add two more attributes, one for the title and one for a short description.

2. Select **Text** in the drop-down at the bottom and hit **Go**. Enter `title` for **Handle** and `Title` for **Name**. Click on **Add** to add the new attribute.

3. Select **Text Area** in the drop-down and click on **Go** again. Enter `description` for **Handle** and `Description` for **Name**. Leave the type as **Plain Text** and add the new attribute.

4. You should now see four attributes as shown in the following screenshot:

5. Go back to the **File Manager** and select the first file in your gallery set. Open the **Properties** dialog. Scroll down and look for **Other Properties**. Click on the label **Title** and enter a title for the current picture, and click on the little icon with the pen when done. Do the same for **Description** and close the dialog. Do the same for all the pictures in your set.

What just happened?

The new attributes we've created are assigned to every file in the file manager but they don't have a value by default. When filled, we can access them by using a single PHP function, a lot like we did with the pages.

This data you've entered is going to be used in the following *Time for action* section. We're going to use them to show some information about the picture in the gallery by using the ad-gallery jQuery plugin from Andy Ekdahl, which can be found at `http://coffeescripter.com/code/ad-gallery/`.

Time for action – using file attributes in the gallery

Add file attributes to the gallery by following these steps:

1. Create a new directory structure, each directory within each other: `blocks`, `slideshow`, `templates`, and `ad_gallery`.

2. Create a new file called `view.php` which generates the HTML output. It's similar to the one we've created before but the structure is a bit different and we have to access more attributes:

```php
<div class="ad-gallery">
  <div class="ad-image-wrapper">
  </div>
  <div class="ad-controls">
  </div>
  <div class="ad-nav">
    <div class="ad-thumbs">
      <ul class="ad-thumb-list">
      <?php
      defined('C5_EXECUTE') or die('Access Denied.');

      foreach($images as $imgInfo) {
        $f = File::getByID($imgInfo['fID']);
        $fp = new Permissions($f);
        if ($fp->canViewFile()) {

          $fileName = $f->getFileName();
          $picturePath    = $f->getRelativePath();
          $thumbnail = $f->getThumbnail(2, false);
          $fileTitle = $f->getAttribute('title');
          $fileDescription = $f->getAttribute('description');

          echo "<li>";
          echo "<a title=\"{$fileName}\"
            href=\"{$picturePath}\">";
          echo "<img src=\"{$thumbnail}\"
            title=\"{$fileTitle}\" alt=\"{$fileDescription}\"/>";
          echo "</a>";
          echo "</li>";
        }
      }
      ?>
      </ul>
    </div>
  </div>
</div>
```

3. Download the latest plugin from the following address:

```
http://adgallery.codeplex.com/releases/
```

4. In our template directory called `ad_gallery`, create another directory called `css` and extract the CSS files from the `lib` directory along with all the pictures from the downloaded file to this directory. The directory should contain the following files afterwards:

- ❏ `ad_next.png`
- ❏ `ad_prev.png`
- ❏ `ad_scroll_back.png`
- ❏ `ad_scroll_forward.png`
- ❏ `jquery.ad-gallery.css`
- ❏ `loader.gif`
- ❏ `opa75.png`
- ❏ `trans.gif`

5. Create another directory called `js` and extract `jquery.ad-gallery.min.js` to it.

6. For this template, we're not going to create our own CSS file; we simply reuse the one that ships with AD Gallery. It's not going to look perfect on our site but it works and saves us some time for the moment.

7. The AD Gallery plugin comes with a nicely working jQuery function we have to call to initialize. For this, we create another file called `view.js` in the `ad_gallery` directory with the following content; please note that you have to enter the correct size of your pictures in case you're not using the default pictures from concrete5:

```
$(document).ready(function () {
    $('.ad-gallery').adGallery({
        loader_image: CCM_REL +
            "/blocks/slideshow/templates/ad_gallery/css/loader.gif",
        width: 800,
        height: 192,
        animate_first_image: true
    });
});
```

8. Go back to the page where you want to use the new slideshow and add a new slideshow block using our previously created file set. Click on the block and select **Custom Template**, pick **Ad Gallery** from the list, and hit **Save**.

What just happened?

By writing only a few lines of code we were able to use an existing jQuery plugin to add a lot more functionality to the default slideshow block shipped with concrete5.

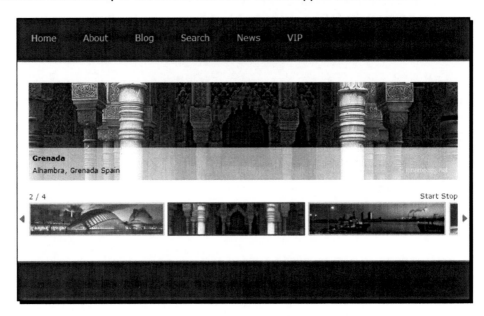

Using such jQuery plugins comes with a few nice things, and it's usually quite easy to embed them as most of them extend jQuery with a single function. Some scripts also have lots of optional options you can use to modify the behavior to suit your needs. **AD Gallery** comes with tons of options to change the animation type, speed, effects, and a lot more.

Right now, with the templates we've created you have to modify `view.js` whenever you want to change something about the gallery, even if you just want to use the template for pictures with a different dimension.

Using advanced tooltips in the content block

By default, HTML displays a simple hint on an element where you've set the title attribute. Have a look at the following code:

```
<a title="CMS concrete5" href="http://concrete5.org/help" target="_
blank">help</a>
```

This code will produce the following result. The exact output might differ depending on your browser and operating system though:

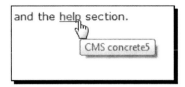

Again, jQuery is going to help us to customize this little information box. There's a nice jQuery plugin called **TipTip** from Drew Wilson which you can find here: `http://code.drewwilson.com/entry/tiptip-jquery-plugin`.

Time for action – creating advanced tooltips

Create a **TipTip** tooltip by following these steps:

1. Create a new directory structure for our template: `/blocks/content/templates/tip_tip`.

2. Create a new file called `view.php` in it. We're going to use the previously described technique again which allows us to extend the existing core template:

    ```
    <div class="content-tip-tip">
      <?php
      $bvt = new BlockViewTemplate($b);
      $bvt->setBlockCustomTemplate(false);

      include($bvt->getTemplate());
      ?>
    </div>
    ```

3. Download the **TipTip** source code from the following location:

    `http://code.drewwilson.com/entry/tiptip-jquery-plugin`

4. Extract the CSS file into a new folder called `css` within our template folder. Extract `jquery.tipTip.minified.js` into a new directory called `js`.

5. We've added all but one file we need. The last file called `view.js` is going to initialize the advanced tooltips:

    ```
    $(function(){
        $(".content-tip-tip [title]").tipTip();
    });
    ```

6. Go to the page where you want the new tooltip to appear. Edit the page and click on a content block of your choice and click on **Custom Template**. Select **Tip Tip** and hit **Save**.

7. Make sure there are links in the content with the `title` attribute set. Click on a link and hit the **Anchor** button in the toolbar; there should be a value next to the label **title**. If not, add one and hit **Update**.

What just happened?

The last template in this chapter works a lot like the ones we've already created. We included the default block template, in this case not by copying the whole file but rather by wrapping the default block template in a new one.

We then added all the files from the jQuery plugin we needed, the CSS and JavaScript files.

Lastly we had to call the jQuery function `tipTip` for all HTML tags with the attribute `title` within all elements having the CSS class `content-tip-tip`. We added the class by surrounding the existing block template with an additional `DIV` element.

Now, when you hover over the link, you'll see a slightly different tooltip:

Summary

We've created several templates to extend the default concrete5 blocks. While we've only looked at the page list, content, guestbook, and slideshow block, the procedure is the same for every block you can find, as well as for blocks downloaded from the marketplace.

While templates are very easy to create, they sometimes lack functionality. In the previous examples you might have seen some values we had to add statically to a JavaScript file. This is one problem you might run into with templates; it's just a template, there's no way to change the block edit interface from a template. If you wanted to change values such as the dimensions of the pictures in a gallery, you'd have to create your own block, exactly what we're going to do in *Chapter 8, Creating Your Own Add-on Block.*

You can find all the templates from this chapter in the accompanying ZIP file, so extract it to `blocks` and all templates will be available.

But luckily, concrete5 is not restricted to custom templates; you can easily build your own block for a more sophisticated user experience. We're going to look at some more templates to improve the **autonav** block, but afterwards, we're going to look at creating blocks.

Keep in mind that you should never make any kind of modifications to files in the `concrete` directory as it's part of the core and would be overridden in case you update to a newer version of concrete5.

7

Adding Site Navigation

In this chapter we'll have a deeper look at the autonav block you use to create dynamic navigation. It basically pulls a selection of pages from the sitemap and prints a hierarchical HTML structure, which represents the navigation.

We're going to start with information about the use of the block. Afterwards we're going to create a series of templates for the block in order to change the look and the behavior of the navigation to explain the process of building a custom navigation in concrete5.

We'll cover the following topics in this chapter:

- An introduction about the autonav block, which is mostly used to build a site's navigation
- An example showing you how to add pictures to the navigation
- Another example that uses CSS3 to add a hover effect
- An example that adds a drop-down navigation using a jQuery plugin
- One last example to show how you can add navigation to improve the usability for visitors using a mobile phone

Introducing the autonav block

Before we start customizing the autonav block, we're going to have a quick look at the different options and the output. It's very helpful to be familiar with all the block options as well as knowing the HTML output that the block generates before you start extending the block.

Preparation

If you have followed the book chapter by chapter, you'll have the autonav block included in your theme, more precisely in header.php of your theme. Since we're going to play with navigation, we should undo this modification; changing the options in header.php would be a bit annoying otherwise. If you're done with this chapter, you might want to put the code back in place; this is mostly to make it easier to work with the custom templates we're going to build.

Time for action – undoing autonav block integration

1. Open header.php from your theme; it's located in the themes/c5book/ elements directory.

2. Since the following code snippet doesn't show the complete file, make sure you replace the correct lines. Everything is underneath the HTML tag with the ID header:

```
<div id="wrapper">
<div id="page">
<div id="header_line_top"></div>
<div id="header">
    <?php
        $a = new GlobalArea('Header Nav');
        $a->display($c)
    ?>
</div>
<div id="header_line_bottom"></div>
```

3. Save header.php and go back to your page. Make sure the navigation is still there; if it isn't, go back to edit the page and add a new autonav block in Header Nav. Please note that you'll see a hint telling you that you're placing the block in a global area. It just means that these changes will have an effect on several pages, though this is not an issue but rather what we want.

4. After you add the block, click on it and select **Custom Template** and select the custom template to **Header** menu and confirm the change by clicking on **Save**.

What just happened?

We had to undo a modification done before this chapter. The code which printed the autonav block directly from the template would be fine if your navigation wasn't going to change. However, since we're working on the autonav block for a whole chapter, we had to remove this code and replace it with the default code for an editable area.

Autonav options

The `autonav` block comes with a bunch of options you can use to create the correct hierarchical output of pages in your navigation.

While you probably have to play around with it for a bit to get used to all the options, we're still going to look at a few possible configurations which we'll need later in this chapter.

Autonav page structure

The example configuration we're going to look at uses the pages of the sitemap shown in the following screenshot.

It doesn't matter if your structure looks different at this point; the examples are easy to understand even if your result looks a bit different.

Page order

By default, the `autonav` block uses the sort order which you can see in the sitemap as well. This usually makes sense because it offers the biggest flexibility. Remember, you can arrange pages by dragging their icon to the place where you want the page to be.

In all our examples you can chose whatever order you like; it doesn't have an effect on our templates. Have a look at the following screenshot to see all the options:

Example 1 – showing all pages

The most basic configuration shows all pages, no matter where we are and no matter how many pages there are. This configuration is useful when you create a JavaScript-based navigation which displays subpages dynamically without reloading the page.

The settings and the result should be obvious; it will show all pages shown in the preceding structure. Have a look at the following screenshot to see what you have to do:

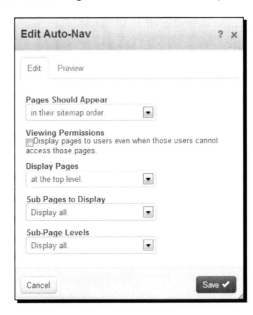

When you create a JavaScript drop-down navigation, you have to generate HTML code for all the elements you want to show, but that doesn't necessarily mean that you want to print all elements. Assuming you've got hundreds of pages, would you like to see all of them in the drop-down menu? Probably not, and this is why you can manually specify the number of page levels you'd like to print. Use the settings shown in the following screenshot for the drop-down navigation we're going to create later in this chapter:

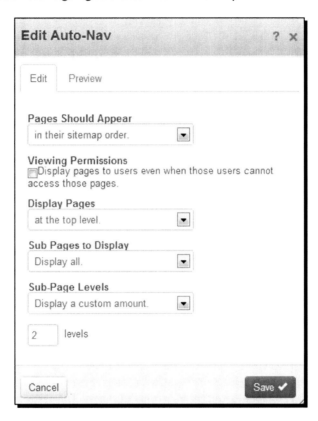

Example 2 – showing relevant subpages

In the structure just shown, assume you're on `About`, which has two direct child pages.
If we wanted to display the two subpages in the left sidebar of our page, we could use
the following settings:

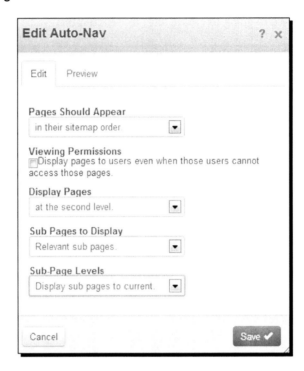

Example 3 – showing relevant subpages starting from the top

For a site where you only have a single navigation, probably on the left-hand side, you
have to start at the top and include all the relevant subpages. The settings are similar,
but this time we start at the top and include the level below the current subpage as well
by using these settings:

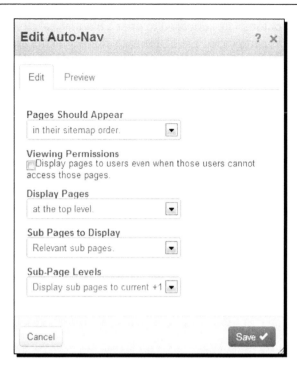

If you're on the About page again, you'd see all pages at the top, along with the About page and its two subpages.

Autonav output

The autonav controller produces an HTML output that is compatible with most jQuery libraries you can find. It uses an UL/LI structure to create a proper hierarchical representation of the pages we show in our navigation.

Before we look at the actual output, here are some words about the process which generates the output. The autonav block controller uses all the settings you make when you add the block. It then creates an array of pages which don't have any children—it's a flat array. Unlike what some of you would expect, there's no real recursion in the structure which you have to process in the block template.

How's an `autonav` block template supposed to print a hierarchical structure? That's not too difficult; there's a property called `level` for each element in the array. You simply have to check what happens to that level. Is the level of the current page element bigger than the one from the previous element? If yes, create a new child to the current page. Does it decrease? If yes, close the HTML tags for the child elements you've created when the level increased. Does this sound a bit abstract? Let's look at a simplified, not working, but commented `autonav` template:

```php
<?php  defined('C5_EXECUTE') or die(_("Access Denied."));

$navItems = $controller->getNavItems();

/*** STEP 1 of 2: Determine all CSS classes (only 2 are enabled by
default, but you can un-comment other ones or add your own) ***/
foreach ($navItems as $ni) {
  $classes = array();

  if ($ni->isCurrent) {
    //class for the page currently being viewed
    $classes[] = 'nav-selected';
  }

  if ($ni->inPath) {
    //class for parent items of the page currently being viewed
    $classes[] = 'nav-path-selected';
  }

  //Put all classes together into one space-separated string
  $ni->classes = implode(" ", $classes);
}

//*** Step 2 of 2: Output menu HTML ***/
echo '<ul class="nav">'; //opens the top-level menu

foreach ($navItems as $ni) {

  echo '<li class="' . $ni->classes . '">'; //opens a nav item
  echo '<a href="' . $ni->url . '" target="' . $ni->target . '"
class="' . $ni->classes . '">' . $ni->name . '</a>';

  if ($ni->hasSubmenu) {
    echo '<ul>'; //opens a dropdown sub-menu
  } else {
    echo '</li>'; //closes a nav item
    echo str_repeat('</ul></li>', $ni->subDepth); //closes dropdown
sub-menu(s) and their top-level nav item(s)
  }
}

echo '</ul>'; //closes the top-level menu
```

The templates we're going to create don't change a lot from the default PHP template. We mostly use the HTML structure the default template generates and only add some CSS and JavaScript. Understanding every detail of the default `autonav` template isn't necessary, but still helps you to get the most out of the `autonav` block.

What we must understand is the HTML structure shown as follows—it's what you'll have to work with when you create a custom navigation or layout:

```html
<ul class="nav">
  <li class="nav-path-selected">
    <a class="nav-path-selected" href="/">Home</a>
  </li>
  <li class="nav-selected nav-path-selected">
    <a class="nav-selected nav-path-selected"
      href="/index.php/about/">About</a>
    <ul>
      <li>
        <a href="/index.php/about/press-room/">Press Room</a>
      </li>
      <li>
        <a href="/index.php/about/guestbook/">Guestbook</a>
      </li>
    </ul>
  </li>
  <li>
    <a href="/index.php/search/">Search</a>
  </li>
  <li>
    <a href="/index.php/news/">News</a>
  </li>
</ul>
```

It should be fairly easy to understand the preceding structure. Each new level added a new `ul` element that contains an `li` element for each page, along with an `a` element to make it clickable. Child pages within a `ul` element belong to their parent, meaning that the `li` element of the parent is closed when all the children have been printed.

The output uses the default template which adds some classes you can use to style the navigation:

- **nav**: The main `ul` tag contains this class. Use it to access all elements of the navigation.

- **nav-selected**: This class is assigned to the elements if they belong to the current page.

- **nav-path-selected**: This class can be found on pages that are above the current page. They belong to the path of the current page, and are thus called `path-selected`.

Adding navigation images

If you add a new `autonav` block, it will always print text links, no matter which template you use or which option you select.

We're going to assign the navigation pictures as we did with the pictures attribute used in the page list template where we've added a thumbnail. For this we have to create two new attributes, one for the picture in the normal state and one displayed when the page is active.

Time for action – creating page attributes for navigation pictures

1. In the dashboard, go to **Attributes** in the **Pages & Themes** section.

2. At the bottom, in the **Add Attribute** area, select the drop-down, select **Image/File**, and click on **Add**.

3. Enter `navigation_pic_off` for **Handle** and **Navigation Picture Off** for **Name**.

4. Create another attribute of the same type with `navigation_pic_on` as the **Handle** and **Navigation Picture On** for the **Name**.

5. If you intend to use this for all navigation items, you might want to assign the new attributes to the page types by default. Go to **Page Types** and click on **Settings** for each page type. Select the two new attributes and click on **Save**.

What just happened?

By following the steps given in the *Time for action* section, you created two attributes which allowed you to assign two pictures to every page. Attributes in concrete5 are very flexible—you can create and connect them to pages, users, and files in case you have to manage object-specific data.

Attributes can be helpful with a variety of different problems; make sure you know how to use them.

Time for action – creating a block picture navigation template

1. Copy the default `autonav` template `concrete/blocks/autonav/view.php` to `blocks/autonav/templates/picture_nav.php`.

2. We have to modify a few lines toward the end of the new template where the comment `Step 2 of 2` starts. You have to insert two lines (see highlighted lines in the following code) to get the two pictures and replace the line that starts with `echo '<a href="'` . `$ni->url`... with the second highlighted code block shown in the following code:

```
//*** Step 2 of 2: Output menu HTML ***/
echo '<ul class="nav">'; //opens the top-level menu

foreach ($navItems as $ni) {

    $navigationPicOff = $ni->cObj->getAttribute('navigation_pic_
    off');
    $navigationPicOn = $ni->cObj->getAttribute('navigation_pic_
    on');

    echo '<li class="' . $ni->classes . '">'; //opens a nav item
    echo '<a href="' . $ni->url . '" target="' . $ni->target . '"
    class="' . $ni->classes . '">';

    // menu item is active or in path
    if ($ni->inPath || $ni->isCurrent) {
        if ($navigationPicOn) {
            echo '<img src="' . $navigationPicOn->getURL() . '"
                alt="' . $ni->name . '"/>';
        } else {
            echo $ni->name;
        }
    }
    else {
        if ($navigationPicOff) {
            echo '<img src="' . $navigationPicOff->getURL() .
                '" alt="' . $ni->name . '"/>';
        } else {
            echo $ni->name;
        }
    }

    echo '</a>';

    if ($ni->hasSubmenu) {
        echo '<ul>'; //opens a dropdown sub-menu
    } else {
        echo '</li>'; //closes a nav item
        echo str_repeat('</ul></li>', $ni->subDepth); //closes
        dropdown sub-menu(s) and their top-level nav item(s)
    }
}

echo '</ul>'; //closes the top-level menu
```

Pop quiz – parts of image navigation

Q1. In order to assign a picture to a page, we've added an attribute; out of the following statements about attributes, which is correct?

1. The handle of the attribute is used by developers in the code to access the attribute.
2. Page attributes assigned to a set can be reordered.
3. Page attributes not assigned to a set can be reordered.
4. There's a restriction in the number of attributes a page can have.

Q2. In the autonav output handled in `view.php` we've used some functions properties, what is correct?

1. `$ni->isCurrent` is true if the current page in the loop is identical to the page the user is looking at.
2. `$ni->inPath` is true if the page in the loop is a subpage and therefore has a path.
3. `$ni->inPath` is true if the page in the loop is a parent page of the current page the user is looking at.

What just happened?

Using the two new attributes, we created another block template. We had to insert a few new lines of code, but the logic behind it is rather simple.

First, we try to get the values of the two attributes from the page we need. We then check if the current page object in the loop is either active, `$ni->isCurrent`, or in the path of the active path, `$ni->inPath`. If it is, we try to print the picture assigned to the attribute `navigation_pic_on`. In case there's no picture, we print the page name like the default template does. Everything else in the template is identical to the original template.

Adding a CSS3 hover effect

While CSS3 isn't supported in every browser yet, it allows us to do things for which we previously needed JavaScript. The use of JavaScript would have been possible for most effects as well, but we're going to look at a CSS3-only effect to get a quick impression to see how easy it is to integrate upcoming web technologies. Make sure you're using a browser with CSS3 support, such as the latest version of Chrome or Firefox, to see the effect.

The effect we're going to use is just a bit more than a classic CSS hover effect which you've probably used before. It starts with something similar to this:

```
a {
  color: silver;
}
a:hover {
  color: black;
}
```

This CSS file would display all the links in silver and, when you hover over them, it would display them in black. With CSS3, things get a bit fancier, but let's create the new template first; we'll see how it looks very quickly.

Time for action – creating a CSS3 transition autonav template

1. Create the directory structure for our new template `autonav/blocks/templates/css3_hover`.

2. Our template works a lot like the existing header menu; copy `concrete/blocks/autonav/templates/header_menu.php` to `blocks/autonav/templates/css3_hover/view.php`.

3. In our template directory, create another file called `view.css`:

```css
.nav-header li {
    list-style-type: none;
    float: left;
}
.nav-header a {
    display: inline-block;
    padding: 4px;
    border: 2px solid transparent;
    -moz-transition: 0.25s -moz-transform;
    transition: 0.25s transform;
    -webkit-transition: 0.25s -webkit-transform;
    -webkit-transform: scale(1) rotate(0);
    -moz-transform: scale(1) rotate(0);
    transform: scale(1) rotate(0);
}
.nav-header a:hover {
    background: #e64116;
    text-decoration: none;
    color: #ffffff;
```

```
        -webkit-border-radius: 4px;
        -moz-border-radius: 4px;
        border-radius: 4px;
        border: 2px solid white;
        -webkit-transform: scale(1.2) rotate(-3deg);
        -moz-transform: scale(1.2) rotate(-3deg);
        transform: scale(1.2) rotate(-3deg);
    }
    .nav-header li:nth-child(2n) a:hover {
        -webkit-transform: scale(1.2) rotate(3deg);
        -moz-transform: scale(1.2) rotate(3deg);
        transform: scale(1.2) rotate(3deg);
    }
```

4. Save the files and go back to your page, edit it, and click on the navigation block in the previously modified area. Select **Custom Template**, select **Css3 Hover**, and **Save** the block.

What just happened?

Here's another quite simple template, which looks as follows:

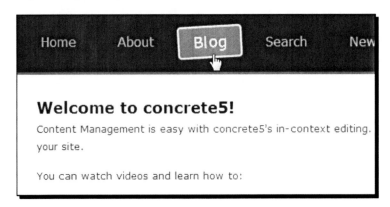

This template is only about the CSS that we have created. The PHP file is an exact copy of the header menu template that is part of the concrete5 core. We will have a few quick words about the CSS rules used in the preceding example without going too much into the details of CSS3. We had to use some browser-specific extensions because it's a rather new feature. If you remove those, things are easier to read; for example:

```
.nav-header a {
  display: inline-block;
  padding: 4px;
  border: 2px solid transparent;
  transition: 0.25s transform;
  transform: scale(1) rotate(0);
}
```

The `transition` property sets the duration for the effect and specifies the element we want to use for the effect. In the case of the `transform` property, the simplified rule relevant when the link is hovered over would look as follows:

```
.nav-header a:hover {
  transform: scale(1.2) rotate(-3deg);
}
```

Here we can see that the `transform` property has a different value than the one in the first example. It's scaled and rotated a little bit which will cause the effect.

In short, `transition` sets the CSS property which we want to use to smoothly change the object from its normal state to its hover state specified with `:hover`. You can also use `transition: 0.25s all`, which would make sure that all CSS properties transform from their original state to their second, in this case hover, state.

Have a go hero – create more transitions

Instead of the `transform` property, you can access all kinds of CSS properties to create a smooth transition effect.

`transition: 0.25s color` would gradually fade the color of the link to the color you have specified in `:hover`. It works with the location, dimension, color, background, and a lot more; there are lots of possibilities and it takes only a few lines of code.

Building a drop-down navigation

Drop-down navigations have been around for quite some time. When graphical user interfaces got popular, they were everywhere. With more advanced web technologies available, they also found a way onto the Internet.

We therefore have to create one in concrete5 as well using the jQuery library. There are lots of scripts available and most of them can be used, but we're going to use **SooperFish** by Jurriaan Roelofs from `http://www.sooperthemes.com`. It's a great little plugin—easy to work with and easy to integrate in concrete5.

Time for action – creating a SooperFish template

1. Go to `https://github.com/jjroelofs/jQuery-SooperFish` and download the latest version by clicking on the **ZIP** button.

2. Create a new directory structure for our template `blocks/autonav/templates/sooperfish`. Create a new sub directory called `js` and extract `jquery.sooperfish.min.js` from the downloaded ZIP file to it. Create another subdirectory underneath `sooperfish` called `css` and extract `sooperfish.css` from the ZIP in it.

3. In the `sooperfish` directory you created, add a new file called `view.php` and insert the following content:

```php
<?php  defined('C5_EXECUTE') or die('Access Denied.');
$navItems = $controller->getNavItems();

/*** STEP 1 of 2: Determine all CSS classes (only 2 are enabled by
default, but you can un-comment other ones or add your own) ***/
foreach ($navItems as $ni) {
  $classes = array();

  if ($ni->isCurrent) {
    $classes[] = 'nav-selected';
  }

  if ($ni->inPath) {
    $classes[] = 'nav-path-selected';
  }

  $ni->classes = implode(" ", $classes);
}


//*** Step 2 of 2: Output menu HTML ***/
echo '<ul id="nav" class="nav sf-menu">'; //opens the top-level
menu

foreach ($navItems as $ni) {

  echo '<li class="' . $ni->classes . '">'; //opens a nav item
  echo '<a href="' . $ni->url . '" target="' . $ni->target . '"
class="' . $ni->classes . '">' . $ni->name . '</a>';

  if ($ni->hasSubmenu) {
    echo '<ul>'; //opens a dropdown sub-menu
  } else {
```

```
    echo '</li>'; //closes a nav item
    echo str_repeat('</ul></li>', $ni->subDepth); //closes
dropdown sub-menu(s) and their top-level nav item(s)
  }
}

echo '</ul>'; //closes the top-level menu
```

4. Create another file called `view.js` where we initialize the SooperFish menu:

```
$(document).ready(function() {
    $('#header > ul').sooperfish();
});
```

5. Create another file called `view.css` to change the background color of the submenu by putting the following content in it:

```
.nav ul {
    background: #fff;
}
```

6. If you create a drop-down menu, your HTML code must contain the child pages, even if you only see them when hovering over the parent element. Since JavaScript is responsible for showing and hiding the child elements, we have to make sure the child elements are printed by `autonav`. Edit the page where you want to use the drop-down menu, click on the `autonav` block, and apply these values:

7. After you've changed and confirmed the autonav settings, click on the block again and select **Custom Template** to change the template to SooperFish. Save that change too and publish the changes made to the page.

What just happened?

A new template based on SooperFish has been created. Since our theme works quite well with SooperFish, we do not even have to make any CSS modifications. The only thing that is needed is the SooperFish JavaScript, another super small JavaScript to load the script and the standard template. Depending on the CSS file from your theme, you might have to include a modified version of some CSS rules that you can find in the SooperFish ZIP file. The menu does require a few CSS instructions in order to work properly.

Have a go hero – changing the SooperFish parameters

When we created the `view.js` file, we did not pass any parameters to SooperFish, but there are plenty of things you can configure with this plugin. If we have a look at the example from the author's website, we'll find the following example:

```
$(document).ready(function() {
    $('#header > ul').sooperfish({
        hoverClass:     'over',
        delay:          '400ms',
        dualColumn:     7,
        tripleColumn:   14,
        animationShow:  {height:'show',opacity:'show'},
        speedShow:      '800ms',
        easingShow:     'easeOutTurbo2',
        animationHide:  {width:'hide',opacity:'hide'},
        speedHide:      '400ms',
        easingHide:     'easeOutTurbo',
        autoArrows:     false
    });
});
```

An interesting feature other drop-down plugins don't offer can be configured by `dualColumn` and `tripleColumn`. In the previous example, any submenu with more than seven elements will be divided into two columns.

All the other properties should be fairly easy to understand—they let you specify a custom animation, duration, and some interface-related features such as arrows to indicate the availability of child pages. There's a nice page where you can play with all these properties at http://www.sooperthemes.com/sites/default/files/SooperFish/example. html.

Why not try to build a custom menu using the properties of SooperFish?

 Please note that you have to extract `jquery.easing-sooper.js` from the ZIP to the `js` directory of your new template if you want to use a different easing setting.

Have a go hero – including SooperFish themes

By default, there are four different themes in the SooperFish ZIP that you've downloaded. You can see them if you open the `themes` directory part of the ZIP. Files ending with `.css` located in the `css` directory, like `sooperfish.css` in our example, are automatically included by concrete5.

We can use this fact to include a SooperFish theme, just copy a theme file such as `sooperfish-theme-silver.css` and place it in the `css` directory.

Sliding mobile navigation

In times where lots of people surf the Internet on a mobile device, it doesn't hurt to think about navigation for devices with a small screen. If your site is small and has very few pages, you might be able to display them in the same way you'd show them on a desktop computer, but what happens if you have a lot of content spread over lots of pages?

An often seen approach is to hide a tree like structure which appears from the left if you click on a special navigation link or button. It doesn't take much to build something like that from scratch but we're going to look at a jQuery plugin called PageSlide, available at `http://srobbin.com/jquery-plugins/pageslide/`.

Time for action – building a mobile navigation

1. Create another directory structure for our template `blocks/autonav/templates/page_slide`.

2. Within that directory create a new file called `view.php` with the following content:

```php
<?php
$bvt = new BlockViewTemplate($b);
$bvt->setBlockCustomTemplate(false);

function nav_tree_callback_mobile($buffer) {
```

```
    return str_replace('<ul class="nav">',
        '<ul class="nav-page-slide">',$buffer);
}

echo '<a id="nav-page-slide-link"
    href="#nav-page-slide">Navigation</a>';
echo '<div id="nav-page-slide" style="display: none;">';
ob_start("nav_tree_callback_mobile");
include($bvt->getTemplate());
ob_end_flush();
echo '</div>';
?>
```

3. Create another file called view.js in the same directory and put the following lines in it:

```
$(document).ready(function() {
    $("#nav-page-slide-link").pageslide();
});
```

4. In order to make sure our navigation is readable, put the following content in a new file called view.css:

```
#nav-page-slide a {
    color: white;
    text-decoration: none;
    font-family: verdana, helvetica, arial;
    line-height: 200%;
}
#nav-page-slide ul {
    margin-left: 20px;
}
```

5. In the template directory, create a new subdirectory called css and extract the CSS file called jquery.pageslide.css in it from the ZIP file, which you can download at http://srobbin.com/jquery-plugins/pageslide/.

6. In the template directory, create another subdirectory called js. Unfortunately the file from the ZIP has a problem. There's a fixed version available here http://www.concrete5.ch/jquery.pageslide.min.js; extract it to the new directory.

7. Once you've created all the files, go back to your home page and switch into the edit mode. Add a new autonav block, select Display all for **Sub Pages to Display**, Display a custom amount for **Sub-Page Levels**, and 1 for **levels**. Add the block and click on it again after it has been placed in your page, click on **Custom Template**, and select our new Page Slide template.

8. Publish the changes.

What just happened?

We've created another template for the autonav block which uses a jQuery plugin called PageSlide to add a navigation, which slides in from the left. By using such a navigation, you can make sure that your site still works, even if visitors use a mobile phone to access your site.

You probably have to add some more details to make it look nicer but this template should give you enough information to get started with mobile navigation. By default, it will look like this:

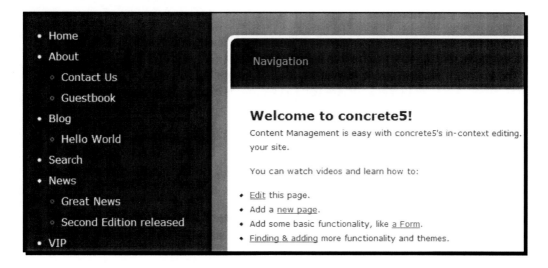

Summary

We had a closer look at the `autonav` block, an element you'll often need when you work with concrete5. While a lot about the `autonav` block is about experience, you should already have gotten an impression about some of the possibilities.

The templates we created are fairly easy to modify or extend with some basic knowledge about the used web technologies. The layout is mostly amendable by adding some CSS rules. Some templates we've created use JavaScript libraries, where you can modify some parameters such as colors and number of columns very easily by changing some easy-to-understand variables.

Try to use the template we've created as a base for your own, custom navigation. You've got examples which show you how to include JavaScript, CSS, and PHP to get the most out of the `autonav` block to create almost any kind of navigation you want. If you need more information, here are two links where you can get more information about autonav and get one more autonav example:

- `http://c5blog.jordanlev.com/blog/2011/12/customizing-the-autonav-template/`
- `http://www.codeblog.ch/2013/03/concrete5-sitemap-like-autonav-block/`

In this chapter we continued what we've learnt in *Chapter 6, Customizing Block Layouts*. Now that we've also mastered the customization of the autonav block template, we're ready to create some blocks from scratch in the next chapter.

8

Creating your Own Add-on Block

In this chapter, we will delve a bit deeper into the actual development of concrete5. In the previous chapters, we mostly copied and modified existing functionality. This worked well for basic tasks and even for some more advanced features. However, there comes a point when you work with concrete5 when you have to create a completely new block to meet your or your customers' requirements.

Let's get started with a simple block, we'll go through this step-by-step and add more functionality to it till we get to the end of this chapter. We'll follow these steps:

- A first block that simply holds discrete values that represent a product
- A few additions to that block to check for mandatory fields as well as an option to categorize the product blocks
- The next block will use the previous product block to build a list
- We'll then look at a block you can use to add a magnifying effect to a picture
- The next block creates a PDF document from the current page by wrapping existing libraries
- The last block shows you how you can create a simple picture gallery on top of the concrete5 file manager sets

Building a product information block

In this section, we're going to create a rather simple block that allows you to enter structured content in order to make sure the output looks identical for all products on your webpage. This block is needed for the second example, which pulls information from every information block to create a list.

While this block is called *Product Information*, it can easily be modified to hold different kind of information, such as news, real estate, FAQ, team members, and more. The input dialog is going to contain three fields, one for the title, a picture, and a rich text editor for the description. The result is going to look similar to the following screenshot:

Steps for creating a block

We already had a first quick look at the files of a basic block in *Chapter 4, Managing Add-ons*. Now, we're going to create these files. To do this, we have to create a new directory as we did several times when we created a new template. However, this time we're not going to use the name of an existing block that you can find in the `concrete/blocks` directory; we're creating a new block and therefore have to use a new, unique name. For this, you have to create a folder named `product_information` in the top-level `blocks` folder.

Every block can have a little icon, which you'll see in the list when adding a new block. For this, you can create a PNG picture, 16 x 16 pixels, and save it as `icon.png` in the new directory.

Adding the database schema

Most blocks have to process and save some kind of data, which is why we create an XML file to describe our database model. We're not going to use traditional SQL commands to create or alter our database tables. This has the advantage that you can easily describe our model in an XML file that creates a new table or updates it if there's an older version of it in the database. The file we're going to create uses an ADOdb library, which is described at `http://phplens.com/lens/adodb/docs-datadict.htm#xmlschema`.

 XML is a standardized textual data format to manage any kind of data structure, whether it's a letter, a configuration, or—as in our case—a description of our database structure.

Time for action – creating the database structure

Carry out the following steps:

1. In our block directory, create a new file named `db.xml`.

2. In this file, you have to add a hierarchical structure of tables and columns. The whole content of the file should look similar to the following code snippet:

```xml
<?xml version="1.0"?>
<schema version="0.3">
    <table name="btProductInformation">
        <field name="bID" type="I">
            <key />
            <unsigned />
        </field>
        <field name="title" type="C" size="255"></field>
        <field name="description" type="X2"></field>
        <field name="fIDpicture" type="I"></field>
    </table>
</schema>
```

What just happened?

The file we created is everything we'll need to tell concrete5 what to create in the database for our add-on. Most of it should be pretty intuitive; it starts with the XML file definition, a root schema element that you have to use in order to tell ADOdb to use the correct version, a table, and a bunch of fields. Not too difficult, but the field types might be a bit difficult to guess. Here's a list of the most common types you'll need: C, character field, capped to 255 characters. Use this for single-line text fields such as the title in our example. This field type needs a `size` attribute where you have to specify the length from 1 to 255.

- X2: It is the largest multibyte varchar data type we've got. Use this for rich-text fields.

- ◆ T: This creates a timestamp field. There are other types for dates, such as D, but always use T to be consistent with the core add-ons.

- ◆ I: It is short for integer; use this for numbers, foreign key references to files, and pages.

This list is not complete, but should be enough for most add-ons. If you're looking for a complete list, you can go to http://phplens.com/lens/adodb/docs-datadict.htm.

> If you want to save a "yes/no" in the database, you might be looking for a Boolean data type. As the SQL 1999 standard does have some inconsistency about that data type, there's no type for this that you can use with all databases.
>
> In concrete5, simply use an integer field and save 0 for false and 1 for true.

There are also a few case-insensitive keywords, which we have to use to create indexes, constraints, and set default values; look at the bID field in the preceding example to see how they are implemented. The following options are available:

- ◆ AUTO / AUTOINCREMENT: It is used for columns where you need an autoincrementing number; often used for primary keys.

- ◆ KEY / PRIMARY: It sets the primary key. Compound keys are allowed; simply set this flag for multiple fields.

- ◆ DEF / DEFAULT: Use this if your column needs a default value. This attribute needs to have a value like this: <default value="0"/>

- ◆ NOTNULL: It marks a field as mandatory.

- ◆ UNSIGNED: It sets a number field to unsigned. Use this for autoincrementing primary keys as there's no need for negative numbers in such a situation.

- ◆ DEFTIMESTAMP: It sets a default function to get today's date and time.

- ◆ NOQUOTE: It disables default string autoquoting.

- ◆ CONSTRAINTS: It is used to specify required relations between fields. Can be manually handled in the controller of your add-on.

There's a column called bID that you must add to every main table of a block. bID is short for **block ID** and is used by concrete5 to connect the proper page version to your block.

There's one behavior which might surprise you: after you've added one block to a page and used it for a while, you might end up having several entries in your block table, even if you just added one block. How does this happen? concrete5 allows you to look at or approve an older version of your page. This works by saving the content of every block from that time; concrete5 automatically creates a new bID in case the block content has changed in a new page version. Nothing to be worried about at this point, but we'll have to keep this in mind when creating more complex blocks.

Time for action – creating the block controller

Carry out the following steps:

1. Create another file named `controller.php` in our new add-on directory.

2. Add the following content in it:

```php
<?php
defined('C5_EXECUTE') or die('Access Denied. ');
class ProductInformationBlockController extends BlockController {

    protected $btTable = 'btProductInformation';
    protected $btInterfaceWidth = "590";
    protected $btInterfaceHeight = "450";
    protected $btCacheBlockRecord = true;
    protected $btCacheBlockOutput = true;
    protected $btCacheBlockOutputOnPost = true;
    protected $btCacheBlockOutputForRegisteredUsers = true;
    protected $btCacheBlockOutputLifetime = CACHE_LIFETIME;

    public function getBlockTypeDescription() {
        return t("Embeds Product Information in your web page.");
    }

    public function getBlockTypeName() {
        return t("Product Information");
    }

    public function view(){
        $this->set('bID', $this->bID);
        $this->set('picture', $this->getPicture());
    }

    public function save($data) {
        parent::save($data);
    }

    public function getPicture() {
        if ($this->fIDpicture > 0) {
            return File::getByID($this->fIDpicture);
        }
        return null;
    }

}
?>
```

What just happened?

The file we created is the one that contains all the logic, the data processing. It's still very small, but this is a file which can quickly grow. With this file, we start going into object oriented programming. Let's go through this file step-by-step:

- The line with `defined` simply checks if we're running the correct way from `index.php` in order to make sure the security checks have been executed.

- The next line is derived from our directory named `product_information`. The result `ProductInformationBlockController` is created by the following rules:
    - Start with a capital letter
    - After every underscore, start with a capital letter again
    - At the end, add `BlockController` to the name and derive the class from it as well

- `btTable` sets the main table the block controller has to work with; it must match with the table name in `db.xml`.

- `btInterfaceWidth` and `btInterfaceHeight` set the size of our block edit dialog.

- The functions `getBlockTypeDescription` and `getBlockTypeName` return a string to describe our block. Please note that the value returned is processed by the function `t` as well. This function is used to translate that value into other languages. In our case, it will return the value we passed to the function, since we don't have any translations yet, but that's okay for now.

- The function `view` isn't necessary in our block at the moment. It's only to show you how to pass values to the view, in case you have to process your data before rendering them.

- `save` is similar, not necessary in our case. The block controller saves discrete values automatically by matching the form field names with the field names of the table we specified in `btTable`. However, if you wanted to save data from a child table or add some checks to this method, this is where you could hook into it.

- The last method `getPicture` is used because we only save a reference in the form of a number when we work with files from the concrete5 file manager. Since we have to work with this file reference several times, we add a new function which returns the file object and not only the numeric reference to it.

Right now, this is everything we need to get our data in the database and back.

Time for action – creating the editing interface

Carry out the following steps:

1. As adding and editing a block is pretty much the same, we're going to create a file named `form_setup_html.php`, which is shared by both, `add.php` and `edit.php`.

2. First, let's create `add.php` and `edit.php`; both are rather simple and identical because everything is located in `form_setup_html.php`:

```php
<?php
defined('C5_EXECUTE') or die('Access Denied.');
$this->inc('form_setup_html.php');
?>
```

3. In a new file `form_setup_html.php`, save the following content:

```php
<?php
defined('C5_EXECUTE') or die('Access Denied.');

$al = Loader::helper('concrete/asset_library');

echo '<div class="ccm-block-field-group">';
echo '<h2>' . t('Title') . '</h2>';
echo $form->text('title', $title, array('style' =>
    'width: 550px'));
echo '</div>';

echo '<div class="ccm-block-field-group">';
echo '<h2>' . t('Picture') . '</h2>';
echo $al->image('ccm-b-image', 'fIDpicture', t('Choose File'),
    $this->controller->getPicture());
echo '</div>';

echo '<div class="ccm-block-field-group">';
echo '<h2>' . t('Description') . '</h2>';
Loader::element('editor_config');
Loader::element('editor_controls', array('mode' => 'full'));
echo $form->textarea('description', $description, array('class' =>
    'ccm-advanced-editor'));
echo '</div>';
?>
```

What just happened?

Our code is getting bigger but we're also coming closer to finishing the first block. Let's go through all the new steps:

- `Loader::helper` is often used to include functionality from the concrete5 core. In this case, we're loading the `asset_library`, which contains functions to include the file manager.

- Next we use a `DIV` element with a built-in class named `ccm-block-field-group`. This class adds a line to make our dialog look a bit nicer.

- The next line uses the function called `t` again; and again, this is just to make the block translatable.

- The `$form` refers to the form helper from which we use several methods. In this case, the `$form->text` method uses the following parameters:
  - ID of your input box.
  - A variable to process. Please note, this has been added automatically by the controller because the table specified in `btTable` contains a column with this name.
  - An array where you can pass any HTML attribute to the input element. In this case, a style to specify the width of the control.

- `$al->image` adds a selector, which pops up a dialog to select an image from the file manager. There's another method you can use to select any kind of file; just use `$al->file` instead. In the example, we'll use a few parameters as follows:
  - The ID of your form field.
  - The name of your column, must match with the blocks table.
  - Text to display when no file has been selected.
  - A reference to the currently selected file. Must be a file object and not just the reference in form of a number.

- `$form->textarea` prints a plain-text, multi-line input field. If you include some PHP elements in front of it and add the proper CSS class, you'll get access to the built-in rich text editor. `Loader::element` pulls files from `concrete/elements` where you can find a bit more about the details of the rich text editor, in case you want to know what's going on under the hood.

Time for action – printing block output

Carry out the following steps:

1. Last but not least, we have to make sure the data we save in the block gets printed on the page. For this, we have to create a file named `view.php` in our new add-on directory.

2. We've got to access and print the file object along with some basic commands to print the value of our variables. The content of the file has to look like this:

```php
<?php defined('C5_EXECUTE') or die('Access Denied.'); ?>
<div class="product-information">
<h2><?php echo $title?></h2>
<?php
if ($picture instanceof File) {
    $html = Loader::helper('html');
    echo $html->image($picture->getURL());
}
echo $description;
?>
</div>
```

What just happened?

The last part, the actual rendering of the content, is rather short:

- We did use another helper, `html`, to print our image element. We could have built this string manually; which option you chose is up to you.

- We're accessing `$picture` which has been set in the block controller in the method `view`. If it contains a file, we show it to the user.

Time for action – installing a block

Now that we've created all the files, we can install our block.

1. Focus the **Intelligent Search** box and type `Block Types`.

2. You should see your new block on top of the list. Click on the **Install** button next to it and concrete5 will install it.

3. Edit a page of your choice and add a new instance of our block, enter the necessary data and you'll get a structured output of the three fields.

What just happened?

We created all the files needed for a custom block, installed it and added it to an existing page. That's all it takes to build a basic concrete5 block.

Checking for mandatory fields

If we wanted to make sure there were no products without pictures, we could add a few more lines of code.

Time for action – adding a check for mandatory fields

Carry out the following steps:

1. In the previously created file `controller.php`, add the following method right after the function `getBlockTypeName`:

    ```
    public function getJavaScriptStrings() {
        return array(
            'image-required' => t('You must select an image.')
        );
    }
    ```

2. Create a new file named `auto.js` in your block directory where you've created controller.php; it will automatically be included when you add or edit a product information block instance. Put the following content in it:

    ```
    ccmValidateBlockForm = function() {
        if ($("#ccm-b-image-fm-value").val() == '' ||
            $("#ccm-b-image-fm-value").val() == 0) {
            ccm_addError(ccm_t('image-required'));
        }
        return false;
    }
    ```

What just happened?

We created a JavaScript file, which is automatically included and called before the data is saved.

The method `ccmValidateBlockForm` is a built-in method, which you can use to interact with the field checking process.

`ccm_addError` adds an error to an internal array based on texts processed by `ccm_t`, which is looking for values generated by the method `getJavaScriptStrings` in the controller. This is necessary because JavaScript strings can't be translated; we have to fetch them from our PHP-based block controller.

Please note that we're accessing a field called `ccm-b-image-fm-value`, which is created by `echo $al->image('ccm-b-image'...)`. We have to append `-fm-value`. That's because the image helper needs several fields to manage its data. The Chrome developer console is usually the easiest way to find these fields.

Adding product categories

We're going to make one more modification to this block before we start with another one. Whether you want to manage products, news or anything else, you might want to split these entries into categories.

For this, we're going to add another table to our block from which we're pulling all the categories to add a drop-down menu to our block.

Time for action – adding product categories

Carry out the following steps:

1. Open `db.xml` for your block; we've got to make a few modifications. The file should look like the following afterwards:

```xml
<?xml version="1.0"?>
<schema version="0.3">
    <table name="btProductInformation">
        <field name="bID" type="I">
            <key />
            <unsigned />
        </field>
        <field name="title" type="C" size="255"></field>
        <field name="description" type="X2"></field>
        <field name="fIDpicture" type="I"></field>
            <field name="categoryID" type="I"></field>
            </table>
        <table name="btProductInformationCategories">
            <field name="categoryID" type="I">
                <autoincrement />
            <key />
            <unsigned />
        </field>
        <field name="category" type="C" size="255"></field>
        <index name="btProductInformationCategories_IX">
            <descr>Makes sure the categories are unique</descr>
            <col>category</col>
            <unique />
        </index>
    </table>
```

```
<sql>
  <query>REPLACE INTO btProductInformationCategories(category)
      VALUES ('Top-Notch')</query>
  <query>REPLACE INTO btProductInformationCategories(category)
      VALUES ('Junk Goods')</query>
</sql>
</schema>
```

2. Next, open `controller.php` and add a new method that returns a list of categories:

```
function getCategories() {
    $db = Loader::db();
    return $db->GetAssoc('SELECT categoryID,category FROM
        btProductInformationCategories ORDER BY category');
}
```

3. We also have to make sure that the form contains a drop down with our categories, open `form_setup_html.php`, and add the following code just above the closing PHP tag `?>` at the end:

```
echo '<div class="ccm-block-field-group">';
echo '<h2>' . t('Category') . '</h2>';
echo $form->select('categoryID',
    $this->controller->getCategories(), $categoryID);
echo '</div>';
```

4. Since we changed `db.xml` we also have to tell concrete5 to update the database accordingly. To do this, go to the dashboard, select **Block Types** and then select the **Production Information** block. In the block detail screen click on **Refresh** to apply the database changes.

What just happened?

A few modifications to add categories to our product information, starting with the database model:

- ◆ A new column to the existing table, which references to the primary key of our new table `btProductInformationCategories`.

- ◆ The new table with a numeric, incrementing primary key.

- ◆ A single text field to hold the name of the category.

A small piece of code to get the categories from the database—here we have to make sure the array is returned in the correct way.

The PHP array must have the following structure. This is important because the array key (in square brackets) must match the Primary Key of the categories table:

```
Array
(
    [14] => Junk Goods
    [13] => Top-Notch
)
```

The method `GetAssoc` returns this structure if your query only returns two columns. If you haven't worked with ADOdb before, you might want to look at the documentation first at `http://phplens.com/lens/adodb/docs-adodb.htm`.

Next, we did use another method from the form helper to print a drop-down menu using the preceding structure. By modifying the dialog we're already done, have a look at the new dialog and you'll see the new feature in your block.

 If you want to get an overview of the available helper methods you can use to get access to the concrete5 default widgets, you should have a look at the following web pages:

- `http://www.concrete5.org/documentation/developers/forms/standard-widgets`
- `http://www.concrete5.org/documentation/developers/forms/concrete5-widgets`

Have a go hero – getting more information about blocks

We've created our first basic block; if you already have a good feeling about these steps, you might want to dig a bit deeper into the way blocks work. Where can you find more information?

The official developer documentation is always a good start. You can find it at `http://www.concrete5.org/documentation/developers/`. Look at the **Blocks** and **Helpers** sections if you want to get more background information about the topics discussed in this chapter. You'll get more information about helpers during the next few chapters that you can use for blocks as well as other add-ons, such as packages or themes.

It's not everyone's favorite, but the actual source code is more up-to-date than any book or documentation. Try to get a picture of the files found in concrete5. If you remember, we derived all our block controllers from `BlockController`, which you can find in `concrete/libraries/block_controller.php`. You'll then find another derived class called `Concrete5_Library_BlockController`, which can be found in `concrete/core/libraries/block_controller.php`. This is where you'll find all the methods you override in your block controller. If you're working on `view.php`, you should know that you're working on an object instantiated from `BlockView`, which you can find in the same directory too.

Pop quiz – parts of a block

When building a block for concrete5, you have to follow a certain structure in order to get it working. Try to decide which questions are correct and which aren't:

1. `db.xml` is used to describe the structure of the table(s) used by the block

2. The controller of a block in a directory called `my_block` would be named `MyBlockController`

3. The controller of a block in a directory called `my_block` would be named `MyBlockBlockController`

4. In the block controller, you have to specify the main block table in a property called `btTable` if the block needs to work with database tables

5. In `db.xml` you have several data types you can use, mostly `C` for characters/short strings, `I` for integer, `T` for dates and `X2` for long strings

6. In `db.xml` you have several data types you can use, mostly `S` for characters/short strings, `I` for integer, `D` for dates and `X2` for long strings

Building a product list

Wouldn't it be handy if we could create a list of all product information blocks in our website, a list of products or news? Just as we can with the page list block which comes with the core? Sure we can, but we have to create another block.

Handling multiple block versions

However, before we can start building this block, we have to make a few more modifications to our product information block. Remember the explanation about `bID` at the beginning of this chapter—every time a block content is updated, a new data record is created. This means that, after a few updates, we've got more table records than actual blocks we'd like to show in our list.

There are several options to get around this problem:

♦ We could dig into the database model of concrete5 and see where it stores the information about page and block versions. This would certainly work, but as we wouldn't be using an official API, it's possible that our code would be broken in a future version of concrete5. Bad idea, but in case you still wonder, have a look at the `BlockRelations` table.

◆ There's an attribute in the block controller that we can set to disable the concrete5 version control. This works by setting `btIncludeAll` to 1, just as you set the table name by using `btTable`. This would certainly work as well, but users of concrete5 are quite likely going to expect that you don't break any core functionality such as the version control—let's ignore this idea and look at a more sophisticated way.

Time for action – handling multiple block versions

We're going to add an attribute to our table to manage the replacement of block versions. In our product list, we can check for this attribute to see if a block has been replaced.

1. Add a new table column by adding the following modification to db.xml, please note, the code only shows a part of the actual file:

```
<table name="btProductInformation">
<field name="bID" type="I">
   <key />
   <unsigned />
</field>
<field name="title" type="C" size="255"></field>
<field name="description" type="X2"></field>
<field name="fIDpicture" type="I"></field>
<field name="categoryID" type="I"></field>
    <field name="replacesBlockID" type="I"></field>
    <index name="btProductInformation_IX1">
      <descr>Makes sure replacement lookups perform well</descr>
      <col>replacesBlockID</col>
      <unique />
    </index>
</table>
```

2. In `controller.php`, add the following duplicate method to the block controller class:

```
function duplicate($newbID) {
   parent::duplicate($newbID);

   $db = Loader::db();
   $db->Execute('UPDATE btProductInformation SET replacesBlockID=?
WHERE bID=?',array($this->bID,$newbID));
}
```

3. Since we changed `db.xml` again, we also have to tell concrete5 to update the database accordingly. To do this go to the dashboard, select **Block Types** and then select the **Production Information** block. In the block detail screen click on **Refresh** to apply the database changes.

If you already inserted product information blocks, you should remove and re-insert them. The existing blocks are missing some values in the `replacesBlockID`, which could lead to some unexpected results.

What just happened?

We had to add a column to our block to be able to fetch the correct block version, the one which is currently active on the page. The internal method `duplicate` is called when a block is edited. In order to make sure the old version isn't removed, the block content ID is duplicated before it's presented to the user to make changes.

Open phpMyAdmin at `http://localhost/phpmyadmin/`; it has been installed with your Bitnami stack. You can have a look at the content of the table `btProductInformation`:

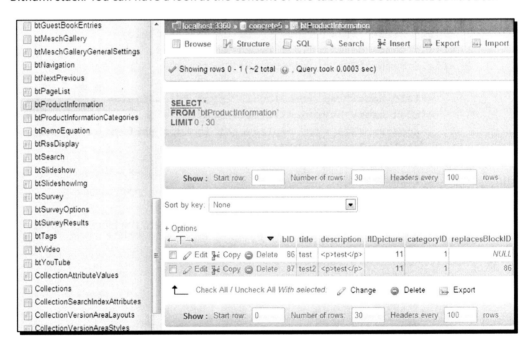

In the preceding screenshot, you can see that the block with the ID 86 has been replaced. This ID has been saved in the column **replacesBlockID** for each corresponding successor. We are going to use this information to present a list of all active block versions, in this case the entry with the bID 87.

Creating a product list block

In this part, we're going to create another block from scratch that depends on the first block. It simply pulls information from it and creates a list. At the end, we're going to have a block which creates a simple list along with a link to get to the detail that looks similar to the following screenshot:

Time for action – creating the product list block

Carry out the following steps:

1. Create a new directory in `blocks` named `product_list`. We start with the database model, create a new file named `db.xml` in the new directory with the following content:

```xml
<?xml version="1.0"?>
<schema version="0.3">
    <table name="btProductList">
        <field name="bID" type="I">
            <key />
            <unsigned />
        </field>
        <field name="categoryID" type="I"></field>
    </table>
</schema>
```

2. Create another file named `controller.php`:

```php
<?php
defined('C5_EXECUTE') or die('Access Denied.');
class ProductListBlockController extends BlockController {

    protected $btTable = 'btProductList';
    protected $btInterfaceWidth = "250";
    protected $btInterfaceHeight = "110";

    public function getBlockTypeDescription() {
        return t("Embeds a Product List in your web page.");
    }

    public function getBlockTypeName() {
        return t("Product List");
    }

    public function getCategories() {
        $db = Loader::db();
        return $db->GetAssoc('SELECT categoryID,category FROM
            btProductInformationCategories ORDER BY category');
    }

    public function getProducts() {
        $db = Loader::db();
        $blocks = array();

        // select all block instances which haven't been replaced
        $rs = $db->Execute('SELECT bID FROM btProductInformation bpi
          WHERE categoryID = ? AND NOT EXISTS (SELECT 1 FROM
          btProductInformation bpi_sub WHERE
          bpi.bID=bpi_sub.replacesBlockID)', array($this-
          >categoryID));

        if ($rs) {
            while ($row = $rs->FetchRow()) {
                $blocks[] = Block::getByID($row['bID']);
            }
        }

        return $blocks;
    }

    public function view() {
        $this->set('products', $this->getProducts());
    }
}
```

3. Create another file, `view.php`. It is going to print a list built within the controller:

```php
<hr/>

<?php
defined('C5_EXECUTE') or die('Access Denied.');

$nh = Loader::helper('navigation');
foreach ($products as $product) {
    $pageLink = $nh->getLinkToCollection(
        $product->getOriginalCollection());

    echo "<h2>{$product->instance->title}</h2>";
    echo "<a href=\"{$pageLink}\">more...</a>";
    echo "<hr/>";
}
```

4. Create two more files, `add.php` and `edit.php`. Both of them have identical content:

```php
<?php
defined('C5_EXECUTE') or die('Access Denied.');
$this->inc('form_setup_html.php');
```

5. Create another file named `form_setup_html.php` with the following content. It's the actual form which is used by `add.php` and `edit.php`:

```php
<?php
defined('C5_EXECUTE') or die('Access Denied.');

$al = Loader::helper('concrete/asset_library');

echo '<div class="ccm-block-field-group">';
echo '<h2>' . t('Category') . '</h2>';
echo $form->select('categoryID',
    $this->controller->getCategories(),
    $categoryID,
    array('style' => 'width:235px;'));
echo '</div>';
```

What just happened?

Let's go through the last section step-by-step:

- ◆ `db.xml`, this file is rather simple. There's the mandatory `bID` because we're linking this table to the block controller. And there's a numeric field to reference the category for which we'd like to show the products.

- ◆ `controller.php`. Besides the already known methods and properties at the beginning, there are only two methods: `getCategories` and `getProducts`, which returns an array of blocks matching our selection. We're not only getting the values from the database, but also using using `Block::getByID` to get a PHP object instead because it allows us to call any block method we like.

- ◆ `view.php`, this file loops through the array of blocks generated by the controller method `getProducts`. There's another helper, `navigation`, which has been used several times in our autonav templates. We use it to create a link to the page object where our block has been inserted. The method `getOriginalCollection()` returns that page.

- ◆ `add.php`, `edit.php`, and `form_setup_html.php` are almost identical to the previous block. The form is just simpler since we only have one element in it.

Don't forget to install the block in the **Block Types** screen in your dashboard.

Have a go hero – extending the product list

The blocks we've created work fine, but they aren't really finished. There are lots of features we could add to improve them. It's not part of this book to go into every possible detail; you just have gotten a first idea about blocks. Now it's time to be creative and add some more features—a few ideas:

- ◆ Create more templates, a product list that prints a thumbnail, and maybe show the first few words from the description

- ◆ Add or modify the fields and turn the blocks into a news, calendar, FAQ application, and so on

- ◆ Allow the user to change the sort order of the product list

Creating a picture magnifier

We've looked at several jQuery plugins when we created block templates. Let's create an add-on from scratch which is based on a jQuery plugin named jQZoom by Marco Renzi available at `http://www.mind-projects.it/projects/jqzoom/`.

Time for action – creating the picture magnifier block

Carry out the following steps:

1. Create a new folder named `jqzoom` in `blocks` as we did before.

2. Download the plugin from the preceding link and copy the `images` directory to our new folder. Do the same with the `css` directory and `js` but make sure there's just one file in `js` named `jquery.jqzoom-core-pack.js`.

3. Create two files, `add.php` and `edit.php` with the same content as always:

```php
<?php
defined('C5_EXECUTE') or die('Access Denied.');
$this->inc('form_setup_html.php');
```

4. The database structure file `db.xml` is quite simple:

```xml
<?xml version="1.0"?>
<schema version="0.3">
    <table name="btJqzoom">
        <field name="bID" type="I">
            <key />
            <unsigned />
        </field>
        <field name="title" type="C" size="255"></field>
        <field name="fIDpicture" type="I"></field>
    </table>
</schema>
```

5. The block controller you have to save as `controller.php` also is quite simple:

```php
<?php
defined('C5_EXECUTE') or die('Access Denied. ');
class JqzoomBlockController extends BlockController {

    protected $btTable = 'btJqzoom';
    protected $btInterfaceWidth = "590";
    protected $btInterfaceHeight = "450";


    public function getBlockTypeDescription() {
        return t("Embeds a picture magnifier in your page.");
    }
```

```php
    public function getBlockTypeName() {
        return t("jQZoom Picture");
    }

    public function getJavaScriptStrings() {
        return array(
            'image-required' => t('You must select an image.')
        );
    }

    public function getPicture() {
        if ($this->fIDpicture > 0) {
            return File::getByID($this->fIDpicture);
        }
        return null;
    }

    public function view() {
        $this->set('picture', $this->getPicture());
    }
}
```

6. Next, we have to create the form used by add.php and edit.php by putting the following content in form_setup_html.php:

```php
<?php
defined('C5_EXECUTE') or die('Access Denied.');

$al = Loader::helper('concrete/asset_library');

echo '<div class="ccm-block-field-group">';
echo '<h2>' . t('Title') . '</h2>';
echo $form->text('title', $title,
    array('style' => 'width: 550px'));
echo '</div>';

echo '<div class="ccm-block-field-group">';
echo '<h2>' . t('Picture') . '</h2>';
echo $al->image('ccm-b-image', 'fIDpicture', t('Choose File'),
    $this->controller->getPicture());
echo '</div>';
```

7. And of course, `view.php` that prints the HTML structure used by jQZoom:

```
<div class="ccm-jqzoom">
<?php
$image = Loader::helper('image');

if ($picture) {
    $bigPicture = $image->getThumbnail($picture,800,800)->src;
    $smallPicture = $image->getThumbnail($picture,200,200)->src;

    echo "<a class=\"jqzoom\" title=\"{$this->controller->title}\"
     href=\"{$bigPicture}\">";
    echo "<img src=\"{$smallPicture}\" alt=\"\"
     title=\"{$this->controller->title}\"/>";
    echo "</a>";
}
?>
</div>
```

8. Since we've included a jQuery plugin, we have to make sure it's loaded as well. Create `view.js` with the following content:

```
$(document).ready(function(){
    if (!CCM_EDIT_MODE) {
        $('.jqzoom').jqzoom({
            showEffect: 'fadein',
            hideEffect: 'fadeout',
            fadeinSpeed: 'slow',
            fadeoutSpeed: 'normal',
            imageOpacity: 0.25,
            zoomWidth: 200,
            zoomHeight: 200
        });
    }
});
```

9. Save all the files and install the block in the **Block Types** screen in your dashboard.

What just happened?

If you placed the block on your page, you'll see a small thumbnail and a magnified picture on the right if you move your mouse over it. A simple but nice effect to get a closer look at a picture:

There are two files we want to have a closer look at:

- `view.php`. This time there are two thumbnails in it and not just one. Why? Sometimes people upload huge pictures, especially in times when even a cheap camera can take pictures twice as big as your screen. By restricting the size of both pictures, we can make sure they won't cause any problems on your site.

- `view.js`. First, there's a variable `CCM_EDIT_MODE`, which we haven't used before. By checking this variable, we can make sure that the jQuery plugin effect won't cause any problems with the in-site editing concept. This can happen from time to time. Disabling the effect in edit mode is usually the easiest thing to do and doesn't cause any problems.

The jQZoom plugin has several options; in order to keep things simple, we didn't create a user interface for all of them. If you want to change the properties, you currently have to do this by modifying `view.php` and `view.js`. You could create more fields in `form_setup_html.php` to manage all those properties if you want to create a more advanced block.

Creating a PDF-generating block

HTML, and the technologies which you can embed, offer a vast number of possibilities to create almost anything you want. Whether it's a game, an application, or just a website, there's a tool for it. However, even with the growing number of web technologies, printing is still easier and more reliable if you've got a PDF file.

In this part, we're going to create a block which will simply print the word PDF but, in the background, it's going to create a PDF on-the-fly. Let's take a look—you'll be surprised how few steps we're going to need for this block!

Time for action – creating the PDF generation block

Carry out the following steps:

1. Create a new directory called `pdf` in the `blocks` directory of your site. Within that directory, add a new file called `controller.php` and insert the following lines:

```php
<?php
defined('C5_EXECUTE') or die('Access Denied.');
class PdfBlockController extends BlockController {

    protected $btInterfaceWidth = "200";
    protected $btInterfaceHeight = "140";

    public function getBlockTypeDescription() {
        return t("Add a PDF-Generation link in your web page.");
    }

    public function getBlockTypeName() {
        return t("PDF Generator");
    }
}
```

2. Here's a new element. As generating PDF files isn't that easy, we're going to use a library for this. Go to `http://www.mpdf1.com/mpdf/` and download the latest ZIP version (at the time of writing the latest is version 5.6). Extract the ZIP file into `libraries` but make sure it's the one in the root, not in the folder `concrete`.

3. Another new element. We're going to create a tool which we're calling from the block; you'll see how it comes together in the next step. For now, just create a file named `generate_pdf.php` in the `tools` folder in the root of your site, not in `blocks`, and put the following lines in it:

```php
<?php
defined('C5_EXECUTE') or die('Access Denied.');

Loader::library('MPDF56/mpdf');
$fh = Loader::helper('file');

$header = <<<EOT
<style type="text/css">
    body { font-family: Helvetica, Arial; }
    h1 { border-bottom: 1px solid black; }
```

```
</style>
EOT;

$url = $_REQUEST['p'];
$content = $fh->getContents($url);
$content = preg_replace("/.*<body>|<\/body>.*/si", "", $content);
$content = preg_replace("/<!--hidden_in_pdf_start-->.*?<!--hidden_
in_pdf_end-->/siu", "", $content);

$mpdf=new mPDF('utf-8','A4');
$mpdf->showImageErrors = true;
$mpdf->SetCreator('PDF by concrete5');
$mpdf->useOnlyCoreFonts = true;
$mpdf->setBasePath($url);
$mpdf->WriteHTML($header . $content);
$mpdf->Output();
?>
```

4. Next, we have to create `view.php` to print a link which generates the PDF file. In this case, we're printing a simple text link, but feel free to replace it with an icon:

```
<!--hidden_in_pdf_start-->
<?php
defined('C5_EXECUTE') or die('Access Denied.');

$nh = Loader::helper('navigation');
$url = Loader::helper('concrete/urls');

$toolsUrl = $url->getToolsURL('generate_pdf');
$toolsUrl .= '?p=' . rawurlencode($nh->getLinkToCollection(
    $this->c, true));

echo "<a href=\"{$toolsUrl}\">PDF</a>";


?>
<!--hidden_in_pdf_end-->
```

5. When you print a PDF generated from your webpage, you probably don't want to include all elements from the website. An element like the navigation might be useless on a paper; no one can click on links printed on a paper. If you want to hide the navigation in the PDF, you can edit `header.php` from your theme, which in case you followed every chapter is located in `themes/c5book/elements` and insert the highlighted lines:

```
<div id="wrapper">
  <div id="page">
    <!--hidden_in_pdf_start-->
    <div id="header_line_top"></div>
    <div id="header">
```

```
        <?php
        $a = new GlobalArea ('Header Nav');
        $a->display($c);
        ?>
    </div>
    <div id="header_line_bottom"></div>
    <!--hidden_in_pdf_end-->
```

6. Once you've saved all the files, you can place the block anywhere you want and click on it to generate a PDF.

What just happened?

The block we created has only a few lines of code, and doesn't even need a new database table. Since we don't have any options, we also skipped the creation of add.php and edit. php. A block without those files will simply be added to the page after you click on it and will not show you a dialog to enter any options.

The most complicated job of this block is handled by mPDF, the library we are using to convert our HTML code into a PDF file. Our add-on is only a wrapper for it and shows you a simple link where you can dynamically create a PDF file looking like this:

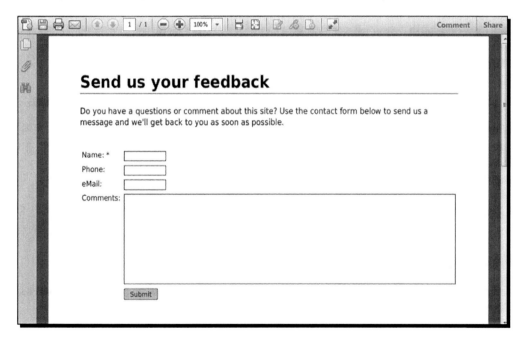

There are a bunch of new files, most of them quite small, but there are a few things we should have a look at:

Using generate_pdf.php

The file that calls mPDF contains two *regex* patterns to filter the content from the page. The first one `/.*<body>|<\/body>.*/si` makes sure we only get the body and ignore the header, as we don't want to include any of the styles from the website layout. This allows us to style the PDF the way we want.

There's another regex pattern `/<!—hidden_in_pdf_start-->.*?<!-- hidden_in_pdf_end-->/siu` to hide everything between the two HTML comments. It's what gets rid of the navigation header in our step-by-step example.

At the beginning of the file are a few CSS rules. The mPDF library supports an impressive number of CSS features. In our example, there's a rule to change the font and one to add a line to the main headings, but there's a lot more you can do with CSS.

There are also a few HTML elements which you can put in the file to add page headers or footers, a PDF table of content, and page breaks. They aren't part of the official HTML standard; unless you've worked with mPDF before, you won't know about them. If you want to get the most out of your PDF, you should probably have a look at the official documentation available at `http://www.mpdf1.com/mpdf/manual`.

Using view.php

The block template starts with the comment we already used to hide the navigation. We also use this to hide the link to generate a PDF from the PDF once it has been created.

There's another helper `urls` that has a function named `getToolsURL`, which we use to generate a link to our PDF-generating tool. Whenever you want to directly call a PHP file in concrete5, you should consider putting it in the tools directory as we just did. While you can certainly call a PHP file directly from concrete5, you won't get access to the concrete5 framework features and you can't use the models, helpers, or anything else offered by the framework.

Creating a simple gallery

Previously, we created a template for the slideshow block to build a simple lightbox such as gallery. In this case, we're going to use the same JavaScript but build a new block with it from scratch.

Time for action – creating the simple gallery block

1. Create a new directory called `simple_gallery` in the root directory `blocks`.

2. In the new directory, add a new file called `db.xml` which describes the table structure of our block. Put this content in it:

```xml
<?xml version="1.0"?>
<schema version="0.3">
    <table name="btSimpleGallery">
        <field name="bID" type="I">
            <key />
            <unsigned />
        </field>
        <field name="fsID" type="I">
            <unsigned />
        </field>
    </table>
</schema>
```

3. In the same directory, create another file called `controller.php` with the following content:

```php
<?php
defined('C5_EXECUTE') or die('Access Denied.');

class SimpleGalleryBlockController extends BlockController {

    protected $btTable = 'btSimpleGallery';
    protected $btInterfaceWidth = "250";
    protected $btInterfaceHeight = "120";

    public function getBlockTypeDescription() {
        return t("Simple picture gallery block.");
    }

    public function getBlockTypeName() {
        return t("Simple Picture Gallery");
    }

    protected function setFileSets() {
        Loader::model('file_set');
        $fileSetsList = FileSet::getMySets();
        $fileSets = array();
        foreach ($fileSetsList as $fileSet) {
            $fileSets[$fileSet->getFileSetID()] =
                $fileSet->getFileSetName();
        }
        $this->set('fileSets', $fileSets);
    }
```

```php
public function edit() {
    $this->setFileSets();
}

public function add() {
    $this->setFileSets();
}

public function view() {
    $fs = FileSet::getByID($this->fsID);
    $fileList = new FileList();
    $fileList->filterBySet($fs);
    $fileList->filterByType(FileType::T_IMAGE);
    $fileList->sortByFileSetDisplayOrder();

    $images = $fileList->get(1000, 0);

    $this->set('images', $images);
}

}
```

4. Still in the same directory, create a new file called `view.php` which will display the actual gallery:

```php
<?php
defined('C5_EXECUTE') or die('Access Denied.');

echo '<div class="simple-gallery">';

foreach ($images as $image) {
    $fileName = $image->getFileName();
    $picturePath = $image->getRelativePath();
    $thumbnail = $image->getThumbnail(2, false);

    echo "<a title=\"{$fileName}\" href=\"{$picturePath}\">";
    echo "<img src=\"{$thumbnail}\" />";
    echo "</a>";
}

echo '</div>';
```

5. In the same directory, create two more files `add.php` and `edit.php`; both have the same content:

```php
<?php
defined('C5_EXECUTE') or die('Access Denied.');
$this->inc('form_setup_html.php');
```

6. Both files `add.php` and `edit.php` include another file that has to be in the same directory and is called `form_setup_html.php` with the following content:

```php
<?php
defined('C5_EXECUTE') or die('Access Denied.');
```

```
echo $form->label('fsID', t('File Set: '));
echo $form->select('fsID', $fileSets, $fsID);
```

7. Still in the same directory, create one more file called `view.js` with the following content:

```
$(document).ready(function() {
  $(".simple-gallery a").lightBox({
    imageBtnPrev: CCM_REL +
      "/blocks/simple_gallery/images/lightbox-btn-prev.gif",
    imageBtnNext: CCM_REL +
      "/blocks/simple_gallery/images/lightbox-btn-next.gif",
    imageLoading: CCM_REL +
      "/blocks/simple_gallery/images/lightbox-ico-loading.gif",
    imageBtnClose: CCM_REL +
      "/blocks/simple_gallery/images/lightbox-btn-close.gif",
    imageBlank: CCM_REL +
      "/blocks/simple_gallery/images/lightbox-blank.gif"
  });
});
```

8. Next, we have to copy a number of files from the previously created slideshow template. Copy the three directories **css**, **images**, and **js** from `/blocks/slideshow/templates/gallery` into the directory **simple_gallery**. The final structure should look like this:

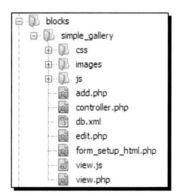

9. Type **block types** in the intelligent search box and select the first entry. You'll see your block on top of the list. Click on the **Install** button next to it.

10. Navigate back to your site and switch into edit mode. If you now click on **Add to ...** in an area of your choice, you'll see your new block at the end. Select your block and you'll see a small dialog where you can select a file set. If you haven't created one yet, go to the file manager, click on a file you want to put in a set, and select **Set** from the menu that shows up. Enter the name of the new set, update the file, and go back to your gallery.

What just happened?

The block we just created is a nice example that shows you how you can integrate an existing jQuery plugin. Compared to the solution shown in the previous chapter where we only created a new template, we had to create a `db.xml` to describe the table we need to save our gallery's data as well as `add.php`, `edit.php`, and `form_setup_html.php` to make it possible to select a file select when adding or editing the block. The main file is `controller.php` though; it connects everything and forwards the correct data to each element.

There are three methods you might want to have a closer look at:

◆ `public function view`: This method is called when a block is rendered, right before `view.php` is processed. You can create variables visible in `view.php` by using `$this->set('hello', 'world')` which would create a variable called `$hello`. We mainly use this method to keep `view.php` clean, thus making it easier to create additional templates.

◆ `public function add`: This method is called when the user wants to add a new instance of your block. You can use it to add data available in `add.php`.

◆ `public function edit`: This method works the same way as the method above but it is used when the user edits an existing block.

Have a go hero – adding more gallery options

If you add or edit a gallery block, you'll see that there's just one option to select a file set. However, there are lots of small features you could add. Here are a few ideas:

◆ An option to specify the maximum thumbnail width and height.

◆ An option to sort the images in a random order.

◆ Some options to use more options of the jQuery plugin. Have a look at this page to get an overview: `http://leandrovieira.com/projects/jquery/lightbox/#extend`.

Summary

We created a few blocks; you should have gotten a first impression about the way to build a block. Whether you build simple or more complicated blocks, the process we've looked at stays pretty much the same. Depending on your background, things might be a bit confusing at this point but take some time to go through these examples and you'll realize they all work more or less the same way. You can also go and download some add-ons from the marketplace or anywhere else on the Internet. There are always a few common elements in concrete5 blocks. Once you understand them, it shouldn't be too difficult to use your PHP and jQuery skills to come up with more advanced blocks.

Please note, we haven't looked at every method available, it's not a reference book. This chapter was merely a collection of explanations about building blocks. If you're eager to understand every detail of the concrete5 API, you have to dig a bit deeper. If you don't, just remember the basic elements of a block—db.xml, which describes the structure of your tables, add.php, and edit.php that are used when you're editing the block, controller.php for the logic, and view.php for the visible things. These are the things you have to understand before we continue in the next chapter and combine all these blocks in a single package.

The complete source code created in this chapter can be found in the 9314_08_c5book_blocks.zip folder on the Packt Publishing website.

9
Everything in a Package

We created lots of different additions for concrete5 in the previous chapters. The page layout has changed, as well as the block layout, and we even created some completely new functionality from scratch.

While we were able to create and improve a lot of different things in concrete5 without touching the actual core files in the concrete directory, we might have had to manually install several elements to get our functionality into a new site. By using a package, we can wrap all the previously created elements into a single directory, which can be installed with a single click on the dashboard.

We'll cover the following topics in this chapter:

- A few words about packages in general, why you might want to build one, what benefits they have, and so on
- An example package based on the previously built blocks
- A basic example about events to show you how to hook right into the core
- Another example showing you how to add a job, a task which is periodically executed
- A final example that shows you how you can inject some JavaScript from a package into every page

What's a package?

Before we start creating our package, here are a few words about the functionality and purpose of packages:

- They can hold a single or several themes together
- You can include blocks which your theme needs
- You can check the requirements during the installation process in case your package depends on other blocks, configurations, and so on
- A package can be used to hook into events raised by concrete5 to execute custom code during different kinds of actions
- You can create **single pages** for custom functionality and dashboard pages
- You can create jobs that run periodically to improve or check things in your website

These are the most important things you can do with a package. Some of what you can do doesn't depend on packages, but is easier to handle if you put it in packages. It's up to you, but putting every extension in a package might even be useful if there's just a single element in it—why?

- You never have to worry where to extract the add-on. It always belongs in the `packages` directory.
- An add-on wrapped in a package can be submitted to the concrete5 marketplace, allowing you to earn money or make some people in the community happy by releasing your add-on for free.

Package structure

We've already looked at different structures and you are probably already familiar with most of the directories in concrete5. Before we continue, here are a few words about the package structure; it's essential that you understand its concept before we continue.

A **package** is basically a complete concrete5 structure within one directory. All the directories are optional though. No need to create all of them, but you can create and use all of them within a single package. The directory `concrete` is a lot like a package as well, it's just located in its own directory and not within packages.

The package controller

As with the blocks we've created, the package has a controller as well. First of all, it is used to handle the installation process, but it's not limited to that. We can handle events and a few more things in the package controller; more about that later in this chapter.

For now, we only need the controller to make sure the dashboard knows the package name and description.

Time for action – creating the package controller

Carry out the following steps:

1. First, create a new directory named c5book in packages.

2. Within that directory, create a file named controller.php and put the following content in it:

```php
<?php
defined('C5_EXECUTE') or die('Access Denied.');

class c5bookPackage extends Package {

    protected $pkgHandle = 'c5book';
    protected $appVersionRequired = '5.6.0';
    protected $pkgVersion = '1.0';

    public function getPackageDescription() {
        return t("Theme, Templates and Blocks from concrete5 for
            Beginner's");
    }

    public function getPackageName() {
        return t("c5book");
    }

    public function install() {
        $pkg = parent::install();
    }
}
?>
```

3. You can create a file named icon.png 97 x 97 pixels with 4 px rounded transparent corners. This is the official specification that you have to follow if you want to upload your add-on to the concrete5 marketplace.

4. Once you've created the directory and the mandatory controller, you can go to your dashboard and click on the link **Extend concrete5**. Please note that we previously created a block we had to install in a screen called **Block Types**; both screens add new functionality but one installs the block and one the packages. You can see the latter on the following screenshot.

Our package doesn't have any functionality but you can try to install it if you want; there's an option to uninstall it too.

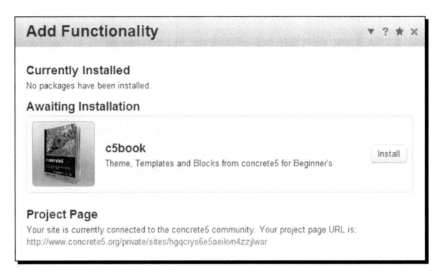

What just happened?

The controller we created looks and works a lot like a block controller, which you should have seen and created already. However, let's go through all the elements of the package controller anyway; it's important that you understand them:

- ◆ pkgHandle: This is a unique handle for your package. You'll need this when you access your package from code.

- ◆ appVersionRequired: This is the minimum version required to install the add-on. concrete5 will check that during the installation process.

- ◆ pkgVersion: This is the current version of the package. Make sure that you change the number when you release an update for a package; concrete5 has to know that it is installing an update and not a new version.

- ◆ getPackageDescription: This returns the description of your package. Use the t-function to keep it translatable.

- ◆ getPackageName: This returns the name of your package. It's the same as getPackageDescription, just a bit shorter.

- ◆ install: You could remove this method in the preceding controller, since we're only calling its parent method and don't check anything else. It has no influence, but we'll need this method later when putting blocks in our package. It's just a skeleton for the following steps at the moment.

Pop quiz – what does a package do?

Q1. In order to know if you have or want to build a package, you should know what you can do with a package. Decide which elements you think should be part of a package.

1. A package can contain one or several blocks as well as block templates.

2. You can include themes and their page types in a package.

3. A package can contain a maintenance job which is executed regularly for periodic checks, updates, and so on.

4. You can include a third-party library in a package.

Q2. Which of the following things can you do within a package?

1. You can catch events by concrete5 to hook into core processes such as executing custom code on user additions and page modifications.

2. You can create a custom installation method to make sure all dependencies are met before the add-on is installed. You can also use it to add objects needed by your add-on such as page types, sample pages, attributes, and a lot more.

3. You can extend the uninstallation method to assure that all traces of your add-on are deleted properly.

Moving templates into a package

Remember the templates we've created? The templates were placed below their respective folders in the top level `blocks` directory: `slideshow`, `guestbook`, `content`, `page_list`, and so on. Worked like a charm but imagine what happens when you create a theme which also needs some block templates in order to make sure the blocks look like the theme? You'd have to copy files into the `blocks` directory as well as `themes`. This is exactly what we're trying to avoid with packages.

It's rather easy with templates, they work almost anywhere.

Time for action – moving templates into a package

1. In the root of your site, create a new directory structure `/packages/c5book/blocks`.

2. Move the directory `slideshow` from the top level `blocks` directory to the newly created directory `/packages/c5book/blocks`. The following screenshot shows this step:

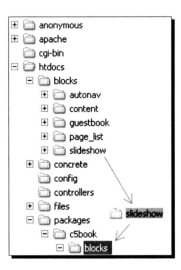

3. Two JavaScripts in the `slideshow` directory contain paths that won't work anymore. We have to change them. First open `/packages/c5book/blocks/slideshow/templates/gallery/view.js` and make sure it looks like the code shown here:

```
$(document).ready(function() {
    $(".ccm-slideshow-gallery a").lightBox({
        imageBtnPrev: CCM_REL + "/packages/c5book/blocks/
        slideshow/templates/gallery/images/lightbox-btn-prev.gif",
        imageBtnNext: CCM_REL +  "/packages/c5book/blocks/
        slideshow/templates/gallery/images/lightbox-btn-next.gif",
        imageLoading: CCM_REL +  "/packages/c5book/blocks/
        slideshow/templates/gallery/images/lightbox-ico-loading.
        gif",
        imageBtnClose: CCM_REL +  "/packages/c5book/blocks/
        slideshow/templates/gallery/images/lightbox-btn-close.
        gif",
        imageBlank: CCM_REL + "/packages/c5book/blocks/slideshow/
        templates/gallery/images/lightbox-blank.gif"
    });
});
```

4. Next, open `/packages/c5book/blocks/slideshow/templates/ad_gallery/view.js` and make sure it looks like this:

```
$(document).ready(function () {
    $('.ad-gallery').adGallery({
        loader_image: CCM_REL + "/packages/c5book/blocks/
        slideshow/templates/ad_gallery/css/loader.gif",
        width: 800,
        height: 192,
        animate_first_image: true
    });
});
```

What just happened?

This step was even easier than most things we did before. We simply moved our templates into a different directory and just had to change some JavaScript to reflect the new location of the templates.

concrete5 looks for custom templates in different places such as:

- `concrete/blocks/<block-name>/templates`
- `blocks/<block-name>/templates`
- `packages/<package-name>/blocks/<block-name>/templates`

It doesn't matter where you put your templates, concrete5 will find them.

Moving a theme and blocks into a package

Now that we've got our templates in the package, let's move the new blocks we created into that package as well. The process is similar, but we have to call a method in the installer which installs our block. concrete5 does not automatically install blocks within packages.

This means that we have to extend the empty `install` method shown earlier.

Before we move the blocks into the package, you should remove all blocks first. If we don't do this, we'll have the same blocks in our site twice.

Time for action – uninstalling blocks

1. To uninstall the existing blocks, go to your dashboard, and click on **Block Types**.

2. Next, click on the block called **Product Information**. Click on the **Remove** button in the next screen and the block will be removed.

3. Do the same for all other blocks we created, **Product List**, **jQZoom Picture**, **PDF Generator**, and **Simple Gallery**.

What just happened?

We did some cleaning in order to avoid some potential problems that might occur if we keep the old blocks where they are. Having a block at two locations confuses concrete5; it's better to get rid of them right now.

 Please note; removing a block will, of course, remove all the blocks you've added to your pages. Content will be lost if you move a block into a package after you've already used it.

Time for action – moving the jQZoom block into a package

Carry out the following steps:

1. As mentioned a few lines before, make sure the JQZoom block isn't installed in your site by removing it in the **Block Types** screen.

2. Create a new directory called `blocks` in our package directory `c5book`.

3. Move the directory `blocks/jqzoom` to `packages/c5book/blocks`.

4. Open the package controller we created a few pages before, you can find it at `packages/c5book/controller.php`. The following snippet shows only a part of the controller, the `install` method. The only thing you have to do is to insert the highlighted line:

```
public function install() {
    $pkg = parent::install();

    // install blocks
    BlockType::installBlockTypeFromPackage('jqzoom', $pkg);
}
```

5. Save the file and go to your dashboard again. Click on **Extend concrete5** and locate the `c5book` package. Click on **Edit** and then **Uninstall Package** if it's already installed and confirm the action on the next screen. Go back to the **Extend concrete5** screen and reinstall the package again, which will automatically install the block too.

What just happened?

Besides moving files, we only had to add a single line of code to our existing package controller. This is necessary, because blocks within packages aren't automatically installed. When installing a package, only the `install` method of the controller is called, exactly the place where we hook into and install our block.

The `installBlockTypeFromPackage` method takes two parameters: the block handle and the package object to connect the two.

You've seen that we had to remove and reinstall the package several times while we only moved a block. At this point, it probably looks a bit weird to do that, especially as you're going to lose some content on your website.

However, when you're more familiar with the concrete5 framework, you'll usually know if you're going to need a package and make that decision before you start creating new blocks. If you're still in doubt, don't worry about it too much and create a package and not just a block. Using a package is usually the safest choice.

Don't forget that all instances of a block will be removed from all pages when you uninstall the block from your website. Make sure your package structure doesn't change before you start adding content to your website.

Time for action – moving the PDF block into a package

Some blocks depend on helpers, files, and libraries, which aren't in the block directory. The PDF generator block is such an example. It depends on a file found in the `tools` directory in the root of your concrete5 website as well as a file in the `libraries` directory. How do we include such a directory in a package? Here are the steps that you need to follow:

1. Move the `pdf` directory from `blocks` to `packages/c5book/blocks` since we also want to include the block in the package.

2. Locate the `c5book` directory within `packages` and create a new subdirectory named `tools`.

3. Move `generate_pdf.php` from `tools` to `packages/c5book/tools`.

4. Create another directory named `libraries` in `packages/c5book`.

5. Move the `MPDF56` directory from `libraries` to `packages/c5book/libraries`.

As we've moved two objects, we have to make sure our code looks for them in the right place. Open `packages/c5book/tools/generate.php` and look for `Loader::library` at the beginning of the file. We have to add a second parameter to `Loader::library` as shown here:

```php
<?php
defined('C5_EXECUTE') or die('Access Denied.');

Loader::library('MPDF56/mpdf', 'c5book');
$fh = Loader::helper('file');

$header = <<<EOT
<style type="text/css">
    body { font-family: Helvetica, Arial; }
    h1 { border-bottom: 1px solid black; }
</style>
EOT;
```

6. Next, open `packages/c5book/blocks/pdf/view.php`. We have to add the package handle as the second parameter to make sure the tool file is loaded from the package.

```php
<!--hidden_in_pdf_start-->
<?php
defined('C5_EXECUTE') or die(_('Access Denied.'));

$nh = Loader::helper('navigation');
$url = Loader::helper('concrete/urls');

$toolsUrl = $url->getToolsURL('generate_pdf', 'c5book');
$toolsUrl .= '?p=' . rawurlencode($nh->getLinkToCollection(
    $this->c, true));

echo "<a href=\"{$toolsUrl}\">PDF</a>";

?>
<!--hidden_in_pdf_end-->
```

7. After you've moved all the files, add a new line in the package controller to install the second block. To do this, open `controller.php` in your package and insert the highlighted line:

```php
public function install() {
    $pkg = parent::install();
```

```
// install blocks
BlockType::installBlockTypeFromPackage('jqzoom', $pkg);
BlockType::installBlockTypeFromPackage('pdf', $pkg);
}
```

8. If you go back to **Extend concrete5** and uninstall and then install the package again, you'll find the PDF block again.

What just happened?

In the preceding example, we put a file in the `tools` directory and a PDF generator in the `libraries` directory, which we had to move as well.

Even at the risk of saying the same thing several times: A package can contain any element of concrete5—libraries, tools, controllers, images, and so on. By putting all files in a single package directory, we can make sure that all files are installed at once, thus making sure all dependencies are met.

Nothing has changed apart from the small changes we've made to our code that access or load an element. A helper behaves like a helper, no matter where it's located; you just have to make sure your code looks for it in the right place.

Have a go hero – moving more add-ons

We've moved two different blocks into our new package, along with the slideshow block templates. These aren't all the blocks we've created so far. Try to move all add-ons we've created into our new package. If you need more information about that process, have a look at the following page:

`http://www.concrete5.org/documentation/developers/system/packages/`

Hooking into core events

You've made it through a lot of different concrete5 features if you got to this point. We've changed the layout, added new styles, added new functionality, and even wrapped these things in a package.

However, what if you wanted to react on things happening in the concrete5 core? You want to know when a page has been added, a group deleted, or a new user added? All of that can be achieved by using events and concrete5 will tell you what's going on and let you execute custom code and even interrupt some processes.

Event types

There are a lot of different events you can use to extend some core functions. The following table shows all the different events you can catch, along with their parameters described with their number and the data type, and a short description:

Event	Parameters	Description
on_group_delete	1: Group	Fired when a group is deleted. You can add some checks and return false if you don't want the group to be deleted.
on_user_add	1: UserInfo	Fired when a new user is added.
on_user_delete	1: UserInfo	Return false if the passed UserInfo object shouldn't be deleted.
on_user_update	1: UserInfo	Fired when a user is updated, passed UserInfo object contains the updated values.
on_user_change_password	1: UserInfo 2: String	Hook into this event if you want to replicate user accounts including their password (passed as a string in the second parameter) to another system.
on_user_enter_group	1. User 2. Group	Fired when a user gets assigned to a group.
on_user_exit_group	1. User 2. Group	Fired when a user is removed from a group.
on_user_friend_add	1. User 2. User	Fired when two users connect as friends.
on_user_friend_remove	1. User 2. User	Fired when two users lose their friendship.
on_page_update	1: Page	The passed argument contains the page object of the updated page.
on_page_move	1: Page 2: Page 3: Page	Fired when the page passed in the first argument is moved. The second parameter is the old parent and the third parameter is the new parent page object.
on_page_duplicate	1: Page 2: Page	Catch this event if you want to know when a page has been duplicated. The first parameter is the new parent, the second one the page to be duplicated.
on_page_delete	1: Page	The first argument contains the page to be deleted. Return false to cancel the process.

Event	Parameters	Description
on_page_add	1: Page	Fired for every new page added.
on_page_view	1: Page 2: User	Fired for each page view. Think twice before hooking into this event as you'll get a lot of calls and probably a lot of overhead.
on_page_version_ approve	1: CollectionVersion	Fired when a page version is approved.
on_user_login	1: LoginController	Fired when a user logs in.
on_before_render	1: View	Hook into this event if you want to execute some code before a page is rendered.
on_render_complete	1: View	Fired if the page rendering process has been complete.
on_file_set_ password	1: File 2: String	Fired when a password is set for a file.
on_file_add	1. File 2. FileVersion	Fired whenever a new file is added to the file manager.
on_file_download	1. FileVersion 2. User	Fired when a file is downloaded; the second parameter can be empty.
on_file_version_add	1. FileVersion	Fired when a new file version is added.
on_file_version_ duplicate	1. FileVersion	Fired when a new file version is duplicated.
on_file_version_ update_title	1. FileVersion 2. String	Fired when the title is changed; the second parameter contains the new title.
on_file_version_ update_tags	1. FileVersion 2. String	Fired when the title is changed; the second parameter contains the new tags.
on_file_version_ update_description	1. FileVersion 2. String	Fired when the title is changed; the second parameter contains the new description.
on_file_version_ approve	1. FileVersion	Fired when a file version object is approved.
on_file_version_ deny	1. FileVersion	Fired when the approval of a file version object is denied.

 Page-related events are fired for every action on a page. Because the concrete5 dashboard has been built using pages too, an event is fired for every action happening on a dashboard page as well. You might want to exercise caution if you really want to execute an event for dashboard pages.

Extending an event

The process to extend an event is pretty much the same for all events. There are different places where you can include the code to hook into an event but, as we're dealing with packages, we're going to include it in our package controller as well.

Time for action – hooking into an event from a package

1. Open the package controller from `packages/c5book/controller.php` and insert a new method called `on_start` as shown in this snippet:

    ```
    public function on_start() {
      $html = Loader::helper('html');

      // inform about new users
      Events::extend('on_user_add',
        'UserInformation',
        'userAdd',
        'packages/' . $this->pkgHandle .
          '/models/user_information.php');
    }
    ```

2. Our event needs an attribute where we're going to save some data; you could add it manually but let's have a look at how we can add it from our package installer. Open `/packages/c5book/controller.php` and make sure the `install` method contains the following highlighted line:

    ```
    public function install() {
        $pkg = parent::install();

        UserAttributeKey::add('text', array('akHandle' => 'ip_address',
        'akName' => t('IP Address')), $pkg);
    }
    ```

3. The last file we're going to create is the file which handles the event. Create a file named `user_information.php` in the new directory structure `/packages/c5book/models`. Open the new file and put the following content in it:

    ```
    <?php
    defined('C5_EXECUTE') or die('Access Denied.');

    class UserInformation {
       public function userAdd($ui) {
         $ipv = Loader::helper('validation/ip');
         $ui->setAttribute('ip_address', $ipv->getRequestIP());
       }
    }
    ?>
    ```

What just happened?

Our code extends an event which is fired whenever a new user is added and logs the current IP address in a user attribute.

The call to `Events::extend` is rather simple, there are four parameters:

1. The first parameter is the name of the event you want to catch.
2. The class name where to look for the method to be called.
3. The method name which has to be called.
4. Location of the file where the class and method can be found.

In the preceding example, we created a new file to handle the event. However, in some cases it's easier if you don't have to create a new file and put all the code in the package controller. The following code shows you how you can use an anonymous function in the package controller to handle an event. The result is the same, there's just no need for an additional file:

```
public function on_start() {
    Events::extend('on_user_add', function($ui) {
        $ipv = Loader::helper('validation/ip');
        $ui->setAttribute('ip_address', $ipv->getRequestIP());
    }, '', '');
}
```

Pop quiz – what can you do with events?

Q1. What can you do by hooking into events? What kind of events can you catch?

1. You can interact on all kinds of actions executed on pages, such as creation, deletion, and duplication.
2. You can add additional checks and disallow certain actions if your additional requirements aren't met.
3. You can ensure consistency in your website by making sure depended objects are deleted once the core object such as a page has been removed.
4. It allows you to hack into the core while still keeping the option to upgrade to a newer version of concrete5 without modifying any core files at all.

Q2. Thinking of a real life example, which of the following tasks can you achieve using events?

1. Actions executed on user and group modifications, including password changes, can be used to synchronize user accounts between different systems.

2. Every time a job is executed or an event is fired you can use it to write a custom protocol.

3. You can monitor page changes and generate an e-mail on every page modification to stay up-to-date with all the changes.

4. You can monitor changes made in the dashboard **Sitewide Settings** section.

Working with maintenance tasks and jobs

Some features in concrete5 depend on automated jobs, which have to be periodically executed if you want to use them. By default, there are four jobs installed. You can find them if you type `Jobs` in the intelligent search box and click on the first entry in the search result:

◆ **Index Search Engine**: The full text search engine uses the Zend Lucene search library, which has to be updated by a maintenance job. If you don't execute this job regularly, the website's users will only find old, outdated content.

◆ **Generate the sitemap.xml file**: This job writes a file named `sitemap.xml` in the root of your website, which helps search engine crawlers to index your site.

◆ **Process Email Posts**: concrete5 has the ability to handle incoming e-mails. The included community-like messaging system depends on it.

◆ **Remove Old Page Versions**: If you keep working on a site for a while, you'll create a lot of versions. If you don't need the history of your changes, run this job and you'll get rid of unused data very easily.

The following screenshot shows you how these jobs look in the dashboard:

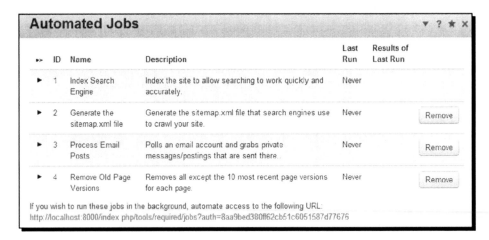

By default, these jobs aren't executed. It's your responsibility as a website administrator to use a scheduler available on your hosting system to make sure the jobs run as planned. As operating systems, web hosting companies, system configurations, and interfaces all differ greatly, no general solutions exist. If you aren't familiar with that, get in contact with your hosting partner.

For now, you can simply execute the jobs manually by clicking on the arrow on the left of each job or the double arrow to run all jobs.

Time for action – executing concrete5 jobs periodically

Carry out the following steps to enable the scheduler on a Windows system:

1. Download the binaries of `wget` from the following URL:

   `http://gnuwin32.sourceforge.net/packages/wget.htm`

2. Extract `wget` into a directory without blanks.

3. Press the *Windows key* + *R* to open the run dialog and type `cmd` and confirm it by clicking on **OK**.

4. In the command prompt window, enter this command but modify the path to `wget` according to the path where you've installed it as well as the job URL which you can see in your dashboard. The preceding screenshot shows the URL too.

   ```
   schtasks /create /tn "concrete5 Jobs" /tr "C:\wget.exe
       http://your-site.com/index.php/tools/required/jobs?
       auth=9499e773311ba4305d5b4b7f35b2c115" /sc daily
   ```

5. Confirm the command with the *Enter* key. You should get a confirmation that the job has been created.

What just happened?

The preceding steps installed a task to make sure that all concrete5 jobs run daily. If you want to test the command before you use it, open the console window again, and run `wget` appended by the URL of your concrete5 job, as follows:

```
C:\wget.exe http://your-site.com/index.php/tools/required/jobs?auth=94
99e773311ba4305d5b4b7f35b2c115
```

This command should return without an error and your jobs in concrete5 should all be executed. The date in the column **Last Run** should be updated for every job afterwards.

Please note: The scheduler runs on your local computer, which means that it will only work as long as your computer runs. If you run a website on a server, you shouldn't use your local computer to run jobs periodically, but instead use the solution from your hosting company.

If you want, you can execute the jobs right now; it shouldn't take long and you should see an updated screen. The number of indexed pages should be higher if you haven't run the job before since we created a few new pages.

For those familiar with Linux, you can use **cron**, the standard tool to manage periodical tasks on Linux. An example based on this that executes all the jobs 30 minutes past midnight would look like this:

```
30 0 * * * /usr/bin/wget -O - -q -t 1 http://
your-site.com/index.php/tools/required/jobs?auth=
9499e773311ba4305d5b4b7f35b2c115
```

As you probably already expected, you can easily create your own jobs without touching the concrete5 core. You can also put them in a package, which is exactly what we're going to do.

Creating a new job

Jobs are always located in a directory named `jobs` but there are several places where you can find that directory:

- In the root of your site
- In the `concrete` directory
- In every package directory

Our job is going to contain a little more PHP code than our usual examples, but since a job doesn't really produce any output, there's not much besides code. What we're going to do has been done before, but not nicely integrated into concrete5. We're going to create a job, which checks all your pages for broken links. It doesn't look professional if your visitors click on links and get an ugly 404 error page.

The script is going to go through the following steps:

1. Get a list of all pages and loop through them.
2. Make sure the current page in the loop is accessible by the guest group, as we don't want to check hidden pages to keep the output compact.

3. If the page is accessible, we get a list of all blocks on that page.

4. We check the block type for every block we find and skip all but the content blocks.

5. The content block output is processed and every link is extracted using a `regex` pattern.

6. As links can be absolute and relative, we have to prepend the server name in case it isn't there.

7. We then check the HTTP status code for every link and save its result in a table.

There are going to be more than a hundred lines of code; if you don't want to type this, you can find a download link at the end of the chapter.

Time for action – creating a job to check for broken links

Carry out the following steps:

1. A package can depend on database tables just as a block does. The procedure is the same, create a `db.xml` file, but this time it's located right in the package directory. Therefore, create a file at `packages/c5book/db.xml` and put the following content in it:

```xml
<?xml version="1.0"?>
<schema version="0.3">
    <table name="LinkChecker">
        <field name="cID" type="I">
            <key />
            <unsigned />
        </field>
        <field name="link" type="C" size="255">
            <key />
        </field>
        <field name="linkStatusCode" type="I"></field>
        <field name="linkStatusName" type="C" size="255"></field>
    </table>
</schema>
```

2. Make sure the directory `packages/c5book/jobs` exists. It's where we're going to put our new job file.

3. In that new directory, create a file named `link_checker.php`. You can find the complete code on the Packt publishing website in the archive called `9314_09_ c5book_packages.zip`. The following is a partial code that explains the basic steps:

```php
<?php
defined('C5_EXECUTE') or die('Access Denied.');

class LinkChecker extends Job {

 public function getJobName() {
  return t("Link Checker");
 }

 public function getJobDescription() {
  return t("Checks your site for broken links.");
 }

 /**
  * Returns the HTTP status text for the URL
  * passed in the first argument. Uses cURL
  * with a 5 second timeout by default and
  * get_headers as a fallback in case cURL
  * isn't installed
  */
 protected function getHttpStatus($url) {
  // ...see code on packt website...
 }

 public function run() {
  // ...see code on packt website...

  $regexLinkPattern = 'href=\"([^\"]*)\"';
  $regexStatusPattern = '(.*) ([0-9]{3}) (.*)';

  $pages = $pl->get();

  // delete data from previous runs
  $db->Execute('DELETE FROM LinkChecker');

  // 1. get all pages
  foreach ($pages as $page) {
    // ...see code on packt website...
```

```
// 3. get all blocks
$blocks = $page->getBlocks();
foreach ($blocks as $block) {

    // 4. only process the output of content blocks
    if ($block->getBlockTypeHandle() == 'content') {
     $bi = $block->getInstance();

     // 5. get all links in the block output
     if(preg_match_all("/{$regexLinkPattern}/siU", $bi->content,
       $matches, PREG_SET_ORDER)) {
      foreach($matches as $match) {
       $link = $match[1];

       // 6. only track external links
       if (substr($link,0,4) != 'http') {
        break;
       }

       // 7. check link status and save it in LinkChecker

       // ...see code on packt website...
      }
     }
    }
   }
  }

  return t('Found %d links, out of which %d are broken.',
    $linksFound, $brokenLinksFound);
 }
}
```

4. In order to make sure our job is installed during the package installation, open packages/c5book/controller.php and modify the install method to match the following code:

```
public function install()
{
 $pkg = parent::install();
```

```
// install blocks
BlockType::installBlockTypeFromPackage('jqzoom', $pkg);
BlockType::installBlockTypeFromPackage('product_information',
  $pkg);
BlockType::installBlockTypeFromPackage('product_list', $pkg);
BlockType::installBlockTypeFromPackage('simple_gallery', $pkg);
BlockType::installBlockTypeFromPackage('pdf', $pkg);


// install link checker job
Loader::model("job");
Job::installByPackage("link_checker", $pkg);
}
```

5. We've added two elements to our package which are processed during the
installation. Go to **Extend concrete5** in your dashboard and remove and install
our package again. This will create the database table and add a new job, which
you'll see when you go back to the screen with the **Automated Jobs** again.

What just happened?

After installing the package, you will see a new job named **Link Checker**. If you run the
job as shown in the following screenshot, you should get a message telling you how
many broken links are there on your site:

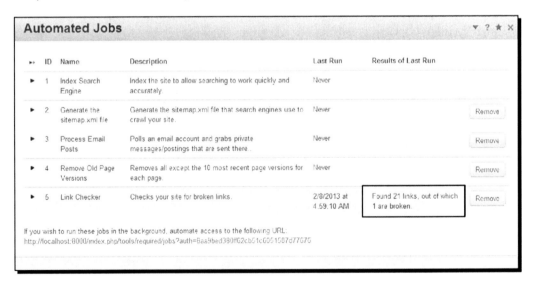

However, what if there's a message saying that there are broken links on the website? For now, there's no nice way to get access to that information, but have a look at phpMyAdmin by opening `http://localhost/phpmyadmin/`. Select the **concrete5** database and scroll down till you see the table **LinkChecker**. Click on it and make sure you're on the **Browse** tab. You should see something like the following:

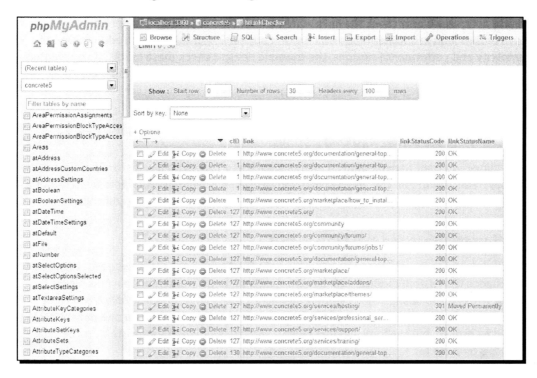

We're going to create a nice interface for this table, but before that a few words about the data you can find in the table:

Here you either see an entry with a **404** status code or an empty (**NULL**) value. As 404 is returned by a web server, it means that the domain is available, but the page isn't. If the domain isn't available at all, you won't get anything back since there's no web server returning your requests, hence the NULL value.

If you found a link which isn't working, you have to know where this link is located in your website. This works by using the `cID` and appending it to `index.php`, which would look like this: `http://localhost/index.php?cID=127`. Using the internal collection ID and not the path to the page has one big advantage: If you rename the page, you'll still be able to access the page and fix the link because the collection ID doesn't change if you move or rename a page.

Anything else in the table output doesn't really hurt and is mostly informational. There's just one thing which you can check: Entries with a **301** status code indicate that the site owner has moved a page and you could check the link to see where you actually end up and replace it. By doing this, your links stay up-to-date and you save an additional redirection when your visitors click on the links, even if they probably won't notice the difference.

Please note; as we only check the links within content blocks, it might happen that you have broken links in another block which won't appear in the table of this add-on. Due to simplicity and performance reasons, the example doesn't check these blocks. If you wanted to extend it, look for the `getBlockTypeHandle` check and extend it by the blocks you want to include as well.

Injecting header items

Sometimes you want to make sure an element, such as a JavaScript file, is shared in the header of your HTML document. concrete5 allows you to inject any element, such as a JavaScript or a CSS file, into the head of your HTML document from your block or package controller.

Adding tooltips for every title tag

Remember the content block template we created in *Chapter 6, Customizing Block Layouts* to enhance the custom tooltips with a more stylish version? The template works nicely, but it only works if you change the custom template for every content block where you want this tooltip to appear. Now, let's say you forget to change the template on one page. Nothing would be broken, but the look and feel of your website wouldn't be consistent, something we'd like to avoid.

What options are there?

- We could create a block for this which would use the content of the whole page. This means that you wouldn't have to modify every content block but you'd still have to place that block on every page.

- We could also place it in the theme. This is an easy option which would work just fine but has one little disadvantage. If you want to use this tooltip feature on other sites, you have to modify the page theme in order to get the functionality on another page. This is not a big deal but can we avoid this?

We can!

Time for action – creating global tooltips

Carry out the following steps:

1. We're going to use the same script again. Download the TipTip source code from the following URL:

   ```
   http://code.drewwilson.com/entry/tiptip-jquery-plugin
   ```

2. Extract `jquery.tipTip.minified.js` to `/packages/c5book/js`. You have to create the `js` folder first.

3. Extract `tipTip.css` to `/packages/c5book/css`; you have to have the `css` folder too.

4. Now, we've got to make sure these files are loaded and properly called. To do this, open the package controller `/packages/c5book/controller.php` and insert the highlighted lines, as follows:

   ```php
   <?php

   defined('C5_EXECUTE') or die('Access Denied.');

   class c5bookPackage extends Package {

       protected $pkgHandle = 'c5book';
       protected $appVersionRequired = '5.6.0';
       protected $pkgVersion = '1.0';

       public function getPackageDescription() {
         return t("Theme, Templates and Blocks from
             concrete5 for Beginner's");
       }

       public function getPackageName() {
         return t("c5book");
       }

       public function install() {
         $pkg = parent::install();
   ```

```
            // install blocks
            BlockType::installBlockTypeFromPackage('jqzoom', $pkg);
            BlockType::installBlockTypeFromPackage('pdf', $pkg);
            BlockType::installBlockTypeFromPackage('simple_gallery',
                $pkg);
            BlockType::installBlockTypeFromPackage('product_information',
                $pkg);
            BlockType::installBlockTypeFromPackage('product_list', $pkg);

            // install link checker job
            Loader::model("job");
            Job::installByPackage("link_checker", $pkg);
        }

        function on_start() {
            $html = Loader::helper('html');

            // inform about new users
            Events::extend('on_user_add', 'UserInformation',
                'userAdd',
                'packages/' . $this->pkgHandle .
                '/models/user_information.php');

            // replace native tooltip with TipTip
            $v = View::getInstance();
            $v->addHeaderItem(
                $html->javascript('jquery.tipTip.minified.js',
                'c5book'));
            $v->addHeaderItem($html->css('tipTip.css', 'c5book'));
            $v->addHeaderItem('<script type="text/javascript">
                $(function(){ $("[title]").tipTip(); });</script>');
        }

    }
?>
```

What just happened?

The preceding code basically replaced the `tipTip` content block template we've created before. However, the new code replaces every tooltip, not only those in the content block. If you don't want that behavior, you might want to keep using the previous template instead of this package controller but if you want to have a consistent look of all tooltips across your site, use this example.

How does the preceding code work? The method `on_start` is automatically called for every installed package during the page rendering process. This allows you to inject code into any page on a website without actually modifying any pages. Simply get the current view instance and call `addHeaderItem` on it. Do it once, use it everywhere!

There's a rather simple, but neat add-on in the concrete5 marketplace, which uses the same technique to include a little JavaScript check to detect old browsers ; if any are found, it also displays a small toolbar that tells website visitors to update to a newer and more secure browser version. You can find it at the following URL:

`http://www.concrete5.org/marketplace/addons/scala-it-browser-update-notification/`

JavaScript browser fixes

A lot of web designers still make sure their website works for old browsers such as Internet Explorer 7.0, even if version 10.0 is already released. It's painful, but even for something like this, a package can make things a bit easier.

There are different projects you can use to help old browsers behave at least partially like they should. One example can be found at `http://www.dustindiaz.com/min-height-fast-hack/` but there are a lot more out there. There's a complete package of fixes available at `http://code.google.com/p/ie7-js/`. What if you wanted to use this for all your websites? You could put this in your theme, but why not create a package for this?

Let's have a look at how easily we could integrate such a browser fix script in our c5book package.

Time for action – integrating a CSS fix in a package

Carry out the following step:

1. Open the controller from `packages/c5book/controller.php` and modify the `on_start` method to match the following code:

```
function on_start() {
  $html = Loader::helper('html');

  // inform about new users
  Events::extend('on_user_add', 'UserInformation',
    'userAdd', 'packages/' . $this->pkgHandle .
    '/models/user_information.php');
```

```
        // replace native tooltip with TipTip
        $v = View::getInstance();
        $v->addHeaderItem($html->javascript('jquery.tipTip.minified.js',
            'c5book'));
        $v->addHeaderItem($html->css('tipTip.css', 'c5book'));
        $v->addHeaderItem('<script type="text/javascript">
            $(function(){ $("[title]").tipTip(); });</script>');


        // include MSIE fix
        $v->addHeaderItem('<!--[if lt IE 8]><script src="
         http://ie7-js.googlecode.com/svn/version/2.1(beta4)/IE8.js">
         </script><![endif]-->');
    }
```

What just happened?

We've included a simple JavaScript file to fix some issues with older browser versions. The same works for different elements, such as a CSS reset script to reduce inconsistency among different browsers. Check the following URL if you want to start working with HTML5:

```
http://meyerweb.com/eric/tools/css/reset/
```

Or,

```
http://www.modernizr.com/
```

Include one of these scripts using the technique described earlier and parts of HTML5 will work in browsers that aren't HTML5-ready.

Pop quiz – benefits of addHeaderItem

Q1. What are the benefits of using `addHeaderItem` to include CSS and JavaScript files?

1. Using `addHeaderItem` in your package or block controller makes sure the elements are included in the head of your HTML document.

2. Putting CSS files in the header allows the page to render progressively, which can improve the user experience.

3. CSS and JavaScript files are easier to cache if they are saved in an external file which is included by `addHeaderItem`.

4. All of the above

Have a go hero – creating a new package

We've included a lot of functionality in a single package. This simplifies a few things because we don't have to create new packages all the time, but it comes at a price—unnecessary overhead.

Try to move some of the created functionality into new packages. Having a package for a single JavaScript fix seems a bit extreme as it contains some overhead, but is easier to work with, as installing an additional package is only a matter of seconds.

Summary

In this chapter, we have learned about the things we can do with a package. We started by moving some of our previous add-ons into a package, making it easier to handle and install. Creating a package is often about the installation process, which is one reason why you have to wrap add-ons in a package if you want to publish them on the concrete5 marketplace.

We also had a quick look at events, a nice but advanced feature that you can use to execute custom code upon certain events happening in the concrete5 core. An example: Being able to hook into actions happening on your user database allows you to synchronize accounts with another system. Think about third-party forum software you want to use—if you already have a concrete5 website, you could create an interface to keep both user databases up-to-date without having your website's users register twice.

Next, we created a maintenance job, which checks for broken links on your website. This was just one example. Maintenance jobs or tasks can be used to optimize databases, index pages, start an interface, and a lot more.

At the end of the chapter, we've looked at a way to include JavaScripts in the header of every page. A simple but effective way to include JavaScripts to improve the look as well as usability and compatibility with older browsers.

In the next chapter, we're going to work with something called single pages. Single pages are used in the dashboard as well as in a website where a certain functionality exists just once.

Dashboard Extensions

In this chapter, we're going to look at extensions which add more pages and functions to the dashboard. As concrete5 uses the MVC pattern to do this, we're also going to have a quick look at the theory behind this pattern. Since this is a beginner's guide, we're only going to scratch the surface of the topic, to ensure that a person who hasn't worked with MVC before gets enough information to understand the pattern and use it in concrete5.

In this chapter we're going to look at these topics:

- A quick introduction to **Model-View-Controller** (**MVC**) to get an understanding of what actually happens when building a single page
- An interface for the broken links job we created in the previous chapter
- An extension which adds an interface where you can make some quick changes to files right in the dashboard

Working with the MVC pattern

You might not have noticed but, we did use parts of the **MVC** (Model-View-Controller) pattern before when we built our first block. A block consists of a controller located in a file named `controller.php` and a view, by default named `view.php`. There can also be more views in the `templates` directory, which are called custom block templates in concrete5.

In concrete5, most pages are created from a page type. It's what you mostly do when you add a new page in the sitemap, but there are single pages such as `/login` and `/dashboard` as well. Their functionality is usually unique, and thus called a single page. A single page is what we're going to create when we print output from an application in concrete5, which follows the MVC pattern.

Why MVC? What are the problems MVC tries to solve?

- ◆ Different elements of the application have been included in a single file: the application logic, as well as the layout. There's no obvious structure in the application, therefore making it hard to get an understanding of it.

- ◆ MVC allows different outputs for different devices, such as mobile phones.

- ◆ It's hard to assign tasks to different people if there's no common structure in the application. Without following a pattern, it's not clear which files have to be modified when changing the database access, layout, or logic of the application.

- ◆ Modularizing the application before MVC was tricky. Modifying a single part (logic, output, and model) has been more time-consuming than necessary.

There are different approaches to achieving these things, but MVC has proven to be a solid and popular choice for lots of web, as well as desktop, applications.

How does the MVC pattern do this? It does this mostly by splitting the view (output), the model (database access), and controller (logic, parsing, and so on) into different files. This helps to keep a clean structure in your application. This makes it easier for a new developer to understand your application, even if he hasn't worked with it before. The following diagram illustrates how these units work together. There are some additional elements to explain the use of these MVC elements:

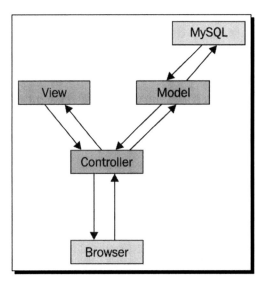

Don't expect that an application will follow this MVC pattern in every case. There are situations where you'll have to break the pattern, but there has to be a good reason for that. Don't give up the pattern too quickly, it's worth the effort.

Let's look at some situations which might happen during the lifecycle of a web application and their solutions when working with MVC. If you have ever created PHP applications where you had the logic, database access, and output in one file, think how you'd have done that.

- ♦ **Database tuning**: Assume that your application has progressively become slower at retrieving and storing data. You get a database expert who knows everything about the database you're using, but there are some queries he cannot tune without rewriting the query. By using a model, he'll quickly get access to the query without having to read through lots of code related to the business logic or output of your application. There's no HTML, AJAX, or CSS interfering with the database access. He can use his full skills without wasting any time on things he's not familiar with.

- ♦ **Mobile phone layout**: On a lovely Monday morning, two days before the project deadline, your boss tells you that the customer realized that the stunning web application you created doesn't work on his kid's Smartphone. Thankfully, you're using MVC and don't have to recreate the whole application; you just have to add another view to your application, add a check to detect mobile devices, and switch to that layout (or theme, in the case of concrete5).

- ♦ **New layout**: You are asked to change the application to skip particular registration screens in a sign-up process if a user meets certain criteria. By being able to keep this kind of processing logic in controller files, you are able to modify the application and succinctly see the logic involved, without the clutter of interface or database code.

Can you see how MVC can make your life a lot easier? Splitting an application into different files and objects allows you to use the skills of people the right way and keeps your application more solid, extendable, easier to test, read, and maintain.

Adding the broken link interface

The first example is a bit simplified in order to start as easy as possible. The maintenance job we've created in the previous chapter searches for links in our website and checks if they are still working. However, there's no interface to see the broken links in the dashboard yet. We're going to use the data from the link checker job as a basis for our first dashboard extension. We are starting with a controller and a single page (view), but no model for now. We're going to add that later in this chapter.

At the end we're going to have an additional child page underneath **Reports** where the broken links are listed, as shown in the following screenshot:

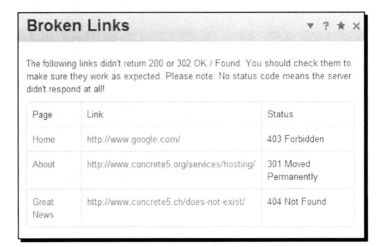

Time for action – creating the broken links dashboard extension

Carry out the following steps:

1. In our package c5book, create a new directory structure `controllers/dashboard/reports`.

2. Within the new directory, create a file named `broken_links.php` and put the following content in it to fetch the data, and pass it on to the single page by using `$this->set`:

```php
<?php
defined('C5_EXECUTE') or die('Access Denied.');

class DashboardReportsBrokenLinksController extends Controller {

    public $helpers = array('form', 'html');

    public function view() {
        $db = Loader::db();

        $brokenLinks = array();
        $result = $db->Execute('SELECT * FROM LinkChecker WHERE
        linkStatusCode NOT IN (200,302) OR linkStatusCode IS NULL');
        while ($row = $result->FetchRow()) {
```

```php
        $row['page'] = Page::getByID($row['cID']);
        $row['status'] = $row['linkStatusCode'] . ' ' .
        $row['linkStatusName'];
        if (trim($row['status']) == '') $row['status'] = 'Server
          not found';
        $brokenLinks[] = $row;
      }
      $this->set('links', $brokenLinks);
    }


  }
  ?>
```

3. In our package c5book, create a new directory structure `single_pages/`
    `dashboard/reports`.

4. Create a new file called `broken_links.php` again. It has to have the same name as
    the controller as they are automatically connected. Once you've created the file, put
    the following lines it:

```php
<?php
defined('C5_EXECUTE') or die('Access Denied.');

echo Loader::helper('concrete/dashboard')->
    getDashboardPaneHeaderWrapper(
    t('Broken Links'), t('Check your site\'s broken links.'),
    false, false
);
?>
<div class="ccm-pane-body">
  <p><?php echo t('The following links didn\'t return 200 or 302
  OK / Found. You should check them to make sure they work as
  expected. Please note: No status code means the server didn\'t
  respond at all!')?></p>

  <table class="table table-bordered table-striped" >
   <tr>
    <td class="header"><?php echo t('Page')?></td>
    <td class="header"><?php echo t('Link')?></td>
    <td class="header"><?php echo t('Status')?></td>
   </tr>
   <?php foreach ($links as $link): ?>
    <tr>
     <td>
      <a target="_blank" href="<?php echo
         $link['page']->getCollectionPath()?>/">
      <?php echo $link['page']->getCollectionName()?>
      </a>
```

```
      </td>
      <td>
       <a target="_blank" href="<?php echo $link['link']?>">
       <?php echo $link['link']?>
       </a>
      </td>
      <td>
       <?php echo $link['status']?>
      </td>
     </tr>
     <?php endforeach; ?>
   </table>
 </div>
 <?php
 echo Loader::helper('concrete/dashboard')->
    getDashboardPaneFooterWrapper(false);
 ?>
```

5. Single pages aren't automatically installed with the package; we have to modify our package controller to achieve this. Open `packages/c5book/controller.php` and look for the method `install` and insert the highlighted lines:

```
public function install() {
    $pkg = parent::install();

    // install blocks
    BlockType::installBlockTypeFromPackage('jqzoom', $pkg);
    BlockType::installBlockTypeFromPackage('pdf', $pkg);
    BlockType::installBlockTypeFromPackage('ftp_gallery', $pkg);
    BlockType::installBlockTypeFromPackage('product_information',
        $pkg);
    BlockType::installBlockTypeFromPackage('product_list', $pkg);

    // install link checker job
    Loader::model("job");
    Job::installByPackage("link_checker", $pkg);

    // install single pages
    Loader::model('single_page');
    $sp = SinglePage::add('/dashboard/reports/broken_links',
        $pkg);
    if (version_compare(APP_VERSION, '5.6', '>')) {
        $sp->setAttribute('icon_dashboard', 'icon-warning-sign');
    }
}
```

6. Go to your dashboard, click on **Extend concrete5,** and select your package. Uninstall and reinstall it.

What just happened?

After you've reinstalled your package, you should be able to see the new page when you go to the dashboard and look at the **Reports** section.

If you look at the installer, you can see that we've added our own page at `/dashboard/reports/broken_links`; you might wonder how to get that. A dashboard extension is basically a single page located in the right structure. We could have placed our page in the top level and it would appear within our own website using our own theme, but since we placed it underneath dashboard, it automatically looks and behaves like a dashboard page. You can easily get details about the dashboard structure by navigating to the sitemap and ticking the **Show System Pages** checkbox.

Whenever you run the maintenance job Link Checker, you should see an updated list of broken links in this additional report. Please make sure you've run the job at least once to get some data.

The example we created has been simplified to show you a first partial MVC example. The controller we've created, which of course can be found in the `controllers` directory, is responsible for fetching the data from our database, something which should actually happen in the model. We're going to split this part into a model to comply with all the MVC parts right after this block.

In our controller, we've got only one method named `view`. This is a method which is automatically called by the controller upon a page view if there's no other method specified. We then use `$this->set` to pass a value to our single page. If you call `$this->set('weather', 'Lovely & Sunny')`, you can access the content of weather in the single page, as if it was a local variable with a command such as `echo $weather`. This works with discrete values, but also with objects or an array, as we did in our example.

The code we're using to add a new single page has a few lines; let's have a look at them. First, we start with `SinglePage::add` that actually adds the single page. We then check the concrete5 version. You could remove that check if you're sure you'll only use the add-on on the latest version of concrete5. If the add-on is installed on an up-to-date site, we'll assign a dashboard icon to your new single page. You can find a list of available icons on this page `http://twitter.github.com/bootstrap/base-css.html#icons`.

The output, our single page, is rather simple; it basically creates a loop over the array generated in the controller and prints a table. Nothing fancy, just a loop with a few concrete5 methods to get the values of the object the right way.

Moving database access into a model

As mentioned before, the database access should be encapsulated in a model in order to make sure every database query can be found in the same place. While you'll probably find a lot of examples in the wild where all database queries are in the controller, we have to create a model if we want to follow every part of MVC properly.

You'll see that the extra effort is rather small, no big deal to create a model, even if there's just a single method in it.

Time for action – creating a package model

Carry out the following steps:

1. In our package c5book, create a new folder named models if it doesn't already exist. Within that folder, create a new file named broken_links.php. Add the following code to it:

```php
<?php
defined('C5_EXECUTE') or die('Access Denied.');

class BrokenLinks {
  public static function add($cID, $link, $statusCode,
  $statusName) {
      $db = Loader::db();

      $values = array($cID, $link, $statusCode, $statusName);
      $db->Execute('INSERT INTO LinkChecker (cID, link,
      linkStatusCode, linkStatusName) VALUES (?,?,?,?)', $values);
  }

  public static function deleteAll() {
      $db = Loader::db();

      $db->Execute('DELETE FROM LinkChecker');
  }

  public static function getBrokenLinks($includeDetails=true) {
      $query = 'SELECT * FROM LinkChecker WHERE linkStatusCode
      NOT IN (200,302) OR linkStatusCode IS NULL';
      return BrokenLinks::getLinksInternal($query,
      $includeDetails);
  }

  public static function getAllLinks($includeDetails=true) {
      $query = 'SELECT * FROM LinkChecker';
      return BrokenLinks::getLinksInternal($query,
```

```
        $includeDetails);
    }

    private static function getLinksInternal($query,
    $includeDetails=true) {
        $db = Loader::db();

        $brokenLinks = array();
        $result = $db->Execute($query);
        while ($row = $result->FetchRow()) {
            if ($includeDetails) {
                $row['page'] = Page::getByID($row['cID']);
                $row['status'] = $row['linkStatusCode'] . ' ' .
                $row['linkStatusName'];
                if (trim($row['status']) == '')
                    $row['status'] = 'Server not found';
            }

            $brokenLinks[] = $row;
        }

        return $brokenLinks;
    }
}
?>
```

2. Next, we have to make sure our controller uses the model and doesn't contain any SQL queries. Open `packages/c5book/controllers/dashboard/reports/` `broken_links.php` again and make sure it looks similar to the following:

```
<?php
defined('C5_EXECUTE') or die('Access Denied. ');

class DashboardReportsBrokenLinksController extends Controller {

    public $helpers = array('form', 'html');

    public function view() {

        Loader::model('broken_links', 'c5book');
        $this->set('links', BrokenLinks::getBrokenLinks());

    }

}
?>
```

3. The maintenance job we've already created contains some SQL statements as well. Open `packages/c5book/jobs/link_checker.php` and modify the run method to match the following code; the changed lines are highlighted. Please note that the code isn't complete; if you're looking for the complete code, go to the Packt's website and download the file called `9314_10_c5book_packages.zip`:

```php
public function run()
{
 Loader::model('page_list');
 Loader::model('broken_links', 'c5book');

 $nh = Loader::helper('navigation');
 $db = Loader::db();
 // ...see code on packt website...
 $pages = $pl->get();

 // delete data from previous runs
 BrokenLinks::deleteAll();

 // 1. get all pages
 foreach ($pages as $page)
 {
    // ...see code on packt website...

      foreach($matches as $match)
      {
       $link = $match[1];

       // ...see code on packt website...

       // we check for 404 and "NULL" which is returned
       // if there's no webserver responding. 404 is
       // only returned by a running webserver
       if ($statusCode == '404' || !$statusCode)
       {
        $brokenLinksFound++;
       }
          BrokenLinks::add($page->getCollectionID(), $link,
            $statusCode, $statusText);
      }
     }
    }
   }
  }
 }
 return t('Found %d links, out of which %d are broken.',
   $linksFound, $brokenLinksFound);
}
```

4. Save all the files and run the job again. It works as if nothing has changed.

What just happened?

The changes we've made won't be noticed by a person using the website; the output is still the same. All changes are in the background and improve the readability and maintainability of the code by following the MVC pattern.

Remember the example at the beginning of this chapter about database tuning? If you happen to run into a database performance issue, you can quickly send someone your model and it's quite clear what kind of requests you run on the database.

A few words about the number of executions per method and your database expert can tune your application on the database side without knowing a lot of concrete5 or PHP.

The first MVC example is done, no interactions or advanced features, but it already contains every element of MVC. At this point, we're just going to add more features to our files, but we're not going to add new parts such as models, controllers, or views.

Working with multiple controller methods

In the previous example, we've used the `view` method to access our data and pass it on to the single page. This method is the default method which is called when you open your page such as `http://localhost/index.php/dashboard/reports/broken_links/`.

If we wanted to add a second method to display all links, not only the broken ones, we can easily add a new method to our controller. The previously created model contains two methods, `getBrokenLinks` that we already use and `getAllLinks` that simply returns all links found in the content blocks, not only the broken ones.

All we have to do is add a second controller method to switch between the two methods and some basic code to the single page.

The following screenshot shows the way the URL is mapped to a controller method. By default, concrete5 is going to call the `view` method if the URL is ended with a controller. However, if you append a method name, concrete5 will look for a method with that name in the controller.

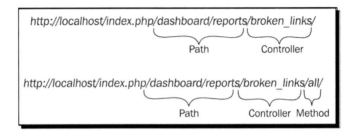

The preceding screenshot maps the following controller code:

```php
<?php
defined('C5_EXECUTE') or die('Access Denied.');

class DashboardReportsBrokenLinksController extends Controller {

    public $helpers = array('form', 'html');

    public function view() {
        Loader::model('broken_links', 'c5book');
        $this->set('links', BrokenLinks::getBrokenLinks());
    }

    public function all() {
        Loader::model('broken_links', 'c5book');
        $this->set('links', BrokenLinks::getAllLinks());
    }
}
?>
```

Time for action – adding a second controller method

Carry out the following steps:

1. Open the controller again `packages/c5book/controllers/dashboard/reports/broken_links.php` and put the preceding code in it. It's pretty much the same, except there's a second method in it to display all links.

2. The output, our single page, needs to handle these two modes as well. We're going to use a method that detects the called method and shows a different output depending on Open `packages/c5book/single_pages/dashboard/reports/broken_links.php.` We'll then alter the content to match the following:

```php
<?php
defined('C5_EXECUTE') or die('Access Denied.');
?>
<h1><span><?php echo t('Broken Links')?></span></h1>
<div class="ccm-dashboard-inner">

   <?php if ($this->controller->getTask() == 'view'): ?>
     <p>
     <?php echo t('The following links didn\'t return 200 or 302 OK
      / Found. You should check them to make sure they work as
      expected. Please note: No status code means the server
      didn\'t respond at all!')?>
     </p>

     <p>
       <a href="<?php
          echo $this->url('/dashboard/reports/broken_links',
             'all')?>">Show All Links</a>
     </p>
   <?php else: ?>
      <p><?php echo t('These are all the links found in the content
      blocks of your site. Click on the link below to display broken
      links only.')?>
      </p>

   <p>
    <a href="<?php echo $this->url
      ('/dashboard/reports/broken_links')?>">Show Broken Links Only
    </a>
   </p>

   <?php endif; ?>

   <table class="entry-form" >
    <tr>
     <td class="header">Page</td>
     <td class="header">Link</td>
     <td class="header">Status</td>
    </tr>
```

```php
<?php foreach ($links as $link): ?>
<tr>
 <td>
  <a target="_blank" href="<?php echo $link['page']->
    getCollectionPath()?>/">
   <?php echo $link['page']->getCollectionName()?>
  </a>
 </td>
 <td>
  <a target="_blank" href="<?php echo $link['link']?>">
  <?php echo $link['link']?>
  </a>
 </td>
 <td>
  <?php echo $link['status']?>
 </td>
</tr>
<?php endforeach; ?>
</table>

</div>
```

What just happened?

The code change that we've made in the single page for our interface uses the two controller methods illustrated earlier. We also added a check on the variable mode to change the output according to the called controller method.

There are two important things to remember:

1. A call such as $this->set('mode', 'allLinks') in the controller creates a variable in the single pages called $mode with the value allLinks. This is the correct way to pass data from the controller to the single page when working with concrete5.

2. When you only specify the controller name in the URL such as http://localhost/index.php/dashboard/reports/broken_links/ the method view is called. In case a different method has to be called, it's simply appended to that URL as in http://localhost/index.php/dashboard/ reports/broken_links/all/.

Embedding a file editor in the dashboard

Here's a topic that has been controversially discussed in the concrete5 community: Some users would like to be able to access and modify all the files on their web space where the concrete5 site is located within the dashboard.

It can be handy to quickly fix an issue with your add-on from your new tablet device while you're on vacation—it could also cause trouble with your partner, though. You don't have to remember an FTP account; getting access to the dashboard is enough to do any work on your website, updating content, fixing bugs in the add-ons, and so on.

Certainly, something that can be handy can also be something that can be a bit dangerous. Changing code on a site that is running on a production server should be well-thought-out. Being able to make modifications very easily can also break things very quickly. Being able to modify all files within a web application also means that the user account you're using to run the web server must have write access to all the files. By default, concrete5 makes sure that it has access to the directories `files`, `packages`, and `config`; this means that you might not be able to change files in the theme directory unless you change the file permissions.

Building this add-on doesn't harm anyone, but think about it before you actually install it on productive site. If you use it, it will look like the following screenshot:

As we're going to create several files for this add-on, we're starting with an overview of the form. It should help you to understand how all the different elements are working together.

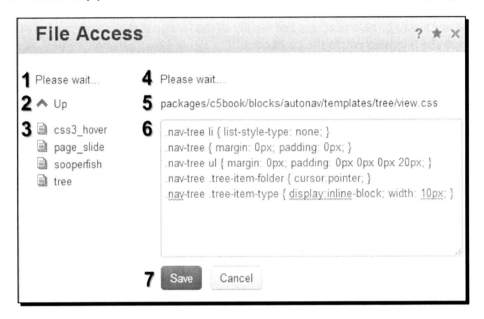

The seven boxes shown in the preceding screenshot are the most important elements in the add-on. To make things easier, all elements are visible, which is not going to happen once you're working with the add-on. There's no point displaying the **Please wait...** box if nothing is going on.

Each of the numbers is given a name, which is the value we're going to use as the ID of the element:

- 1: `directory-structure-waiting`; only shown when we load new data using our AJAX method to update the directory list.
- 2: `directory-structure-up`; this element is shown if we aren't on the top level to get back to the parent directory.
- 3: `directory-structure-content`; the actual list of directories and files, which is always visible.
- 4: `file-access-waiting`; it's the same as the directories, displayed when a file is loading and saving.

- ◆ 5: `file-access-caption`; in this element we're going to show the name of the file that is currently opened. This is especially helpful, as you can change to another directory while you're still working on the file, which you've opened earlier in another directory.

- ◆ 6: `file-access-textarea`; the ID of the textarea where we load the content of the file.

- ◆ 7: `file-access-toolbar`; this element holds all the buttons, which we dynamically show and hide depending on whether a file is loaded or not.

As we're going to create a bunch of files, here's a list with all the files:

- ◆ `packages/c5book/controllers/dashboard/file_access.php`; the second MVC element, our controller that holds everything together.

- ◆ `packages/c5book/single_pages/dashboard/file_access.php`; remember the introduction about MVC? This is the view, which is called single page in concrete5.

- ◆ `packages/c5book/css/file.access.css`; the elements listed earlier need some styles in order to be arranged properly.

- ◆ `packages/c5book/js/file.access.js`; our add-on uses some AJAX calls. This is where you'll find them.

- ◆ `packages/c5book/helpers/page_permissions.php`; a small helper file to ensure the safety of our AJAX files.

- ◆ `packages/c5book/tools/get_file.php`; the file used by the AJAX script to get the content of a file.

- ◆ `packages/c5book/tools/save_file.php`; another file used by an AJAX method to save a file.

- ◆ `packages/c5book/tools/get_structure.php`; the last file, also used by an AJAX method to get the directory list.

Time for action – creating the file editor add-on

We're going to create each file in the order of the preceding list:

1. Create `packages/c5book/controllers/dashboard/file_access.php`
   and put the following content in it:

```php
<?php
defined('C5_EXECUTE') or die('Access Denied.');

class DashboardFileAccessController extends Controller {
    public $helpers = array('form', 'html');

    public function on_start() {
        $html = Loader::helper('html');

        $this->addHeaderItem($html->css('file.access.css',
            'c5book'));
        $this->addHeaderItem($html->javascript('file.access.js',
            'c5book'));
    }
}
?>
```

2. Create the single page `packages/c5book/single_pages/dashboard/file_`
   `access.php` with the following content:

```php
<?php
defined('C5_EXECUTE') or die('Access Denied.');

echo Loader::helper('concrete/dashboard')-
>getDashboardPaneHeaderWrapper(
    t('File Access'), t('Manage your site\'s files.'), false,
        false
);
?>
<div class="ccm-pane-body">
    <div id="directory-structure">
        <div id="directory-structure-waiting">
            <?php echo t('Please wait...') ?>
        </div>
        <div id="directory-structure-up">
            <?php echo t('Up') ?>
        </div>
        <div id="directory-structure-content"></div>
    </div>

    <div id="file-access-container">
```

```
            <div id="file-access-waiting" style="display:none;">
                <?php echo t('Please wait...') ?>
            </div>
            <div id="file-access-content" style="display:none;">
                <div id="file-access-caption"></div>
                <textarea id="file-access-textarea"></textarea>
                <div id="file-access-toolbar">
                    <?php
                    $ih = Loader::helper('concrete/interface');
                    echo $ih->button_js(t('Save'), 'fileSave()',
                        'left', 'primary');
                    echo $ih->button_js(t('Cancel'), 'fileCancel()',
                        'left');
                    ?>
                </div>
            </div>
        </div>

        <div style="clear:both"></div>
</div>
<?php
echo Loader::helper('concrete/dashboard')->
    getDashboardPaneFooterWrapper(false);
?>
```

3. Let's make sure our layout looks as expected and create `packages/c5book/css/`
    `file.access.css`:

```css
.file-access-folder {
  background:
    url('../../../concrete/images/dashboard/sitemap/folder.png')
    no-repeat;
  padding-left: 22px;
  height: 20px;
  cursor: pointer;
}
.file-access-file {
  background:
    url('../../../concrete/images/dashboard/sitemap/document.png')
    no-repeat;
  padding-left: 22px;
  height: 20px;
  cursor: pointer;
}
#directory-structure {
  float:left;
  width:15%;
}
```

```css
#directory-structure-up {
  background:
    url('../../../concrete/images/dashboard/sitemap/up.png')
    no-repeat;
  padding-left: 22px;
  height: 20px;
  cursor: pointer;
  display: none;
}
#file-access-container {
  float:left;
  width:85%;
}
#file-access-textarea {
  width:100%;
  min-height:500px;
}
#file-access-toolbar input {
  margin: 10px 10px 0px 0px;
}
```

4. Next, the file with all the AJAX magic, `packages/c5book/js/file.access.js`:

```javascript
var currentDirectory = '';
var currentFile = '';

function openDirectory()
{
   $("#directory-structure-waiting").show();
   $("#directory-structure-content").hide();
   $("#directory-structure-up").hide();
   $("#directory-structure-content").html("");

   $.post(CCM_REL + CCM_DISPATCHER_FILENAME +
   '/tools/packages/c5book/get_structure', {directory:
    currentDirectory}, function(data) {

      if (data.folders) {
         $.each(data.folders, function(idx, val) {
            $("#directory-structure-content").
               append("<div
               class=\"file-access-folder\">"+val+"</div>");
         })
      }
      if (data.files) {
         $.each(data.files, function(idx, val) {
            $("#directory-structure-content").
               append("<div
```

```
                        class=\"file-access-file\">"+val+"</div>");
               })
           }

           if (currentDirectory != '') {
               $("#directory-structure-up").show();
           }

           $("#directory-structure-waiting").hide();
           $("#directory-structure-content").show();

       }, 'json');
}

function openFile(filename)
{
    currentFile = currentDirectory + filename;

    $("#file-access-waiting").show();
    $("#file-access-content").hide();

    $.post(CCM_REL + CCM_DISPATCHER_FILENAME +
    '/tools/packages/c5book/get_file',
        {directory: currentDirectory, file: filename},
        function(data) {
            $("#file-access-textarea").val(data.fileContent);
            $("#file-access-caption").text(currentFile);
            $("#file-access-content").show();
            $("#file-access-waiting").hide();
        }, 'json');
}
function fileCancel()
{
    currentFile = '';
    $("#file-access-content").hide();
}
function fileSave()
{
    $("#file-access-waiting").show();
    $("#file-access-content").hide();

    $.post(CCM_REL + CCM_DISPATCHER_FILENAME +
    '/tools/packages/c5book/save_file',
        {file: currentFile,
         fileContent: $("#file-access-textarea").val()},
        function (data) {
            $("#file-access-waiting").hide();
```

```
            }, 'json');
   }

   $(document).ready(function() {
       openDirectory();

       $(".file-access-folder").live("click", function() {
           // append selected directory and reload
           currentDirectory += $(this).text() + "/";
           openDirectory();
       })

       $(".file-access-file").live("click", function() {
           openFile($(this).text());
       })

       $("#directory-structure-up").click(function() {
           // remove last directory from path and reload
           currentDirectory = currentDirectory.replace(/[\w]*\/$/,"");
           openDirectory();
       });
   })
```

5. Next, we have to create our helper, which is used in the three PHP files used by AJAX calls. Create packages/c5book/helpers/page_permissions.php and put the following content in it:

```php
<?php
defined('C5_EXECUTE') or die('Access Denied.');

class PagePermissionsHelper {
    public static function exitIfNoReadAccess($path) {
        $page = Page::getByPath($path);
        $permissions = new Permissions($page);

        if (!$permissions->canRead()) {
            die();
        }
    }
}
?>
```

6. Our first PHP file `packages/c5book/tools/get_file.php` used by the AJAX methods:

```php
<?php
defined('C5_EXECUTE') or die('Access Denied.');
header('Content-type: text/json');

Loader::helper('page_permissions', 'c5book');
$jh = Loader::helper('json');
PagePermissionsHelper::exitIfNoReadAccess(
'/dashboard/file_access');

$files = array();
$folders = array();

$directory = './' . $_REQUEST['directory'];
$file = $_REQUEST['file'];

$ret['fileContent'] = file_get_contents($directory . $file);

echo $jh->encode($ret);
?>
```

7. The second file for our AJAX methods, `packages/c5book/tools/save_file.php`:

```php
<?php
defined('C5_EXECUTE') or die('Access Denied.');
header('Content-type: text/json');

Loader::helper('page_permissions', 'c5book');
$jh = Loader::helper('json');
PagePermissionsHelper::exitIfNoReadAccess(
    '/dashboard/file_access');

$file = './' . $_REQUEST['file'];

$ret['returnValue'] = file_put_contents($file,
    $_REQUEST['fileContent']);

echo $jh->encode($ret);
?>
```

8. Finally, the last AJAX file to load the directory and file structure, `packages/`
`c5book/tools/get_structure.php`:

```php
<?php
defined('C5_EXECUTE') or die('Access Denied.');
header('Content-type: text/json');

Loader::helper('page_permissions', 'c5book');
$jh = Loader::helper('json');
PagePermissionsHelper::exitIfNoReadAccess(
    '/dashboard/file_access');

$ret['items'] = array();

$files = array();
$folders = array();

$directory = './' . $_REQUEST['directory'];
if ($dh = opendir($directory)) {

    while (false !== ($file = readdir($dh))) {

        if ($file == '.' || $file == '..') continue;

        if (is_dir($directory . $file)) {
            $ret['folders'][] = $file;
        }
        else {
            $ret['files'][] = $file;
        }
    }

    closedir($dh);
}

echo $jh->encode($ret);
?>
```

9. Open the package controller from `packages/c5book/controller.php` and
insert the highlighted lines in the `install` method:

```php
public function install() {
    $pkg = parent::install();

    // install blocks
    BlockType::installBlockTypeFromPackage('jqzoom', $pkg);
    BlockType::installBlockTypeFromPackage('pdf', $pkg);
    BlockType::installBlockTypeFromPackage('ftp_gallery', $pkg);
```

```
BlockType::installBlockTypeFromPackage('product_information',
    $pkg);
BlockType::installBlockTypeFromPackage('product_list', $pkg);

// install link checker job
Loader::model("job");
Job::installByPackage("link_checker", $pkg);

// install single pages
Loader::model('single_page');
$sp = SinglePage::add('/dashboard/reports/broken_links',
    $pkg);
if (version_compare(APP_VERSION, '5.6', '>')) {
    $sp->setAttribute('icon_dashboard', 'icon-warning-sign');
}
$sp = SinglePage::add('/dashboard/file_access', $pkg);
if (version_compare(APP_VERSION, '5.6', '>')) {
    $sp->setAttribute('icon_dashboard', 'icon-file');
}
}
}
```

What just happened?

If everything worked as planned, you can reinstall the package and a new element **FILE ACCESS** in your dashboard should appear where you can click on the **Home** item to get to the editor. You can see how it should look:

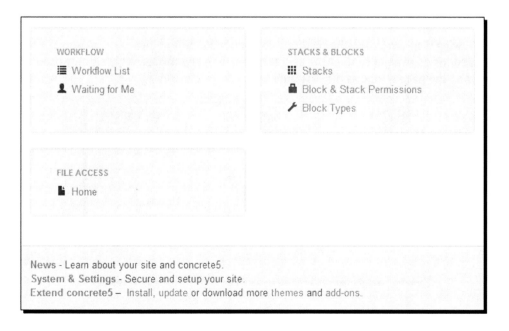

If it doesn't show up, there's an archive called `9314_10_c5book_packages.zip` on Packt's website where you can find the complete code.

If you click on it, the structure should load shortly afterwards and you can navigate around and open text files, edit them, and save the changes. No need to fire up your FTP application for a quick change of the configuration files.

We're going to have a closer look at the controller, as it is a bit uncommon and doesn't completely follow the usual MVC concept.

Controllers without logic

If you look at `packages/c5book/controllers/dashboard/file_access.php`, you'll find very few lines of code. Why is there almost no logic in the controller? Always remember the introduction—the model and the controller contain all the logic of the add-on. As always in life, it's full of exceptions.

The reason for this is simple: instead of reloading the whole dashboard page with every action; we use AJAX to update only the parts which have actually changed. This not only improves the look and feel, but also the performance.

AJAX always needs a different way to fetch data. This could have been a different method in the controller, but this would usually have been linked to a view. In this case, it's easier to create a completely independent file in the tools directory to process the AJAX requests.

What does this mean? The controller is pretty much empty; all the logic has been moved into JavaScript files in combination with some independent tools.

The following diagram shows the relationship of all the different elements. As you can see, all the actions go straight to the AJAX scripts and skip the controller, which is only used once when the page is loaded the first time.

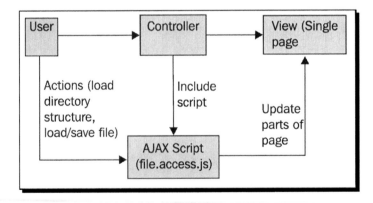

Have a go hero – extending the file editor add-on

This add-on works, but misses quite a few features any end user would expect to find when looking at it. Why not try to add some features?

Here are some ideas:

◆ Add the ability to download files

◆ Detect the file type to make sure no one tries to load a binary file, such as a ZIP or JPG file, into the textarea

◆ A place to upload file, maybe with support for autoextracting ZIP files

◆ Add a breadcrumb navigation to be able to navigate back to a previous directory quicker

◆ Support for different views such as a tree structure, thumbnails, and so on. There are plenty of things to do.

Pop quiz – concrete5 single pages

Q1. When building single pages in concrete5, you have to follow some rules. Try to answer the following questions to test your knowledge:

1. Single pages, as with other elements in concrete5 such as blocks, are built using the MVC (Model-View-Controller) pattern.

2. It's recommended you put code that accesses the database an eponymous model located in the `models` directory.

Q2. When you have a method called `view` in a controller called `Test` in a directory called `dashboard`, what is its URL?

1. `/dashboard/test/view/`

2. `/index.php/dashboard/test/`

3. `/dashboard/test/`

Q3. When you have a method called `show_all` that is in a controller called `Test`, which is in a directory called `dashboard`, what is its URL?

1. `/dashboard/test/show_all`

2. `/dashboard/test/show_all/view`

3. `/index.php/dashboard/test/show_all`

Summary

This has been the last chapter where you actually build something. In the next and last chapter, we're only going to look at how to deploy your site to a different server as well as a few configurations that you can make.

While most customizations and add-ons we created are pretty basic, they should have given you the basic knowledge to build lots of different add-ons. Once you get used to the concrete5 framework, you can build all kinds of add-ons just by knowing what has been discussed so far in combination with some PHP and JavaScript knowledge.

Before the end of this chapter, think about the following things and make sure you know and understand them. These are the basics from this chapter that you should know if you build your own dashboard extension:

- A dashboard add-on is basically a single page like any other single page, with the exception that it's located underneath the dashboard in the sitemap and requires a little stricter HTML/layout to keep visual consistency in the dashboard; on the other hand, normal single pages are more freeform.

- You can put several methods in a single controller to process data or change the behavior of the output.

- Look at the diagram at the beginning of this chapter and make sure you understand the separation of each element in the MVC pattern. Something that is also useful to know if you work with other frameworks.

If you need more information about MVC and the process of creating a controller, including methods with parameters, have a look at the following URL:

```
http://www.concrete5.org/documentation/how-tos/developers/basic-mvc-
in-concrete5/
```

11

Deployment and Configuration

In previous chapters, we created a number of examples, not all of them suited for your website. However, once you clean up everything and add the content you want, you have to make your website available on the Internet.

In this chapter, you'll find information that might be useful but not necessary during the step-by-step examples you've seen earlier in this book. The deployment part is also full of hints and not everything you'll see has to apply to your situation. Keep that in mind.

Deploying a concrete5 site

So far we've done all the work on your local computer, but you'll probably want to publish your website on a web server accessible by the public some day. It's a bit difficult to assume all the possible configurations out there. Every web server is a bit different; there are different operating systems, different web server software, and a lot of parameters your hosting company can change.

In this section, you'll find information that should make the process of deploying your website easier, no matter what hosting company you work with. However, keep in mind that it can vary depending on your situation and you might have to adapt to that.

Preparations for deployment

The following steps aren't necessary in every case but they make the deployment process a bit more solid.

Time for action – disabling pretty URLs and the cache

Carry out the following steps:

1. In your dashboard, go to **System & Settings** and then to **Clear Cache**. Click on the only available button.

2. In your dashboard, go to **System & Settings** and then to **Cache & Speed Settings** to make sure that all checkboxes are set to **Off** and then click on **Save**.

3. In your dashboard, go to the settings again and click on **Pretty URLs**. Make sure the checkbox isn't checked and save the change if necessary.

4. Rename the file named `.htaccess` that is in the root of your site `C:\BitNami\ wampstack-5.4.10-0\apache2\htdocs` to something such as `htaccess- disabled`.

What just happened?

Why did we disable pretty URLs? concrete5 creates a `.htaccess` file to rewrite the URLs that is based on a technology from the Apache web server. If you move your website to a server without support for `.htaccess`, your website might break after this move.

 Please note, without pretty URLs you have to open the login page by using the following address:
`http://localhost/index.php/login`

The cache does not necessarily break things on your website, but since it's quite difficult to predict what objects you will find in the cache, it is safer to disable it. You can enable it once your website has found its new home. You can find the cached files in this directory `C:\BitNami\wampstack-5.4.10-0\apache2\htdocs\files\cache;` some can be read quite easily, others not so readily.

Transferring MySQL databases

concrete5 uses MySQL to store most of its data found in the pages. It's therefore essential to transfer it to the new server. There are plenty of ways to do this; you might even have some bash scripts to transfer a database from one server to another. If you're that guy, this chapter isn't for you.

We're going to use phpMyAdmin, mostly because it's a widely used tool for managing MySQL databases. The Bitnami stack we've worked with also contains a version of phpMyAdmin, which will make it an easy task to export the database.

Time for action – transferring MySQL databases

Carry out the following steps:

1. In your favorite browser, open `http://localhost/phpmyadmin/` and log in
    with the credentials you've used to connect your concrete5 site to the database.

2. In the new phpMyAdmin screen, click on the database named **concrete5**, which
    you'll find in the left-hand side column.

3. A new screen appears where you can activate the **Export** tab on the top. Save the
    data into a plain SQL file including the structure and data. You can see the settings
    in the following screen shot:

4. After you've clicked on **Go** in the bottom-right corner, you'll get a file containing
    all the data in your database.

5. Now it's time to connect to the new website. Open phpMyAdmin on your
    new server; if you don't know where to find it, contact your hosting partner.

6. After you've logged in to phpMyAdmin, locate the database on the left, which you want to use for your website. If there's no empty database, click on the **Databases** tab, enter a database name in the text field in the **Create database** section and select **utf8_general_ci** in the collection list. Once you've selected it, click on **Import** on the right-hand side screen. Select the file you've just downloaded and click on **Go** at the bottom-right corner, as shown in the following screenshot:

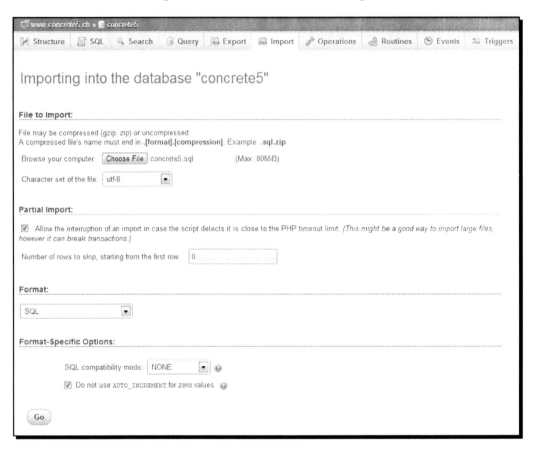

What just happened?

The preceding steps were necessary to transfer the content of our MySQL database to the new server. More experienced users are probably going to skip phpMyAdmin and simply use two commands.

- One to export the database on the Windows computer: `mysqldump -u [user-on-local-computer] -p [database-on-local-server] > sql.dump`

- Another one to import the dump file on the new server: `mysql -u [user-on-new-server] -p [database-on-new-server] < sql.dump`

Not every database is configured the same way. Troubleshooting character sets can be annoying and time-consuming, due to the fact that concrete5 uses utf8 all the time. You should try to make sure your database is set up the same way to avoid possible problems.

In *Chapter 1, Installing concrete5*, we changed the MySQL setting, which made sure that our table names were case-sensitive, even on Windows. Without this setting, we would now have lowercase table names on a Linux server, which doesn't work, unless someone has changed the default setting on the server. If that happened, you'd have to change the server settings or rename every table to its actual name. For example, `areagroupblocktypes` would have to be named `AreaGroupBlockTypes`. In other words, just try to make sure you always work with case-sensitive MySQL server configurations to avoid the hassle.

Transferring files to the server

When you installed concrete5, you probably realized that it needs quite a lot of files. These files have to be copied to the new server as well as the database. Again, there are tons of options to do this.

We're going to use a traditional unencrypted FTP connection because it's enabled on most web servers. You can use almost any FTP client; just make sure it allows you to change file permissions. If you're not sure about it, just go with FileZilla, which you can download at `http://filezilla-project.org/`.

Time for action – transferring files to the server

Carry out the following steps:

1. Open your FTP client and connect to the new server using the credentials you received from your hosting partner.

2. Navigate to `C:\BitNami\wampstack-5.4.10-0\apache2\htdocs` and select all the files in that directory. Before we start the upload process, open the correct target directory on the server. `public_html` is very common but anything is possible such as `htdocs` or `www`. If you can't find anything that looks like a directory to which you have to upload a website, contact your hosting company.

Once you've opened the correct target directory, drag all the files to the right pane or select **Upload** to start the process, as shown in the following screenshot:

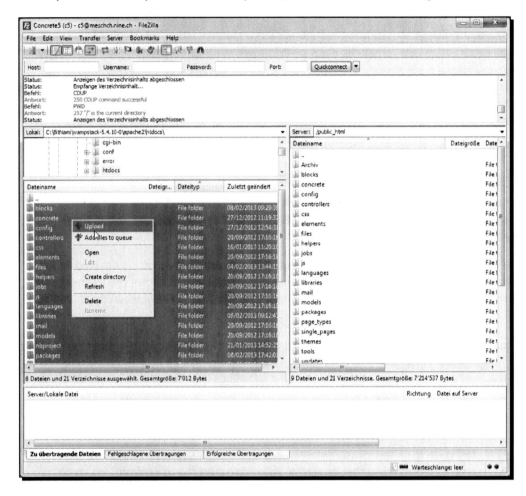

3. Once all the files have been uploaded, it will probably take a while, you can go to the next stage to manage the file permissions.

What just happened?

We uploaded all the files from concrete5, as well as our own files added to the website to the new server by using FileZilla.

Due to the fact that concrete5 contains a lot of files, it took a long time to upload all the files. Even a very fast Internet connection won't change a lot. The FTP protocol has some overhead on every file transferred to the server, making the process slow as soon as you transfer lots of single files.

If you can extract a ZIP archive or something similar on your server, you should compress all the files into a single file first and upload that and then extract it. For example, **cPanel** offers such a functionality.

Time for action – updating the configuration file

The URL to access your website changed and so did probably the username and password to access the MySQL database. We have to update the configuration file to match the new values by performing the following steps:

1. Open `config/site.php` and locate each of the following parameters.

2. DB_SERVER: This parameter has the value `localhost`, which quite likely will work on your new server as well. Check your hosting information to be sure and modify the value according to your information.

3. DB_USERNAME: This parameter has very likely changed; enter the username you want to use to access your MySQL database.

4. DB_PASSWORD: Another parameter that has probably changed; replace it with the new password to access your MySQL database.

5. DB_DATABASE: Another parameter you might have to change. Enter the name of the new database where you've imported the MySQL dump in the previous section.

What just happened?

We modified the configuration file to meet the new values to access your website and MySQL database. Without changing this, your site would still be looking for the database using the credentials from your development environment.

If everything worked as planned, you should now be able to access your website under the new address from your new web server.

Setting file permissions

This part might be unnecessary, depending on your web server configuration. It's all about making sure that your web server can access the files from your website. The following illustration shows a simplified diagram without MySQL involved to illustrate the communication between the web server and the files:

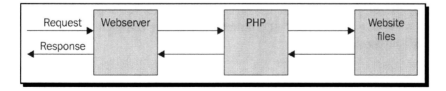

The web server can run under a different user from the PHP and the files can be owned by a different user again. To make things even more difficult, you can use groups instead of users as well. It's pretty hard to predict the configuration of your server; there is therefore not a single solution.

If you're running suEXEC or suPHP on Apache, then all the elements run with the same user' making your web server more secure, and easier to use in this case. The web server can access and write the files by default; no need to change anything.

 Accessing (reading) the files shouldn't be a problem. Files written by the FTP server are almost always readable by the web server, but often not writable. The directories config, files, packages, and updates should be writable by the web server.

Files on a Linux server are usually writable by the user but no one else. If you right-click on the files directory in FileZilla and select **File Permissions**, you'll see a dialog like the one shown in the following screenshot:

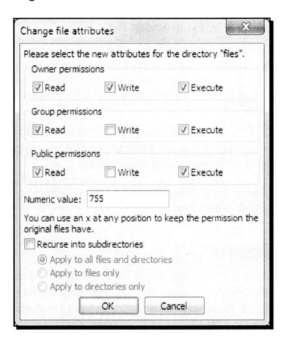

These are the default settings mentioned earlier. The number 755 represents the nine checkboxes in the screenshot. The first number is the owner, the second one the group, and the third one the public.

Each setting has a number that creates the numeric value 755:

- ◆ Execute: 1
- ◆ Write: 2
- ◆ Read: 4

If you add all the selected numbers in the order: user, group, and others, you'll get 755.

- ◆ User: 4 (Read) + 2 (Write) + 1 (Execute) = 7
- ◆ Group: 4 (Read) + 1 (Execute) = 5
- ◆ Others: 4 (Read) + 1 (Execute) = 5

When using FileZilla, you don't really have to care about these numbers, but you'll some day find them very handy when you get into the console.

What do these numbers mean? If your web server doesn't run under the user that owns your files, you won't be able to upload a new file, install a new package, and so on.

Time for action – setting file permissions

1. Try to upload a new file in the file manager. It doesn't matter which method you're using, you can upload a single file or several files by using the advanced multi-file uploader. If it works, you're the lucky one who doesn't has to change any settings. If not, continue with number two.

2. We assume that your web server runs under the same user that is set as the group owner of your files and directory that have to be writable. Go back to FileZilla and select **config**, **files**, **packages**, and **updates** if it exists. Right-click and select **File Permissions** again.

3. Tick the checkbox **Write** in the box of **Group permissions** and click on **Ok**.

4. Try to upload a file again. If it works, you're almost done. If it doesn't work, continue with step five.

5. If your web server cannot even write a file if it's writable by all members of the group, you can only allow everyone to write it and tick the checkbox **Write** in the box **Public permissions**. Click on **Ok** and try to upload a file again.

6. If that still doesn't work, try to mark the directories as **Executable**; some hosts require this in order to make the directories readable. If it doesn't work, you might have to ask for help in the concrete5 forums.

What just happened?

File permissions can be tricky, especially if you're not used to working with them. Hopefully, the preceding steps worked for you but, due to the vast variety of server configurations, you can never be sure.

 There are also some web servers where you can't change the file permissions by using an FTP client, even though the dialog is available. In this case, you will probably have to use an interface offered by your hosting company. Get in touch with them or ask for help in the concrete5 community, but post as many details about your problem as you can!

If you're done with the transfer, you might want to enable the cache again. Have a look at the previous paragraph where we changed the cache setting; you can find it in your dashboard under **System & Settings | Cache & Speed Settings**. Make sure you check your site's load time afterwards; in some rare situations, the cache can make the site slower instead of faster.

Updating production configuration

In this chapter, you'll find lots of different options you can set. You will probably have to change them very rarely. Memorizing every part in this chapter isn't going to help you a lot, but try to remember the things you can change in case you've got a project with special requirements.

Updating the configuration file

While there are several options you can change using the concrete5 interface, there are also lots of values you have to set in your configuration files.

In this part you'll find some code snippets. Make sure you paste them between the PHP tags. The file `config/site.php` looks like the following:

```php
<?php
define('DB_SERVER', 'localhost');
define('DB_USERNAME', 'concrete5');
define('DB_PASSWORD', 'concrete5');
define('DB_DATABASE', 'concrete5');
define('PASSWORD_SALT', 'R3nAjizpVw3AbleCFD2e5fZbXzNACYvnxoq');
?>
```

You have to insert the snippets before the closing PHP tag, as follows:

```php
<?php
define('DB_SERVER', 'localhost');
define('DB_USERNAME', 'concrete5');
define('DB_PASSWORD', 'concrete5');
define('DB_DATABASE', 'concrete5');
define('DIR_REL', '');
define('PASSWORD_SALT', 'R3nAjizpVw3AbleCFD2e5fZbXzNACYvnxoq');
define('BASE_URL', 'http://www.example.com');
?>
```

Base URL redirection

On a site where you have more than one URL, you might want to make sure that one address is used as the primary URL. Let's assume we've got two addresses: `http://www.example.com` and `http://www.beispiel.ch`. As your company is located in the United States, you don't want your visitors to stay on `beispiel.ch`. When you look at the preceding example, you can see an example where the `BASE_URL` constant is in use:

```php
define('BASE_URL', 'http://www.example.com');
```

By default, this constant is turned off, which is fine as long as you just use one URL.

Changing the concrete5 language

You probably understand English if you're reading this book, but you might still want to use concrete5 in another language.

First, make sure your concrete5 has been translated to the language you're looking for. Check the following project on Transifex to see the current state of the translations:

`https://www.transifex.com/projects/p/concrete5/`

Assuming you found your language in an up-to-date state, follow these steps to install the translation.

Time for action – installing a translation file

Carry out the following steps:

1. Open your browser and navigate to `https://www.transifex.com/projects/p/concrete5/`.

2. Look for the language you want to download and navigate to its page. Click on **concrete5 Core** once the page is loaded. Click on **Download** to get the file with all the translations.

3. Rename the file matching your concrete5 version to `messages.po`.

4. Go to `http://www.poedit.net/`, download `Poedit`, and install it.

5. Open the `messages.po` file you've downloaded using Poedit.

6. Save the file in Poedit; this will generate a file named `messages.mo` in the same directory as `messages.po`. You should have a `messages.mo` file now. If you've downloaded `de_DE`, you have to put `messages.po` in the directory `languages\de_DE\LC_MESSAGES`. You have to create the subdirectories manually.

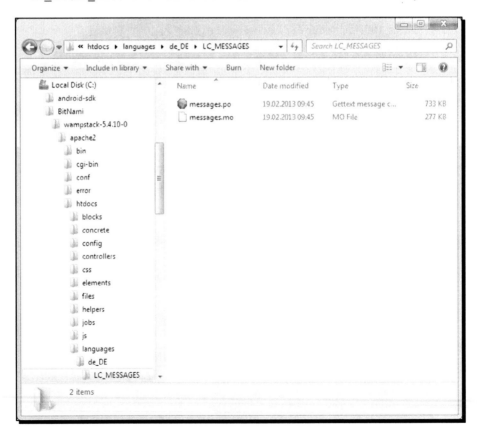

7. Once the files are where they belong, open `config/site.php` in the text editor of your choice.

8. Insert the line `define('LOCALE', 'de_DE');`, it should look like this:

```php
<?php
define('DB_SERVER', 'localhost');
define('DB_USERNAME', 'concrete5');
define('DB_PASSWORD', 'concrete5');
define('DB_DATABASE', 'concrete5');
define('PASSWORD_SALT', 'R3nAjizpVw3AbleCFD22AZkeCuQIzNACYvnxoq');
define('LOCALE', 'de_DE');
?>
```

What just happened?

After you save the file you can reload concrete5.

You should immediately see the changes in the toolbar on the top, as shown in the following screenshot:

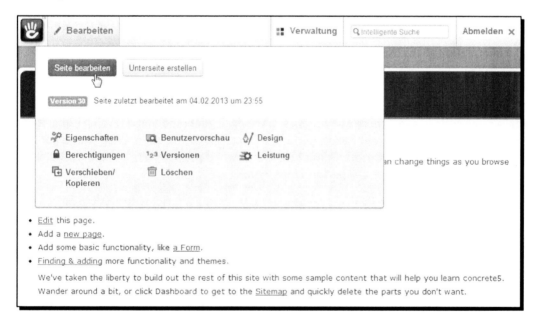

- *Edit* this page.
- Add a *new page*.
- Add some basic functionality, like *a Form*.
- *Finding & adding* more functionality and themes.

  We've taken the liberty to build out the rest of this site with some sample content that will help you learn concrete5. Wander around a bit, or click Dashboard to get to the *Sitemap* and quickly delete the parts you don't want.

Improving performance with a cache

concrete5 uses the Zend Framework for a few things, including caching to improve performance. By using the Zend cache, concrete5 can save the results of complex queries, procedures, and sometimes even complete pages to reduce the number of calls, and therefore improve a website's response time. Thanks to Zend, there are lots of options and backends we can use for our cache.

By default, concrete5 uses a simple file cache but there are other backends you can use:

- **SQLite**: This stores the cached objects in a SQLite database but isn't recommended with concrete5 as you'll probably run into some file-locking problems
- **Memcached**: This uses the distribution caching system daemon memcache
- **APC**: This is a shared memory caching extension for PHP
- **XCache**: This is another shared memory cache extension
- **Zend platform**: This uses an API from the Zend platform product
- **Zend server**: Zend server offers a disk and a shared memory extension that can be used as well
- **Static**: This pulls static files to avoid PHP completely. It uses a complex configuration

The information about the backends has been taken from the following page:

`http://framework.zend.com/manual/en/zend.cache.html`

If your web server supports any of the cache extensions, you should try to enable it and make some tests to see if there's any change in the page generation time. Even if Bitnami should be fast enough for your needs, performance can still be an issue. Once you've got lots of hits or lots of concurrent users, things can slow down. If possible, use a cache extension, even if you don't experience any performance issues.

If you aren't sure about the installed cache extension, create a script with a call to `phpinfo`.

Time for action – getting PHP information

Carry out the following steps:

1. Create a file named `info.php` in this directory: `C:\BitNami\ wampstack-5.4.10-0\apache2\htdocs`.

2. Enter the following lines:

```
<?php
phpinfo();
?>
```

3. Open `http://localhost/info.php` in your web browser.

What just happened?

The PHP information page contains everything about your PHP configuration. If you haven't seen this page before, make sure you get at least a little bit familiar with it as a lot of people will ask for it when you ask questions in the concrete5 community.

If an extension such as APC is enabled, you can find it somewhere in the information page. Bitnami ships with the PHP extension APC but it's not enabled by default. If you want to use APC with Bitnami, you have to remove the semicolon at the beginning of the following line in `C:\BitNami\wampstack-5.4.10-0\php\php.ini: extension=php_apc.dll`.

> When you're looking to get support from a community such as `concrete5.org`, people will often ask you about information you can find in this information page as well. It does reveal lots of information about your configuration, but it helps a lot if you can attach the output of this page to a forum thread if you ask for help.
>
> There's also a dialog in concrete5 that reveals the most important configuration settings of your site. Simply type `environment information` in the search box and click on the first entry displayed in the search result.

Caching with APC

APC is the currently preferred cache backend of a lot of concrete5 developers and does noticeably improve the performance.

The APC backend doesn't have any options. You therefore don't have to set `CACHE_BACKEND_OPTIONS`; only `CACHE_LIBRARY` is needed. The configuration file should look like the following:

```php
<?php
define('DB_SERVER', 'localhost');
define('DB_USERNAME', 'concrete5');
define('DB_PASSWORD', 'concrete5');
define('DB_DATABASE', 'concrete5');
define('PASSWORD_SALT', 'R3nAjizpVw3AbleCFD2exSwiUzKkbXezNACYvnxoq');

define('CACHE_LIBRARY', 'apc');
?>
```

Measuring site performance

If you change the cache backend, you probably want to make sure that it actually improves the performance. It can in fact happen that a cache backend slows down the process instead of improving it. This might be because of a slow file system, an overloaded database server, or anything else that runs on your server. Since concrete5 Version 5.6.1, things have gotten better though.

Bitnami installs Apache with a component named **ApacheBench**, a small executable file named `ab`. On most Linux and Unix-like systems, you already have a copy of `ab` installed on your system. This is a simple but nice way to test a website's performance.

Time for action – measuring site performance

1. If you're running Windows, press Windows key + *R* and enter `cmd`. Confirm it with a click on the **OK** button.

2. Enter `C:\BitNami\wampstack-5.4.10-0\apache2\bin\ab.exe -c 5 -n 100 http://localhost/` and press *Enter* to confirm the command. The parameter `-c` sets the number of concurrent requests to 5 and `-n` sets the number of requests to `100`. After a few seconds, you should see an output with lots of information—most people care about `Requests per second`.

What just happened?

If `ab` was installed and able to analyze your site, you should see an output like this:

```
This is ApacheBench, Version 2.3 <$Revision: 1373084 $>
Copyright 1996 Adam Twiss, Zeus Technology Ltd, http://www.zeustech.net/
Licensed to The Apache Software Foundation, http://www.apache.org/


Benchmarking localhost (be patient).....done


Server Software:        Apache
Server Hostname:        localhost
Server Port:            80

Document Path:          /
Document Length:        5870 bytes
```

```
Concurrency Level:        5
Time taken for tests:     0.324 seconds
Complete requests:        100
Failed requests:          0
Write errors:             0
Total transferred:        624400 bytes
HTML transferred:         587000 bytes
Requests per second:      309.08 [#/sec] (mean)
Time per request:         16.177 [ms] (mean)
Time per request:         3.235 [ms] (mean, across all concurrent requests)
Transfer rate:            1884.66 [Kbytes/sec] received
Connection Times (ms)
               min    mean[+/-sd]  median    max
Connect:        0      0    0.2      0         1
Processing:    11     16    7.1     14        55
Waiting:       11     16    7.0     14        54
Total:         11     16    7.1     14        55


Percentage of the requests served within a certain time (ms)
   50%        14
   66%        15
   75%        16
   80%        17
   90%        23
   95%        33
   98%        44
   99%        55
  100%        55 (longest request)
```

Using this simple tool allows you to quickly and easily compare a cache backend. It also offers you a simple way to see if your new web host performs as well as they are saying. Just replace `http://localhost/` with the address of your server, but keep in mind that you're going to execute a lot of requests. Don't use this tool for productive servers unless it's your server you're benchmarking.

Pop quiz – concrete5 configuration

Before you close this book, try to answer the following questions about the configuration of concrete5.

Q1. What is the constant `BASE_URL` in `config/site.php` used for?

1. It doesn't have any use anymore.
2. It defines the main URL of your site.
3. If specified on a site with multiple domains such as `www.site.com` and `www.site.ch`, it will forward all users to the main domain defined with `BASE_URL`.

Q2. What questions about internationalization are correct?

1. Translations are managed on transifex.
2. The language has to be specified in `config/site.php`.
3. All of the above.

Q3. What's special about directories such as `/config`, `/files`, `/packages`, and `/updates`?

1. They aren't needed by the core.
2. They must be writable by the core.

Where to go next

If you're eager to learn more about concrete5, here are a few links where you can find more information about concrete5.

*   `http://www.concrete5.org/documentation/how-tos/` provides a lot of how-tos targeted at developers, editors, as well as designers
*   `http://www.concrete5.org/documentation/` offers you some detailed videos about various topics for editors, designers, and developers
*   `http://www.concrete5.org/documentation/developers/` is the more technical part of the documentation aimed at developers
*   `http://www.concrete5.org/api/` is not made for beginners but, once you know a few things about concrete5, you can find classes and methods in this API documentation

- `https://github.com/concrete5/concrete5` is the place where you can find the latest code changes to concrete5

- `http://www.concrete5.org/marketplace/addons/?filters[]=free` supplies a number of free add-ons from where you can quickly get some nice examples to learn from

- `http://www.codeblog.ch/category/concrete5/` The author of the book has published a few articles about concrete5 on his blog

- `http://www.concrete5.org/community/forums/` The official forum is always a good place to find answers to questions that haven't been answered yet

Summary

You've made it to the end of this book! We hope you enjoyed it and learned how to work with concrete5 to create your own website with some basic customizations. While we realize that this book does not include the perfect solution for every problem, you now have a few techniques to try out during your investigations.

If there's anything unclear, feel free to contact the author at the following website:

`http://www.c5book.com`

Pop Quiz Answers

Chapter 1, Installing concrete5

Pop quiz – requirements for concrete5

Q1	1
Q2	2
Q3	4
Q4	5 (All of the above, but keep in mind that Apache is the only officially supported webserver)

Pop quiz – the configuration file

Q1	3

Chapter 2, Working with concrete5

Pop quiz – concrete5 inside editing mode

Q1	6
Q2	3

Chapter 3, Managing permissions

Pop quiz – permissions in concrete5

Q1	1, 3, and 5
Q2	1

Chapter 4, Managing Add-ons

Pop quiz – what's a package?

Q1	1, 3, and 4

Chapter 5, Creating your Own Theme

Pop quiz – what are page templates and page types?

Q1	1, 3, and 4

Pop quiz – what are attributes?

Q1	3

Pop quiz – what's a single page?

Q1	2, 3, and 4
Q2	1, 3, and 4
	While you probably won't have several contact forms on your site, you'll have several forms and at the end, there's not much custom functionality in a contact form and therefore not recommended as a single page

Chapter 6, Customizing Block Layouts

Pop quiz – how to include CSS and JavaScript files

Q1	1, 3, and 4

Chapter 7, Adding Site Navigation

Pop quiz – parts of image navigation

Q1	1 and 2
Q2	1 and 3

Chapter 8, Creating Your Own Add-on Block

Pop quiz – parts of a block

Q1	3

Chapter 9, Everything in a Package

Pop quiz – what does a package do?

Q1	1, 2, 3, and 4
Q2	1, 2, and 3

Pop quiz – what can you do with events?

Q1	1, 2, 3, and 4
Q2	1 and 2

Pop quiz – benefits of addHeaderItem

Q1	4

Chapter 10, Dashboard Extensions

Pop quiz – concrete5 single pages

Q1	1 and 2
Q2	2 and 3
Q3	1 and 3

Chapter 11, Deployment and Configuration

Pop quiz – concrete5 configuration

Q1	2 and 3
Q2	3
Q3	2

Index

Thank you for buying
concrete5 Beginner's Guide: Second Edition

About Packt Publishing

Packt, pronounced 'packed', published its first book "*Mastering phpMyAdmin for Effective MySQL Management*" in April 2004 and subsequently continued to specialize in publishing highly focused books on specific technologies and solutions.

Our books and publications share the experiences of your fellow IT professionals in adapting and customizing today's systems, applications, and frameworks. Our solution based books give you the knowledge and power to customize the software and technologies you're using to get the job done. Packt books are more specific and less general than the IT books you have seen in the past. Our unique business model allows us to bring you more focused information, giving you more of what you need to know, and less of what you don't.

Packt is a modern, yet unique publishing company, which focuses on producing quality, cutting-edge books for communities of developers, administrators, and newbies alike. For more information, please visit our website: www.packtpub.com.

About Packt Open Source

In 2010, Packt launched two new brands, Packt Open Source and Packt Enterprise, in order to continue its focus on specialization. This book is part of the Packt Open Source brand, home to books published on software built around Open Source licences, and offering information to anybody from advanced developers to budding web designers. The Open Source brand also runs Packt's Open Source Royalty Scheme, by which Packt gives a royalty to each Open Source project about whose software a book is sold.

Writing for Packt

We welcome all inquiries from people who are interested in authoring. Book proposals should be sent to author@packtpub.com. If your book idea is still at an early stage and you would like to discuss it first before writing a formal book proposal, contact us; one of our commissioning editors will get in touch with you.

We're not just looking for published authors; if you have strong technical skills but no writing experience, our experienced editors can help you develop a writing career, or simply get some additional reward for your expertise.

concrete5 Beginner's Guide

ISBN: 978-1-849514-28-6   Paperback: 320 pages

Create and customize your own website with the concrete5 Beginner's Guide

1. Follow the creation of a sample site, through the installation, configuration, and deployment of a concrete5 site

2. Use themes and add-ons to create a personalized site

3. Part of Packt's Beginner's Guide series – lots of practical examples, screenshots, and less of the waffle

Creating concrete5 Themes

ISBN: 978-1-782161-64-6   Paperback: 160 pages

Create high quality concrete5 themes using practical recipes and responsive techniques to make it mobile-ready

1. Get to grips with the concrete5 architecture

2. Learn how to create a concrete5 theme

3. Discover how to make a theme responsive to improve it for small devices

Please check **www.PacktPub.com** for information on our titles

Joomla! 2.5 Beginner's Guide

ISBN: 978-1-849517-90-4   Paperback: 426 pages

An easy to use step-by-step guide to creating perfect websites with the free Joomla! CMS

1. Create a Joomla! website in an hour with the help of easy-to-follow steps and screenshots.

2. Go beyond a typical Joomla! site to make a website that meets your specific needs.

3. Learn how to secure, administrate, and fill your site with content.

4. Update to the popular Joomla! 1.5 Beginner's Guide by Eric Tiggeler.

Drupal 7 Development by Example Beginner's Guide

ISBN: 9780-1-849516-80-8   Paperback: 366 pages

Follow the creation of a Drupal website to learn, by example, the key concepts of Drupal 7 development and HTML5

1. A hands-on, example-driven guide to programming Drupal websites

2. Discover a number of new features for Drupal 7 through practical and interesting examples while building a fully functional recipe sharing website

3. Learn about web content management, multi-media integration, and e-commerce in Drupal 7

Please check **www.PacktPub.com** for information on our titles

Lightning Source UK Ltd.
Milton Keynes UK
UKOW02f1002310114

225631UK00002B/9/P